Gus Hornsby's Gamble

Gus Hornsby's Gamble

*The Life of Chicago Football's
Founder Turned Fugitive*

LARRY LaTOURETTE

McFarland & Company, Inc., Publishers
Jefferson, North Carolina

ISBN (print) 978-1-4766-9118-3
ISBN (ebook) 978-1-4766-4897-2

LIBRARY OF CONGRESS AND BRITISH LIBRARY
CATALOGUING DATA ARE AVAILABLE

Library of Congress Control Number 2023028003

© 2023 Larry D. LaTourette II. All rights reserved

No part of this book may be reproduced or transmitted in any form or by any means, electronic or mechanical, including photocopying or recording, or by any information storage and retrieval system, without permission in writing from the publisher.

Magnifying glass and silhouette © 2023 Shutterstock; background illustration by Frederic Remington (*Harper's Weekly,* November 26, 1887)

Printed in the United States of America

*McFarland & Company, Inc., Publishers
Box 611, Jefferson, North Carolina 28640
www.mcfarlandpub.com*

To my father (Hi, Dad!)

And in memory of
Robert Cox

"Life without a purpose is oblivion."—Frances Willard[1]

"Why should we long for the next world, before we are fit even for this one?"—Charles Kingsley, *Westward Ho!*[2]

Life without a purpose is oblivion.
Frances E. Willard

Willard occasionally included this phrase when signing autographs. She used this adage as early as 1873 (personal correspondence, Frances Willard, 1873, author's collection).

Acknowledgments

Hornsby's story is relatively obscure, with forgotten fragments and scraps of information strewn across archives, letters, and newspapers—some digitized, many others not. It took a lot of people working together to put together so many of these pieces and help with the research into Hornsby, William Curtis, Frances Willard, early Midwestern football, and the histories of Evanston, Chicago, St. Paul, and Stillwater.

I'm deeply indebted to Kevin Leonard, the archivist of Northwestern University, for his generosity and insights into the school's history. He opened the vaults and provided valuable clues to the story. Janet Olson, archivist for the Frances E. Willard Memorial Library and Archives (and also on the staff of Northwestern's Archives office), provided much-needed research support, as did Rebecca Snyder, the director of research and publishing for the Dakota County (MN) Historical Society. I'm also indebted to Caroline Jones, the Wellington College archivist, and the staffs of the Minnesota History Center, the Chicago Art Institute, the Evanston History Center, and Chicago's Newberry Library.

The relatives of Gus Hornsby helped in this work, particularly Patty Conroy, who tracked down stories among the Hornsby family, and Hugh Evans, who provided information from "across the pond."

Barbara Hague was the first editor to see a draft of this book, and her guidance was critical to the final product.

I'm grateful to McFarland for their work in bringing Hornsby's story to the public, including Gary Mitchem, Adam Phillips, Kristal Hamby, and Sophia Lyons. Mark Durr and the team deserve special recognition for the outstanding cover.

Dr. Kate Andrews van Horne and Jennifer Andrews van Horne also offered their support, as did Vince Adams and Ellise Estes Kingsberg, who served as early readers of the manuscript.

My wife, Carissa Casbon LaTourette, was (as usual) the most vital early reader. She also provided moral support and championed the project alongside me. No thanks are enough.

Table of Contents

Acknowledgments	vii
Preface	1
Introduction: A Gambler at the Rubicon	5
Part One: The Football	**9**
Game Day, 6:30 a.m.	10
Chapter 1. 1846: India	15
Game Day, 9:00 a.m.	23
Chapter 2. 1866: Madras	29
Game Day: A Glimpse of Evanston, Illinois, at High Noon	40
Chapter 3. 1873: America	46
Game Day, 1:00 p.m.	54
Chapter 4. 1875: Chicago	63
Game Day, 2:00 p.m.	71
Chapter 5. 1876: Chicago	78
Part Two: The Fraud	**87**
Game Day, 3:05 p.m.	88
Chapter 6. 1882: St. Paul	91
Game Day, 3:10 p.m.	101
Chapter 7. 1888: Chicago	104
Game Day, 3:25 p.m.	113
Chapter 8. 1892: St. Paul	116

Table of Contents

Game Day, 3:30 p.m.	125
Chapter 9. 1893: Hastings	132
Game Day, 3:45 p.m.	138
Chapter 10. 1893: Stillwater	140
Game Day, 3:55 p.m.	151
Chapter 11. 1895: St. Paul	153
Game Day, 4:05 p.m.	158
Chapter 12. The Precipice of the American Century	163
Game Day, 5:30 p.m.	178
Chapter 13. 1926: Evanston	181
Game Day, Night	189
Chicago Foot-Ball Club : List of Known Members, 1875–1878	193
Chapter Notes	195
Bibliography	214
Index	219

Preface

This book began as a research project exploring early football games in Chicago and surrounding communities, including the first games held at Northwestern University in Evanston, Illinois, which played its first intercollegiate football in 1882. While researching the school's earliest games, I noticed a tantalizing passage in an old sports history book from 1951. In *Tale of the Wildcats*, sports historian Walter Paulison wrote that

> the first evidence of any football activity at Northwestern appeared in an article in [the school's first newspaper] *The Tripod* of February 24, 1876, which said, "The trial game of football on Tuesday last enthused the boys so much that they have formed a Football Association and intend to give the representatives of 'Old Rugby' a hard time to beat them in a scrimmage when they come here again." Just who the representatives of "Old Rugby" were is not known....[1]

Who, indeed, were the representatives of "Old Rugby"? If the 1876 game in Evanston was an American football game, it would be an example of football played three years before the University of Michigan challenged Racine College in Chicago, typically viewed as the first American football game played in the Midwest. A quick search of the *Chicago Tribune* from that day revealed that the team that visited Northwestern was an American football team called the Chicago Foot-Ball Club. A few further searches showed that an Englishman named Augustus H. "Gus" Hornsby organized the Chicago club.

Researching Hornsby quickly became a plunge down a rabbit hole: he was the Forrest Gump of nineteenth-century Chicago, popping up in the least likely settings with a hand in dozens of schemes, projects, and events. The more I read, the more weirdly fascinating Hornsby's life became. I chose to recount his story here for three reasons.

The first, and perhaps the most obvious, reason is that it has never been told. Gus Hornsby's story, the arc of his life and career, is oddly compelling. He was a man with one of the broadest sets of talents and experiences I've come across, and several of his abilities reveal powerful gifts. He was a person who seemed fated for greatness and to make a lasting impact. Instead, his contributions are mostly forgotten; indeed, they amounted to little even during his lifetime. A published book has not even mentioned Hornsby since Alexander Weyland's 1955 work *The Saga of American Football*, in which Weyland noted:

> In 1876, the year that Eastern colleges changed from soccer to rugby, Augustus H. Hornsby organized the Chicago Football Club and claimed credit for introducing rugby into the West. He was born in India, but he learned his football in England where he was educated. On February 22, 1876, his club played a team composed of Northwestern University students and Evanston town boys. The clubmen used fifteen players against thirty, but won.²

I begin this book with Frances Willard's statement that "life without a purpose is oblivion," and no sentiment could better fit Hornsby. At various points in his life he seemed to have everything: fantastic wealth, power, status, respect, and boundless potential. He lacked, however, a passion, a purpose. Instead, he had a nearly fatal flaw: his gambling addiction. I try with this narrative to look at what Hornsby lacked, his shortcomings—including deep-seated prejudices—what he had, and how these assets and disabilities ultimately shaped this occasionally unpleasant but always fascinating person.

My second reason for writing this book is that I remain surprised and intrigued by the sheer number of interesting people who were directly involved in one obscure event (the little-known 1876 football game between Chicago and Northwestern University). Many, including Chicago players, university students, and a handful of spectators, were then unknown and later became famous, either fleetingly or—in a couple of cases—up to the present.

Third, it is interesting to see how the rise of American football and Gus Hornsby's own life paralleled the pivot and growth of America as we have come to know it: powerful, original, arrogant, and seemingly limitless. And now, as I write this book, we are witnessing America reach another social pivot point, coincidentally just as American football, with the legitimate concern over player safety, seems to be on the cusp of its own oblivion.

• • •

Tracking down Hornsby's entire story was challenging. For example, there are only four known photographs of the man, and I included two of them in this work (the other two, taken in the early twentieth century, when Hornsby was middle aged, are in non-digitized newspapers and are so degraded that they are virtually unidentifiable). Only a few of his descendants are alive. Although his distant relatives were very cooperative and wanted to provide details, there weren't many details left, only one photograph, and virtually no records.

Hornsby's partner in putting together the Chicago Foot-Ball Club was William B. Curtis, "the father of American amateur athletics" and a much more famous person than Hornsby. Throughout the 1890s, Curtis was the one person in the country most responsible for keeping records of athletic events, and his collection eventually contained photos, written recollections, and histories of sports across the country, including his early football exploits with Hornsby. Unfortunately, a 1904 fire wiped out the Curtis estate's vast collection.[3] This biography necessarily became a patchwork of sleuthing and some educated guessing.

Another example: in the 1890s, Hornsby edited and wrote for a Minnesota newspaper, providing valuable insights into his life through his column. However, he did so anonymously. Figuring out that the writer and editor was indeed Hornsby involved building a case through the newspaper and its historical archives with circumstantial evidence until I had established his identity without a doubt. I include the details of this evidence in the chapter notes.

• • •

The result of this cobbling is a sprawling story about Hornsby, early football, the players who took part in the Chicago–Northwestern game in 1876, and the groups who crisscrossed Hornsby's journey. One of those groups, unexpectedly, was composed of the women and men who were the "first-wave" movement of American feminism. In fact, the subtitle of this book was initially going to be "Football, *Feminism*, and Fraud." The early feminist movement, with its roots in the religious temperance groups of the 1870s, remains an essential thread in this rambling narrative, a key component among dozens of cultural and social factors that intersected with—and profoundly influenced—Hornsby's life.

The people and events described during the February 1876 game also interwove through Hornsby's life, his early experiences in England, India, and Chicago, and his later exploits in St. Paul, Minnesota. To highlight this, I've intercut Hornsby's story with moments from that pivotal game day in Evanston, Illinois. I've also included several sections throughout the book that describe some of the ideas, people, and events tangential to the narrative, so you, too, can peer down the rabbit hole.

Introduction:
A Gambler at the Rubicon

This is the true story of the immigrant who brought American football to the American heartland for the first time.

I write *American* football to distinguish the game from styles of football that had come before and which mostly children had played in America since before the country's founding. There are several different varieties of the sport that Americans played in the middle and late nineteenth century, and historians refer to them in numerous ways. For simplicity, this narrative categorizes them into four games: the "early kicking game," association football, rugby football, and American football—the earliest version of which was the East Coast college game.

Before the 1870s, football in the United States was predominantly the early kicking game, a nearly rules-free, no-holds-barred schoolyard game. Players simply kicked about a round ball, typically made of an animal bladder (and, later, rubber). By the 1860s, association football, the predecessor of modern soccer, began to appear in the United States on the East Coast, as did rugby football. Association-style football predated the rugby style, but the rugby game began to be formalized in the 1830s, while association football, with its more modern rules, started in earnest in England with the creation of the London Football Association Code, written in 1863.[1]

East Coast colleges, including Princeton, Rutgers, Harvard, Columbia, and Yale, began to modify association football and rugby to suit their own needs. The first recognized game of American football—at least in most histories of the game—is the November 1869 match between Rutgers and Princeton. That game was almost entirely based on association football. If a modern observer were to travel in time back to this game, he or she would think it was more soccer than modern football.

Harvard initially played association, kicking-style football as early as the 1850s, but in 1858 it allowed players to carry the ball in limited sets of plays.² One of the reasons for this change was that Boston schoolchildren started learning English rugby, and many of them eventually enrolled at Harvard, taking the rugby-style of play with them. As will later be shown, this set up a clash with other nearby colleges, which enjoyed playing association football and were resistant to carrying the football at any point in the game.

The divide between association and rugby football eventually led to a mutated form of the game, played by Harvard, Tufts, a handful of Canadian schools, and a small but growing number of other East Coast colleges in the early 1870s. It was this blended version of football that evolved into the forerunner of the modern American football with which we are familiar.

For the first few years of the modified rugby game, it stayed with the Eastern schools. An Englishman named Augustus Hornsby first took the game West. This is his story, and it is also the story of some of the men and women whose vibrant and influential lives intersected with Hornsby during a crucial time for America.

• • •

Hornsby initiated the new style of football in the Midwest in 1876 at the Chicago–Northwestern University game in Evanston, Illinois, just north of Chicago. A greater-than-coincidental number of people linked to this one game led incredible lives, sought risk, and made a national impact. This group of talented men and women speaks to the potential that was bound up in this one place and at one specific time. Chicago, just after the Great Fire of 1871, was bursting with creativity and possibility.

Architects had flocked to Chicago to help with the rebuilding process, and they were developing plans that would revolutionize the modern American city. Chicago, reborn from the ashes, bristled with new, expansive, and breathtaking structures that spoke to the energy and potential of its people (one such building, the vast and imposing rebuilt Tremont House Hotel, is the setting for several key moments in this story). Journalists, including the editor of the Chicago *Evening Journal*, John Jeffrey, were transforming local and national journalism. And men and women in and near Chicago just after the Fire began a drive for women's rights and suffrage that would reap benefits nationwide by the century's end.

Frances Willard, the temperance and early feminist leader who lived in Evanston, Illinois, at this time, also plays an important role in this story. Willard's significance would be felt long after her early death, on her followers and—as will be seen—even on Hornsby. In the 1870s, Willard had a lasting influence across Northwestern's campus and on its students, specifically several who had roles in the game that is the focus of this story.

Frank Casseday is one such student. A player for Northwestern in the 1876 game, Casseday was also a follower of Willard, and her influence and message would transform his life. Casseday's story includes several parallels to Hornsby's life (both would eventually travel from Chicago to St. Paul to seek fortunes). However, there were a couple of notable differences—Casseday had a passion, and he lacked Hornsby's crippling addiction.

• • •

For Hornsby, gambling was a lifelong obsession, and it drove him to ruin two different times in his life. American cities in the nineteenth century were havens for illicit gambling: card games like the new varieties of poker and older games like faro, roulette, betting on horse racing, and wagering on animal fighting (cock fighting and, in some towns, rat fighting) all involved the trading of millions of dollars and occasionally claimed lives when the games produced disagreements. In Chicago, the eastern portion of Randolph Street is in the modern city's Loop and is surrounded by offices, franchise restaurants, and the building that hosts the Goodman Theatre. When Hornsby came to Chicago, that same stretch of Randolph had multiple illegal gambling houses and suffered frequent shoot-outs between aggrieved gamblers.

Not all gambling during this period was the traditional, illicit variety. Speculators were risking huge amounts in stock trades and other businesses. Former professional gambler George H. Devol remarked in 1887:

> What are the members of the Board of Trade but gamblers? The Board of Trade is just as much a gambling house as a faro bank. Do not the members put up their (and often times other peoples') money on puts, calls, margins, and futures? Do not some poor people have to wait a long time in the "future" before they get back the money some rascal has put up and lost? Talk about the morality of gamblers. They are not thieves and swindlers, and I never heard of one who ever served a term in the penitentiary, or was arrested for embezzling money.[3]

The second half of Devol's remarks is dubious at best. However, his point about the Board of Trade was a common view in the late nineteenth century. "Stock gambling" was rife in the 1880s; according to a former trader, "Hundreds of men and women were driven to suicide by their losses, while the insane asylums were filled to overflowing with victims of the stock-gambling mania."[4]

Real estate speculation was another form of gambling; property values skyrocketed in Chicago in the second half of the nineteenth century, primarily due to heavy speculation beginning in 1873 (coinciding with the same year that Hornsby settled in Chicago).[5] Naturally, Hornsby was drawn to this sort of speculation as well, and it compelled him to follow a real estate bubble from Chicago to St. Paul, where his gambling, speculating, and ultimately fraudulent activities took off in earnest.

• • •

Hornsby was from an upper-class family, and he made business and social contacts relatively easily, which helped him eventually break into real estate speculation. Earlier, those connections had also helped him when he took part in creating the Chicago Foot-Ball Club. Most sports clubs in the 1870s through the 1880s were significantly different from modern athletic teams: rather than an assembled group of the best athletes in their fields, the earliest sports clubs were primarily *social* clubs—ones driven by class distinctions and recruited from well-heeled families. Membership in groups such as the New York Athletic Club, the Chicago Foot-Ball Club, and others was a mark of social status and an opportunity for developing business connections and enjoying social events. The use of athletic teams for social status and networking eventually subsided as more directly business-focused clubs began, but it persisted well into the early twentieth century. The Chicago Foot-Ball Club and its members give an insightful glimpse into this period and the culture of privilege that pervaded athletics in America after the Civil War.

One could say the same about most of the members of Northwestern's team. This narrative focuses on Northwestern's football team, highlighting its events in the 1870s, the beginning of the twentieth century, and into the first national heyday of the sport in the 1920s. However, there is nothing unique about Northwestern's football program in this sense: it was typical of the large universities at the time. Northwestern's football program is described here in detail as an example of what was happening across the country, particularly in the American Midwest, as the culture of athletics shifted following the changes in society.

PART ONE

The Football

Game Day, 6:30 a.m.

As Frank Casseday dressed in near darkness, he stared at the dim, suspended image of the grinning human skull that seemed to levitate in the void opposite his bed. Sunrise was still three minutes away, but the first rays were feathering across Frank's small bedroom, sweeping slowly across the wall. Light moved across an old, framed carbon photo of Frank, his half-brothers George and David, and his mother, Ellen.[1] In 1863, when the photo was taken, Frank was seven years old but looked younger in the picture; his mother was thirty-two, but she looked considerably older—haggard, sunken-cheeked, with kind but smoky, tired, shadowed eyes. Frank's father was one year dead when the family posed,[2] thirteen years before, and Frank had trouble remembering the finer details of his father's appearance, despite other photographs—anything beyond his towering presence draped in his minister's robe and cigar smoke.

The light continued to cross the room to the only other wall hanging: a handmade image, painted on wood, a gold Maltese cross, bearing the letters ΦΚΣ on the cross's arms, the phrase *Stellis Aequus Durando*[3] limned under the cross, and—in the middle of the cross—the large, smiling skull with crossbones. The painting had belonged to Frank's half-brother David, who helped found the Phi Kappa Sigma fraternity chapter at Northwestern University.[4] When Frank also enrolled at Northwestern, he had joined his brother's fraternity.[5]

Frank and his brother were close, but there was tension: for his entire life, Frank was quick to point out that he was Ellen's only child.[6] His two older brothers were the children of Frank's father's late first wife. Ellen moved the family to Evanston, Illinois, so that all three of her sons, step and biological, could have an opportunity to attend the college. Phi Kappa Sigma kept a suite of rooms near Northwestern's campus. Frank, however, chose to stay in the family house and his old room during his time at school, to stay close to his mother. Years later, when Frank moved to Minneapolis and, later still, to Oregon, Ellen joined him. As Frank later wrote, his mother was "my guiding star."[7]

The light crept down to Frank's immaculate desk, on which lay two slim volumes, a Greek primer and a book of British oration. Aside from Frank's bed and a wooden chair with a cane seat, the room was bare.

Frank churned through what the day had in store for him. Tuesday was typically a busy day and Frank's favorite: Tuesday afternoons usually included laboratory practice for chemistry and German philosophy.[8] His classes, however, were to be held only in the morning on this day—it was a holiday, and the school closed its classrooms in the afternoon to honor Washington's birthday.

• • •

Washington's birthday would not be signed into law as a permanent holiday until 1879. However, many states already celebrated the day as a holiday, and in early 1876 President Grant signed an executive order to make the 1876 Washington's birthday celebration a national holiday.[9] Northwestern also chose to celebrate the 1876 Washington's birthday holiday by canceling most of its classes.[10]

The upcoming football game was a part of the Washington's birthday celebrations, and it was notably the only event for the occasion in Evanston, contrary to neighboring communities. In Wilmette, Illinois, just north of campus, residents displayed American flags throughout the town, and several houses burned lamps and bonfires through the night.[11] Other towns in the area held parades, dances, and concerts. The festivities weren't limited to America: European nations celebrated the day as well.[12] The *New York Daily Herald* noted that even in London, "that modern Babel where George the Third was King, the triumphs of his rebellious subjects will be applauded and approved in 'dinings and winings' that will take place in honor of the arch rebel's birthday."[13]

• • •

Occasionally Frank would pay a midday visit to one of his mentors, temperance leader Frances Willard, but Willard was visiting the East Coast, and Frank hadn't seen her in weeks. Willard recently left the staff of Northwestern, where she had been dean of the Women's College, and she had taken a leadership role in the Woman's Christian Temperance Union, headquartered in Evanston. Willard's house, on Chicago Avenue in the old part of Northwestern's campus, swarmed with Temperance Union activity. Frank met Willard his freshman year in the fall of 1873, and the W.C.T.U. leader impressed him greatly: "We all learned to love her," he would say decades later. "I look back through all these intervening years with gladness that it was our lot to have contact with such a wonderful woman."[14]

Frank had more contact with Willard in the past year. His brother

David was engaged to a Highland Park, Illinois, singer named Clara Willard, a relative of Frances. Occasionally David and Clara, a budding soprano with a soft, lilting voice, visited Willard, and Frank joined them. Those meetings were festive and included singing, with Clara taking the lead.[15]

Instead of afternoon classes or meetings, Frank had plans to be at the school athletic grounds. He was eager for the spring baseball practice to begin—Frank was a member of the varsity baseball team, the first athletic group to represent the school. However, he wasn't going to the field this afternoon to play baseball. In fact, he wasn't quite sure what he was going to play. The game, as described to him, was football, but it wasn't like the roughhouse children's kicking game he learned as a boy. This version of the game involved using one's hands, running with the ball, lunging with it across the goal, and trying to kick the ball between upright posts to score.

Despite having had a copy of the instructions since earlier in the month and practicing the game with a few other students, it still seemed a jumble of odd rules.

After dressing, Casseday took the slip of paper from his desk drawer and glanced again at the football rules.

A small pin rested in the same drawer. The pin's design matched the cross on Frank's wall, though its gold skull seemed outsized. Frank carefully attached the pin to his lower coat lapel. He pocketed the sheet of football rules.

• • •

At the same time that Frank was dressing, the man who had jotted down those rules for him had been awake for hours. He was running hard through the streets of Chicago.[16]

He was twelve miles south of Frank Casseday's family home. South of the mud- and ice-streaked Evanston roads lined with wood-framed houses, south of the tonier brick houses on Lake and Greenwood avenues. Past the Chicago north-side shops, their owners preparing to open, hanging up American flags and red and blue bunting across the facades. Past the new downtown Chicago construction still sprouting in the once-scarred moonscape left by the Great Fire five years ago. Past the newly rebuilt grand Tremont Hotel, its balconies festooned with seeming acres of red and blue silk, its iron spires sporting American flags the size of train cars.

As he ran, Augustus Hornsby would have drawn the attention of the few pedestrians and horsemen out at this hour and in this weather. They looked at him, baffled, as he rushed by. Most assumed that he was running from someone, that his sprint through the streets was sinister.

Hornsby was exercising, as he did every morning, without fail. He raced past the Tremont, where he had spent much of the night before, dining and playing cards, first pleasantly and discreetly beneath the massive ironwork chandeliers in the grand hotel's vast parlor, then in a tucked-away room on the fourth floor, a queasy, unyielding ordeal.

Occasionally, Hornsby might stop on his runs to enjoy an early breakfast at the Tremont: a typical Tremont breakfast would have entailed cornbread, a cold sausage, coffee. On this morning, however, he raced past the Tremont's arched entrance without stopping, navigating quickly between a pair of carriages already parked outside.

He ran past the offices of the Chicago *Inter-Ocean* newspaper, its entrance the only source of activity yet on this block. Hornsby headed for the Chicago River, and he soaked in the steaming, chilling landscape of urban America on the threshold between a backwoods wilderness and an industrial hive. It was pockmarked with a few old buildings and ruins, but it was mostly new, aggressively rebuilt during the past four years. In Chicago that week, the architect William LeBaron Jenney was developing the idea that would render the world's first skyscraper; he did so less than 300 feet from a smith shoeing horses.

Elsewhere, in bustling St. Paul, Minnesota, General George Armstrong Custer said his goodbyes that morning. He prepared to take his cavalry west to eliminate the problem that the Sioux were posing for miners in Montana. "You can't civilize an Indian any more than you can teach a rooster to lay goose eggs," Custer noted to the St. Paul press the day before.[17] On the morning of February 22, 1876, the country was only a little more than a decade removed from the Civil War; Chicago was only a decade away from the 1886 Haymarket Riot.

Chicago and the rest of the country were gearing up for the nation's centennial in July. This day, Washington's birthday, was the dry run. There were to be flags and fireworks.

America was celebrating its vision of itself.

Hornsby reached the Chicago River and the new Madison Street bridge. To his left, the iron mazework of the Pittsburgh & Fort Wayne train yards billowed steam and stench in the freezing early sunlight. He streaked to the Union House, a hotel that survived the Great Fire, its small rooms enrobed with smells of soot and rot.[18] He walked through the hotel lobby toward the offices of the *Chicago Field* magazine, high-ceilinged, wallpapered with a pattern of bright red diamonds, sparsely furnished.

He only stopped moving once inside his office, which was a blazing contrast to the other rooms in the magazine's apartment. It was a claustrophobic riot of weirdly incongruous artifacts: chessboards piled with wood and ivory pieces, leather bridles and whips, his father's 1822 pattern sword and an enormous ceremonial Indian *katar* dagger crossed in mock combat on the wall. There were stacks of books, volumes in English, French, German, and Hindi. He was, just shy of his thirtieth birthday, an expert swimmer, a crack soldier, an experienced miner, a world-class chess player, an inventor, an explorer, and a journalist. On this day, he was going to add to his list of accomplishments: he would help pioneer American-style football in the American Midwest, during the birthday celebration of the father of America. Hornsby looked up at the Union Jack draped across his mantel—the irony of his position would not have been lost on him. He unfolded his new football jersey, feeling the rough texture of the blue flannel.

His wife and son, in their Hyde Park house eight miles south of downtown Chicago, remained asleep and unaware.

Hornsby ran his hand across his desk, over a crimped deck of playing cards stacked to the side. These stiff slabs of faded paper had brought him unspeakable pleasure, unbridled rage, and tremendous debt.

Chapter 1

1846: India

Captain Henry Hornsby escorted his two children and his new wife from the oppressively hot boat hold and back to the scorching Indian shore. May is the hottest month in Madras,[1] and twenty-two-year-old Eliza felt the heat more acutely than the others: she was nine months pregnant with her first child, and the weeks-long trek from England would have tested her endurance. She reached out to the wooden pier railing to steady herself, guided by her stepson, Henry Jr. The elder Henry strode ahead, giving orders to the servants who had met the boat. Eliza was minutes away from going into labor, and hours from giving birth to her son Augustus.

Augustus Henry Hornsby's parents were both English, and their families had strong ties to India. Britain had controlled India since the late 1700s; for nearly all of that time, the Hornsby and Frend families had been a part of the colonizing forces.

Hornsby's mother, Eliza Frend Hornsby, was raised in England, South Africa, and Madras (now Chennai), India. Her father, John Frend, commanded the British 55th Regiment in Grinqualand West, South Africa, before that territory's annexation by the English. Frend took his family to India, and eventually both he and his wife died in India of cholera, orphaning their nine children.

Hornsby's father, Henry, had been stationed in India since the early 1820s. By 1824, Henry Hornsby was a lieutenant in the 2nd Battalion, 8th Regiment in Madras. He married young, and his first wife (the daughter of a royal artillery captain)[2] died in England in 1840, after the couple had two children together. Henry married Eliza within a year.

Madras was a vital city for the British, and the army maintained a garrison a few miles away. Ringed by palm trees, the old sprawling fort was imposing: stone walls more than twenty feet tall and two feet thick protected the soldiers, their barracks, a depot, and a hospital.

Much of Henry's job required him to keep the peace between the British civilians, soldiers, and the residents of the city, and he resented a great deal of it. The army required soldiers to take part in local religious festivals, marching in processions, and some refused outright.[3] Cultural and racial tensions inflamed already-uneasy relations between Indians and British in the city, and the Hornsbys' views were shaped by this dynamic.

Henry was ambitious and aggressive. He rose in the Madras army and, by 1838, made captain. That same year, the army convicted him of assaulting the territory's magistrate, throwing the man bodily backward and breaking his collarbone. The cause of the fight seems to have been a dispute over the right to use a sidewalk in front of the small garden next to the military hospital. Henry not only threw the magistrate to the ground, but he also challenged the injured man to a duel. The court found Henry guilty of assault and the threat to duel, but fined him only 200 rupees, noting that the magistrate had insulted Henry, after all, when Henry objected to the man using the sidewalk.[4]

Henry, his two children, and Eliza returned to England in the summer of 1845, when he was captain of the 2nd European Light Infantry. During the following spring, he was recalled to Madras. Eliza was eight months pregnant with the couple's first child by then. The family had relatives in Dublin, and Eliza could have made the easier trip to Ireland to have her child. Instead, all four of the family returned to India.

Augustus Hornsby, like his parents, shuttled between India and England, but he spent most of his youth in central and eastern India, inseparable from his younger brother, Raymond. Augustus's older half-brother, Henry Jr., was eleven years older and practically belonged to another generation. Raymond, however, was born just two years after Augustus. Not as popular as the gregarious Henry, nor as mischievous as Arthur, who would be born in 1852, Raymond was, by Augustus's admission, his favorite brother.[5] Together, they learned to speak a smattering of Tamil—at least, its local vernacular—and association-style kicking football from other English children stationed there.

• • •

The family stayed in a house in Tamil Nadu that belonged to a colleague,[6] a vast stone manor with a long veranda overlooking a glen. Augustus, nicknamed Gus, enjoyed running through the house's great hall, sliding across the spacious dining room with its polished teak floor. In one corner of the great room, Henry Hornsby displayed rows of mounted animals—"Forest, hill side, and glen teemed with animal life, and my father was master of all the arts of killing them," Gus wrote as an adult.[7]

When he was five, Gus walked into the great room with little Raymond in tow. His father was putting stuffed birds into an expansive glass case, part of Henry's taxidermy zoo. Gus looked out the window. Coming from the glen, a bear lumbered through the yard, moving slowly toward the manor's walkway.

"A bear, father," Gus whispered. Hornsby later wrote,

> my father finished putting up the birds, then took down his heavy Westley-Richards smooth bore, put in powder and pushed home a greasy patched ball into each barrel. Meanwhile, the bear had commenced feeding; my father placed the gun on the low sill of the open window, knelt and took a sight, then whispered "Would you like to shoot him?"
>
> Need I describe my feelings, or tell my answer, that fell with trembling whispered eagerness on the still air? "Keep quiet, don't be excited, and pull the trigger when I say pull." He steadied the gun with his left hand.... I waited; it seemed a long time coming; my heart beat and my finger quivered on the trigger. At last—and I pulled. My father sprang up gun in hand, but the bear was dead. The steady hand and eye of the trained sportsman had guided the muzzle upwards in the correct line, and given me a certainty.[8]

• • •

In 1854, Henry Hornsby's ambitions seemed to have paid off. Now a major, he was named deputy judge advocate general and began traveling

Eliza Hornsby (sitting, right) and her children in a photograph taken in the mid–1860s. Augustus is sitting on the desk, holding an open book. Arthur is standing, holding a hat. Their older brother Henry stands between them (courtesy Hugh Evans).

throughout the territory. By the end of the year, he was promoted again, to lieutenant colonel. He soon came down with fever but continued to travel and lead his regiment. In early January, the illness outpaced his aggression, and he died in Vizianagaram. Henry Hornsby was fifty-two years old. Gus was eight.

Eliza took the family to Dublin, where fever quickly claimed Hornsby's younger sister, Rachel.[9] Soon after this, India revolted against British occupation, and Henry Hornsby, Jr., Gus's older half-brother, rejoined his regiment in India.

With Henry's departure, Eliza stayed in Dublin with her five younger remaining children and stepchild. The family lived in a spacious townhome in the suburb of Monkstown, just a few blocks from the Dublin Bay shore. Though grieving for Rachel and still coping with the loss of her husband, Eliza did not need to worry about money—her family had resources. And Gus was about to come into a bit of good fortune, an opportunity that would profoundly affect the course of his life.

• • •

In 1858 Wellington College informed Eliza that it had accepted Gus into its founding class. Queen Victoria had helped launch the new public school, initially founded as an elite school for boys of English officers who had died. The campus, just north of Sandhurst, was still wrapping up construction when Eliza took Augustus there in January 1859.

The day of Wellington's opening, January 20, "was as miserable as a winter day could be, sunless, with a steady drizzle intermitted by showers," Hornsby recalled years later:

> The day made the journey into the unknown a dismal hazard, whether you arrived at the little station three quarters of a mile away across the dreary sodden moor, or strove to arrive by vehicle from the nearest towns of Sandhurst and Wolkingham.
>
> Arriving, my mother and I knocked at a door and entered into the presence of Edward White Benson, first head master of Wellington College, afterwards Archbishop of Canterbury, who was then a young man of about thirty, promoted from a mastership at Rugby. A very pleasant voice greeted us as he rose and invited us to be seated. While my mother answered some necessary questions, I took stock of the man ... my future guide, hated enemy, and subsequent very good friend.
>
> Wellington was, I believe, the first and, as far as I know, only school in which every boy had his individual undivided "castle." My dormitory cubicle was about eight feet square, with partitions about eight feet high, open to the front and sides. In it were a single iron bed, comfortably equipped, a desk of painted deal* with shelves and a washstand with necessaries. A single window,

---

* Here, deal refers to pinewood.

single gas jet above the desk, a perforated banquette [a window with a seat, under which there was a heating duct] admitting a well-appreciated gush of air completed my "home."

After my mother had left in the cab that took her back to Sandhurst, I returned to my dormitory. There we answered to our names and became the first fruits of that nurturing mother whose boys have since borne themselves all over the world, even to the uttermost parts.

Then to the great dining hall. There we had supper of bread and butter, cheese and very good small beer, an unstinted meal, as was every other served there.[10]

Hornsby's first full day at the school was, in his words, "startling and weird."[11] His second day began with an even stranger encounter. A visiting instructor approached Hornsby and several other boys in the courtyard and told Hornsby to "give me a back." The man was middle-aged, "lip and chin shaven, showing a very jolly mouth; he wore a black frock coat and top hat."[12] Hornsby bent down, and the man immediately leaped over him, beginning a spontaneous, vigorous game of leapfrog with the dozen or so boys who had gathered. The teacher introduced himself as Charles Kingsley, a visiting rector from Eversley, a couple of miles west of the school.

Kingsley was the author of *Westward Ho!* (he later wrote *The Water-Babies*, the book for which he is now best known), a renowned scholar, and a progressive priest.[13] He was also an unwavering advocate for physical fitness, and one of his goals at the new school was to rouse the boys into habits of exercise and competitive sportsmanship. As he greeted the boys in the courtyard, Kingsley introduced them to another visiting teacher, Frederick Temple, the headmaster of Rugby School. After the introductions, Kingsley jokingly swore Temple to secrecy, forbidding him to tell the Wellington staff about Kingsley's leapfrog antics.[14]

• • •

Frederick Temple was a scholar who had just become Rugby's headmaster after he was recommended to the post by English poet Matthew Arnold. Arnold himself was the son of another Rugby headmaster, the renowned historian Thomas Arnold. The elder Arnold took Rugby's headmaster position in 1828, and he presided over the school during the period when the game of rugby was becoming popular and more structured. Arnold's work reforming education at Rugby helped to propagate its methods and traditions to other schools and contributed to the spread of rugby football throughout the region.

Thomas Arnold and his contribution to rugby would be immortalized in *Tom Brown's School Days*, a book that had a significant influence on Harry Potter author J.K. Rowling. There is some evidence that Arnold, as the benevolent headmaster of Rugby, served as one of the inspirations for Rowling's Dumbledore.[15]

Temple's work at Rugby included reforming several of the school's hallowed sports traditions, which irritated some of the school's more conservative alumni and staff. However, one novel tradition of the school made a lasting impression on him: the school's unique brand of football, which had its legendary genesis in the early 1820s. As opposed to the rough-and-tumble all-kicking style of football that would eventually morph into association football and, still later, modern soccer, the rugby style involved running with the ball and scoring tries and goals. The school's students had played primitive forms of kicking-style football for decades. In 1823, however, the students added their distinctive twist. As football historian Parke Davis described it in 1911:

> Over a hundred boys had gathered.... The game was in action and backward and forward surged the ball, but without a score. The time wore on until at last the school-bell trembled on the stroke of five, the hour which terminated the game. A long sailing punt was sent down the field, the last effort of one side to effect a score. Suddenly out from the mass of players upon the other side sprang a young Rugbeian by the name of William Webb Ellis. With arms outstretched and eyes keenly on the spinning ball he swiftly ranged into position to catch the punt.... With the ball tightly held beneath his arm, he dashes into the ranks of his opponents, who, angered by this flagrant violation of the rules, roughly seize him and endeavor to throw him to the ground.[16]

Initially dismissed as a foolish foul, Ellis's run later inspired the students to craft the new game.

• • •

Temple shared the Rugby School's game with Kingsley, and together they shared rugby football with the new students at Wellington College. Hornsby was thrilled to learn rugby directly from the headmaster of Rugby School. "Most of us took to rugby football as naturally as a duck to water,"[17] he later noted. The football field at Wellington was makeshift and roughly plowed, but the students made do with the conditions.

Kingsley also introduced the students to paper chases, the children's game of chasing one person, typically through a large, wooded area, as the child who was "it" leaves a small trail of paper bits. Hornsby also loved this game, calling it "a factor in the making of manhood."[18] Hornsby, still dressed in his blue sack coat and plaid uniform trousers, a blue and red hat sporting the crown emblem of the school, raced through the nearby woods, his hands full of shredded paper. He was so far ahead he could not hear the other students, but he knew they were in the woods, searching for the paper trail that he was—not too judiciously—leaving for them.

Hornsby sprinted through the mossy patchwork of weeds and branches, happily sprinkling too much paper behind him, then scrambling into a bush, dirty, panting, and pleased in the certainty that he had eluded his inferiors.

• • •

Hornsby recalled his time at Wellington with fondness for the rest of his life. He was particularly proud of having met Queen Victoria, who visited the school during its first year. He was an adept and successful student, and he saw himself as belonging among the top of the students, even at Wellington: at thirteen, he was named a prefect, one of the youngest at the school.[19]

At Wellington, Hornsby began to play chess competitively. He became a passionate, nearly obsessive player, and he took that enthusiasm for the game with him for the rest of his life, occasionally playing professionally. The strategy of chess, situating the game's various pieces, each with its unique strengths and peculiar advantages, mirrored the excitement that football would later give Hornsby. For him, football was another kind of chess match, with endurance and tactics layered exquisitely on the strategic framework.

At the beginning of his competitive chess career, Hornsby started to challenge older students at Wellington and even the staff. When he was sixteen, Hornsby had a chance to play against a true master. Johan Löwenthal, a Hungarian exile, was among the world's leading chess players in the 1850s, during which time he lived and taught in London. In 1862, while Löwenthal was coordinating a tournament, the school invited Hornsby to play the master as one of a group of twenty who would play simultaneously against Löwenthal. Hornsby was among a handful of challengers who achieved a draw.[20] He later wrote that the night he returned to Wellington, he dreamed of the game. In his dream, Hornsby changed one of his moves, winning the game. "Next day I suggested the change and its results to Herr Löwenthal, who gave it careful analysis and pronounced the move sound and forceful of a win as followed out."[21]

• • •

After several pleasant years at Wellington College, Hornsby gained admittance into the Royal Military College at Sandhurst, situated just east of the town and a couple of miles from Wellington. His acceptance here was no surprise: even if he had not been an excellent student at Wellington (and, by surviving accounts, he was[22]), he had the advantage of having an uncle who was governor of the College. Hornsby's aunt had married Sir Harry Jones. Jones was a famous career officer who fought the Americans in New Orleans, participated in the Crimean War, and was eventually wounded in battle in 1855. A year later, he became governor of the College at Sandhurst.

At Sandhurst, Hornsby also found comfort in rugby football, learning additional tactics of the sport while teaching the cadets what he learned from Rugby's headmaster. Sandhurst had organized athletic teams since 1812, one of the earliest—if not the first—schools with structured sports.[23] Rugby became ingrained in the Sandhurst culture, and Hornsby was soon an expert at the game.

Game Day, 9:00 a.m.

Hornsby left his office at the Union House a few minutes after 9:00. He carried his football uniform, bundled under his arm, and a new leather football he purchased for the occasion.[1]

In Chicago, it was just above freezing, warmer than earlier. The sun was still out, but clouds gathered to the west. Hornsby headed east again, toward the Chicago River. To Hornsby's right, the Pittsburgh & Fort Wayne depot continued to belch steam and smoke. Farther south, whistles from the Union Star Line pierced the calm. Hornsby turned and headed north, onto Wells Street, crossing the bridge and walking past a barren steamers' landing on the river. There were no boats; the pier looked deserted. In fifty years, the site would hold the art deco colossus Merchandise Mart, the largest building in the world constructed to that time. In 1876, however, it was the scene of a few boat houses, a dilapidated carriage house hastily built after the Fire, and a mostly vacant lot. Across the river activity increased. Chicago Republicans were taking advantage of the holiday to stage their regional meetings to prepare for the Republican state and national conventions later that year. The party's headquarters was on the corner of Lake and Clark streets. There, the party had constructed a mammoth speaker's platform decked out with bunting, flags, and a large portrait of Washington.[2] They erected a banner, half a block long, that read, "Illinois, Home of Lincoln and Grant." The group planned to close the sessions with a party at the Tremont that night.

Hornsby passed the carriage house and piles of stone and made his way to the Wells Street Station of the Chicago & Northwestern Railway, with plenty of time to spare for the 9:45 train to Evanston. On a weekday morning, most of the passenger traffic headed the other way—dozens of Evanston commuters taking trains to their downtown offices. Most took a pre-dawn train, hauling hand lanterns with them in the dark, leaving the lanterns at Evanston's Davis Street station on a cement ledge, only to collect them in the evening for the walk back to their houses.[3] Some commuters took cabs, but roads from Evanston were still somewhat rough, and a twelve-mile trip by horse and carriage through Chicago and South Evanston was a bit arduous.

Hornsby, along with a handful of others, boarded. Because of the holiday, there were fewer passengers than usual. Most, like Hornsby, were not traveling north for work, but were heading for Washington's birthday festivities, or were taking advantage of the holiday to visit nearby family. Hornsby leaned into the green velvet seat and watched the landscape outside the slowly-moving train shift from stone to wood.

• • •

At Northwestern University, Frank Casseday sat in declamations class in a tiny room in University Hall. Professor Robert Cumnock held court with the junior class. Cumnock's was among the most popular courses at Northwestern, particularly with the women students.[4] Casseday's devotion to Cumnock and elocution, combined with his friendship with feminist leader Frances Willard, placed him in an unusual position for a male student in the 1870s. Casseday's upbringing, combined with his views on women's issues, gave him a perspective that was relatively progressive.

Northwestern was founded in 1851, but it had only been open to students since 1855. It took the bold step of admitting women in 1869. At the same time, the Evanston College for Ladies, located in a building on the outskirts of Northwestern's campus, was run by Willard. Willard became Northwestern's first dean of women and taught philosophy and other classes. In 1874, Willard left to devote herself to the temperance movement, but by then women were becoming an integral part of Northwestern life—academic and social. Some of the male students, however, were still flummoxed by the presence of women on campus. "The young ladies who intimidated a certain bashful senior," a note released on campus earlier that week admitted, "are very sorry, and they have promised not to chew gum at him anymore."[5]

Northwestern was proud of its newly open policy on admissions and campus diversity, going so far as to claim in its 1876 catalog for admission, **"The University recognizes neither sex nor race**. It asks the candidate, 'What do you know?'" (emphasis and italics are the university's).[6] While the sentiment was commendable, the school had not yet put it into full practice. The student body by 1876 had but a handful of women, and no minorities at all. Years later, Frank described the surprise the Northwestern baseball team felt in 1876 when one of their opposing teams turned out to be all–Black:

> Another time a [team of] nine composed of colored boys appeared in Evanston to play with us by appointment. When the arrangement was made by mail we did not know they were negroes. But we never played with a more gentlemanly

set of boys. They simply played ball and said nothing. They left us in a dazed condition, wondering what had happened to us.[7]

Northwestern brought in its first Black football player in 1893, when George Jewett transferred from the University of Michigan to Northwestern. Jewett, the first Black player for any Big Ten university (and the second-ever Black player at a historically White American college[8]), earned his medical degree from Northwestern, as well as his football letter—the school's first to a Black athlete.[9] In the 1870s, however, Black athletes were a head-turning novelty.

• • •

Simon Douthart was another Northwestern junior who would play in the game that afternoon, although he did not know it that morning. Douthart took Professor Cumnock's declamations class alongside Frank Casseday, but Douthart was considerably older than Frank. A blond farmboy who stood nearly a foot taller than most of his colleagues, Douthart had served in the 45th Iowa Regiment in the Civil War.[10] According to Douthart's recollection, which he wrote decades later, he guarded rail bridges near the battlefields, "and I saw the wounded being brought back lying on the floor of box cars, with the blood dripping from the cars. The military fever left me, and I afterwards belonged to the Peace party, not at any price, but war as a last resort."[11] Douthart was not planning to participate in the afternoon's football game, despite being larger and stronger than most of the other students. On the previous Saturday evening, Douthart had wrestled Walter Lee Brown, another member of the new Northwestern football team, inside of the school's new gymnasium. The match drew a large crowd; it was one of the first events for the recently opened gym. Douthart easily won.[12]

Douthart presented his oration to Cumnock's class, a speech he had prepared meticulously. The day after his wrestling victory, Douthart had hastily written a presentation for Sunday chapel exercises, at Professor Cumnock's request. Afterward, Cumnock took Douthart aside to let him know that "as an oration the effort was a failure, but as a vaudeville it was a success."[13] Simon wanted to be sure not to repeat his vaudeville triumph in front of the class.

Frank was Cumnock's star pupil in 1876. In January, he had won Northwestern's Mann Prize, given to the best orator in the university.[14] However, Frank was not paying attention to this morning's speeches. He was preoccupied with the upcoming football game, having removed the slip of paper from his pocket and surreptitiously inspecting the East Coast football rules again.

Compared to the virtually rule-free kicking game he had previously played, this version of football was a labyrinth of rules. The sheet was titled "Concessionary Rules." Concessionary to what? Frank had to have wondered.

• • •

Football's Concessionary Rules

The November 1875 Concessionary Rules brought together the rugby style of play favored by Harvard and Canadian schools with elements of the association game played by the other schools. Yale initially preferred the more soccer-oriented game, but the school's administration stymied its influence. The faculty ruled that Yale could only play home games.[15] With no chance to play on the road, Yale could not showcase its kicking-only version of the game, and American football took on a rugby-heavy dynamic. Princeton, one of the first college football teams in America, switched its style to that of Harvard later in 1876, and Yale followed suit.

Harvard and Yale drew up the Concessionary Rules as a compromise due to the teams' different football styles. The rules mix association football and traditional rugby into what became the foundation for American football.[16] These rules are vital to understanding how schools like Harvard and Yale were developing the game, and the state of the sport on the East Coast at the end of 1875:

CONCESSIONARY RULES.
- I. The grounds shall not be more than 400 feet nor less than 300 feet long, and one half the length in width.
- II. The goal-posts shall be 20 feet apart.
- III. The number [of players] for match games shall not exceed 15 nor be less than 11.
- IV. Time of game shall be left to the discretion of the captains, but shall in no case exceed two hours, and that side shall be declared victor which, at the end of the allotted time, shall have secured the majority of goals. To secure a goal the ball must pass between the goal-posts and over a cross line 10 feet high.
- V. After a goal has been won sides shall be changed and the losing side shall kick off. In the event of no goal being won at the lapse of half an hour, ends shall be changed.
- VI. The ball may be caught on the bounce or fly, and carried; the player, so carrying the ball, may be tackled or shouldered, but not hacked, throttled, or pummeled. No player may be held unless he be in actual possession of the ball. No batting with the hands is allowed.
- VII. When the ball passes out of bounds the player first touching it shall

advance to the point where the ball went out and throw it in at right angles to the line.
VIII. Every player is on-side, but is put off-side if he enters a scrimmage, upon his opponents' side, or, being in a scrimmage, gets in front of the ball, or when the ball has been kicked, touched, or is being run with by any of his own side behind him (that is, between himself and his goal line). Every player when off-side is out of the game, and shall not touch the ball in any case whatever, or in any way obstruct or interrupt any player until he is on-side.
IX. A player being off-side is put on-side when the ball has been kicked by, or has touched the dress or person of any one of the opposite side, or when one of his own side has run in front of him either with the ball or having kicked it when behind him.
X. In kick-offs, the winners of the toss shall have the choice of side or kick-off. The ball must be fairly kicked, not babied, from a point—(to be decided by the captain).
XI. Until the ball is kicked off no player shall be in advance of a line parallel to the line of his goal and distant from it (to be decided by the captains).
XII. The two judges and a referee shall be determined upon by the two captains of the contesting sides.
XIII. In match games a No. 6 ball shall be used, furnished by the challenging side and becoming the property of the victor.
XIV. The ball cannot be taken from off the ground except for a kick, and it must be kicked from the point where it was taken from the ground.
XV. No hacking, throttling, tripping up, or striking shall be allowed under any circumstances. No one shall be allowed to wear projecting nails, metal plates, or gutta-percha on any part of his shoes.
XVI. In case of foul the referee shall throw the ball perpendicularly into the air to a height of at least 12 feet from the place where the foul occurred, and the ball shall not be in play until the ball has touched the ground. On continued transgression of these rules by any player, the side to which he belongs shall lose him.[17]

• • •

The winning team was the one with the most goals, scored by kicking the ball between the uprights. But the ball could also be carried, and a player running with the ball could be tackled, "but not hacked, throttled, or pummeled." Well, that was good to know: no pummeling. Also, there was to be "no hacking, throttling, tripping up, or striking," and players' shoes could not contain "projecting nails, metal plates, or gutta-percha." Frank likely wondered: just what kind of football were they used to playing on the East Coast?

Despite what the players from Chicago had told Frank, the "Concessionary Rules" said nothing about touchdowns, which somehow counted in the game, but did not determine the game's winner. The object, the

Chicago players had told the students, was to carry the ball past the opponent's goal, scoring a touchdown, which would give the scoring team a better chance at kicking a goal.

Frank, still confused, repocketed the paper. This sport was nothing like what he had played as a child, and even less like the association football game the Northwestern students had been playing on campus informally since before he arrived. He would discover soon enough the dynamics of the new sport.

CHAPTER 2

1866: Madras

After his time at Sandhurst, Hornsby received a commission as an ensign in the British army and, in March 1866, prepared to be sent back to India to join his brother, Henry. Gus returned to Madras that spring as a member of the 102nd Regiment.[1]

The 102nd Regiment of Foot was a recent addition to the British army proper, having transitioned from the Honorable East India Company four years before. Already a member of the 102nd, Henry had fought against the Indian rebellion the year after Gus left with his mother for Dublin. An orderly officer who saw battle nearly constantly for two years, Henry received a medal with two clasps and a promotion to captain, serving under General Sir Robert Vivian, colonel of the Royal Madras Fusiliers. The Hornsby brothers' colonel was well known for his military exploits, having fought in the 1824 Burmese War and surviving appalling injuries at Rangoon. During Vivian's service in Crimea, he organized and led 20,000 Turkish soldiers.[2] The 102nd, however, had not engaged in combat since 1857.

The only guns that Hornsby fired during his time in eastern India, however, were in pursuit of game. For the next four years Hornsby explored and hunted throughout the region with Henry, enjoying the privileges of the British officer class. The brothers traveled with an entire team of local guides, drivers, and gun and cargo bearers.

Soon after his arrival, Gus Hornsby and his brother embarked on a bison hunt in the Dinah Valley.[3] That morning, the brothers walked through the valley's pass with their carriers, including one who carried the men's breakfast in a sacked bundle on his head. One of their escorts, a British forest ranger, told them about a tiger that had been terrorizing the local village. The ranger amused Gus Hornsby, who considered him a "non-shooter, particularly compared to two such violent destroyers as his guests were."[4] The brothers set off immediately to track down the tiger. They moved toward the village, watching out for the tiger. Midway there, the group found a heifer, dead for some time, with its throat torn out. Gus and Henry decided to hide nearby and wait for the tiger. Henry reasoned that the tiger would return to feast again on the animal.

"Let's come back at sunset. The tiger's not likely to come before then," Henry offered, and the ranger agreed.[5] Gus was against the plan, wanting to keep constant watch on the heifer instead. Henry walked away from his younger brother and shouted over his shoulder, "Well, you pig-headed little brute, you may stay if you like, but we are off."[6] Gus found a tree about forty yards from the dead animal and climbed up with his carrier, watching his brother and the ranger walk to the village.

Early that afternoon, Gus drifted in and out of consciousness on his perch, drowsy from the heat. Gus's carrier spotted the tiger first, gently prodding Gus and pointing to the tiger's head, moving from the bushes nearby. Gus raised his twelve-bore rifle and took aim, but he rustled the branch as he did so. The tiger, slinking toward the heifer, froze and stared at the tree. Gus fired, and the tiger dropped at once. "Every sportsman knows the keen pleasure and tingling excitement of 'my first' anything worth capturing, or killing, so I need not dilate upon my feelings," he later wrote.[7]

The tiger hunt had thrilled Hornsby, but he was most excited at the prospect of hunting wild boar, or—as the Indians and officers called the practice—"pigsticking." The men went into the hunt on horseback and attempted to take down the animals with a boar spear rather than a gun. "There are few sports, if any, that can rival that of 'pig-sticking,' for excitement or danger," Hornsby later wrote. "That which must be most like to it [in America] is a wild rush among the buffaloes of the western wilderness; but of this sport I have not yet tasted, though my hopes are that I may get far enough west to have just one dash at the ponderous game."[8] Hornsby gave a detailed account of his pigsticking adventure several years later in the magazine *Chicago Field*:

> Long before dawn of the eventful day, H---- [his brother Henry; Gus Hornsby wrote anonymously], Jack P----, and myself were jogging along through the crisp frosty air on borrowed "hacks." Shortly we were overtaken by P----a and P----n, two mighty hunters of the artillery, and betimes arrived in camp to find 15 men already gathered under the mangoe trees of the hunt bungalow compound.
>
> Every eye was on P----a; "now gentlemen," and eighteen horsemen dashed out of cover with a wild whoop, the last of the herd had a good 300 yards start, and the course of the nearest jungles was about four miles. J---- on his English mare took the lead across the level field in front of us.... I found myself among the first flight over the ravine into the sieve-like black soil. At first I gained very little, but I did gain and knew that this was good work, for a wild pig gets away over the first half mile at a terrific pace, but when pressed hard, tires.
>
> The moment I had cleared the black soil and landed on some solid stuff beyond, I drove in the spurs, shouted to Paul [Hornsby's horse], and raced up

to Mr. Pig in fine style, but when half way across, I became aware of a horseman close behind, again I pricked my Paul, but we got the go-by from S---- on his $1,250 Arab. I now took a pull at Paul, as I saw S---- must beat me in the run up, which he did, the pig swerving right across his front sent him and horse into a clear somersault, whilst I let Paul out again after the now panting pig.

We soon closed on him, and he jinked again, but Paul showed himself an old hand, for, open mouthed, he swerved with the pig, nearly unseating me and causing me to lose the chance of spearing the game, but Paul stuck close to him, and on the pig jinking again, I drove my spear in between his ribs turning him right over with the impetus of our rush, but it did not finish him. He was on his legs in an instant, but P----n coming up at this moment, gave him the finishing touch just between his shoulders.[9]

The English hunters did not traipse through India, however, without casualties. Hornsby's colleague, whom he identifies in the pigsticking hunt only as "S----," died just two weeks later. Hornsby later revealed S---- as Frank Sharkwell.[10] Henry Hornsby, Sharkwell, and several other officers again joined in a hunt for a tiger. They didn't find a tiger, but they managed to rouse a nearby panther, which struck out at Sharkwell before the officer could fire his weapon. The panther sank its jaws onto Sharkwell's leg, flinging him nearly eighteen feet. As Sharkwell again tried to shoot the panther, the cat pounced onto him and mauled him before the rest of the party could kill it. Sharkwell suffered fifty-six separate wounds to his arms, chest, and legs, and died later that night.[11]

Another of Hornsby's colleagues, titled "G----," accompanied him on a quail hunt and misfired his gun, shooting into a crowd of people and taking out the eye of an elderly woman. What followed demonstrated the contempt with which Hornsby and his peers treated the local Indian communities at the time. The woman clutched at her eye, shrieking, as the crowd around her, appalled, shouted at the pair. "G---- was in a great way," Hornsby wrote at the time, more concerned for his colleague than the woman he had shot. "He did not know the best salve for the injury; I did. 'Give her five rupees' ($2.50), I remarked, 'and send her up to the dispensary. If there is any serious harm beyond the loss of her eye you can see to it afterwards.' G---- accepted the situation, dived into his pockets for coin, and changed the wailing of the crowd into jubilant exclamations of 'Thank you, oh, Protector of the poor!' Each old woman of that crowd would have had an eye knocked out for that sum."[12]

• • •

Hornsby continued to play rugby, teaching his fellow officers the differences between the sport and the loose version of association football they'd grown up with, and playing it continuously with makeshift teams he developed throughout eastern India. Hornsby's athletic abilities brought him the respect of his unit. He later claimed that he could run a mile in four minutes and thirty-two seconds and had achieved a broad jump of nineteen feet and two inches.[13] These claims are suspect, and Hornsby enjoyed puffing up the stories of his athletic talent.

Typical of Hornsby's self-aggrandizement is the following passage he wrote in 1875, in which he recounts an 1868 bet he accepted to run a mile in under five minutes. In this brief column, he succeeds in displaying his callousness to Indians, letting his self-image run wild, and providing the reader with a taste of the gambling culture that was rampant in the army:

> In 1868 there was very considerable amount of athletics going on all over India, and even this has since been accelerated by the introduction and popularization of foot-ball, of all games the most arduous in a hot climate like that of India. Foot-ball is well enough in the winter in the high lands of the interior, where in the early morning the thermometer is down below the forties of Fahrenheit, but at the coast stations it surely requires pluck and abundant vitality.
>
> My object now, however, is not to write a regular dissertation on athletics, but to relate to my readers one incident in particular which will show first the ability of the European to stand the climate:
>
> My regiment was quartered in Lucknow.... At that time I happened to be doing some training to get myself into better than my usual very good trim, to run in the open mile race at the—Lancer's sports—not to win the prize, as it was only open to the men of the garrison—but to tally first past the post, if possible, for my regiment. It was at this period that another regiment arrived in Lucknow, and, according to military etiquette, its officers were invited to dine *en masse* with us.... The evening arrived, our table groaned with silver plate and candelabra. Our sideboards glistened with silver plate and fine glass; all displayed to impress the "enemy" with our style.
>
> [During the dinner], I received a note scrawled on the back of a bill of fare: "They want to bet I cannot name a man to run a mile in five minutes; what do you say? Yours, B----"
>
> Elated perhaps by the good wine, which as a rule I seldom tasted, I scrawled a hasty answer: "All right: I'll do it to-night, if they want it. Yours, -----"
>
> B---- said, "Very well, gentlemen, I will bet you what you please, when the cloth is off the table." This proviso was necessary, as according to military mess etiquette as adopted by most regiments, no bets can be made till the [table] cloth has been removed.... The moment this proviso was complied with, and the cloth had been removed, the betting began, and I received a reply from B: "We are on for 11:30 to-night; shall I put on anything for you?" I answered: "Fifty will do." I went straight home and made my boy rub me down with a flesh brush from head to heel, to set me into a good glow and lay down at once, having given orders for my Jersey running drawers and shoes to be ready by 11:15, at which hour I should be called for a bath. I had an hour and a quarter for digestion, and as I had eaten sparingly I had only to work off the effects of the wine, and this I hoped the cold bath would do.

Chapter 2. 1866: Madras

I lay quietly awake till my boy came to call me, then sprang up and into my bath-room and poured four vases of cold water over my head. I was dried, and again rubbed down with the flesh brush, and slipped on my running gear. B— met and asked me how I felt. "All right," was my reply. "Can you do it, for we have put the pot on quite strong, and between us stand to win or lose over 800 rupees."

"Never fear; put on another fifty for me and as much more for yourself as you please." Several buggies were on the ground, and in one the judge and referee took post with a chronograph and huge dark lantern. The moon shone clear, the road lay white and clear before me, and the narrow strip of grass between the road and the riding track was smooth and springy.

I went very slowly at first to gain my wind, and quickened up after going half a mile. B—'s voice was heard, "Too slow!" At this I let out like a hound from a leash, feeling full of running; faster I flew, and faster, till I caught sight of the little crowd standing on the white road, and then I let out my last reef and rattled in the last 100 yards just as fast as I could go. The judge had to gallop his nag, and as I dashed past the post cried out "4:57." B made me drink a pint of champagne, and I was carried home to bed on the shoulders of a dozen enthusiastic winners and losers.[14]

• • •

Hornsby's skill at chess continued to improve. He eventually beat all comers and was the unofficial champion of the regiment. He later claimed that from 1868 to 1870 he regularly visited the local Indian ruler, the Nawab of Awadh, and played chess with him.[15]

Hornsby's passion for sports and games extended to other table games, and with this obsession came his other, more insidious compulsion: gambling. Hornsby was soon betting on games of *teen patti* and American-style poker (a variant that had not yet been introduced to Europe), occasionally getting into serious debt. He considered himself an expert at most games, and he tended to underestimate anyone around him. The combination, taken with his love of gambling, led Hornsby to repeated financial crises.

By early 1869, Hornsby's gambling debts had become severe, and he cast about for a quick way to get money. He found it with a horse race in northern India. Hornsby had earlier purchased a horse, Grey-Friar, which was not qualified for the race—it was over the height limit.[16] As Hornsby, his brother Henry, and a friend named Jock walked from the stables, Hornsby thought of a scheme.

"I've got it," Hornsby shouted.

"The devil you have," his brother replied,[17] and Hornsby explained his plan. Grey-Friar would be a favorite in the race; it would have a distinct advantage. However, Hornsby knew that other racers would protest the horse, and it would likely be disqualified after the race. Jock, whose own horse, Lamplighter, was qualified for the race, would likely be a longshot. Hornsby would ride Grey-Friar himself and throw the race.

The plan started well. As expected, Lamplighter was down in the pack when the odds were released, at 13–3 against. A horse named Orion was the favorite, with Grey-Friar close behind. Other riders initially protested Hornsby's horse, but he defended it. The three men pooled their remaining money.

Hornsby rode the horse hard, digging in his spurs to give it "a rib-warmer."[18] He took an early lead, and proceeded to block the other horses except for Jock's, which took advantage of Grey-Friar's path. Hornsby, seeing Lamplighter close in, pulled up to slow the other horses. However, the plan almost fell apart at that point: Grey-Friar's sudden swerve came close to spooking Lamplighter, which veered hard to the right and nearly off the track, slamming Jock's right leg into the judge's box. Grey-Friar took first, with Lamplighter in second.

As expected, the event's judges disqualified Grey-Friar for its unfair advantage, and Jock's horse won—providing the group with ill-gotten winnings of over $3,000.[19]

• • •

Gus Hornsby's conscience might not have bothered him outright over the horse racing and other scams. However, he was becoming increasingly anxious in the summer of 1869 and began having sleepless nights and bouts of indigestion.[20] He had disturbing dreams, culminating in an otherwise sleepless, hot evening in August, when Hornsby was visited in a dream by his beloved brother Raymond. Raymond, like Hornsby, had gone to Sandhurst's academy and had joined the army.[21] Since 1868 he had been stationed in the West Indies. Now, as Gus dreamed while lying in his bed in India, Raymond silently walked toward the bed and passed through the gauzy mosquito netting that surrounded it.[22] He was dressed in full uniform, crisp, flawless. He put a white-gloved hand to Gus's forehead and looked into his eyes, smiled, and vanished. Gus woke to find the room still dark, the white netting undisturbed.[23] Three weeks later, Gus learned that his brother had died in August in Nassau; the cause of Raymond's death was not known. He was twenty-one years old.[24] Gus was convinced that Raymond died at the same moment that his apparition visited him in his dream.

• • •

After nearly four years in Madras, Hornsby rose to lieutenant. His rugby teams flourished across the region,[25] and his reputation for both rugby and chess grew. By 1870, Hornsby could speak and write five

Chapter 2. 1866: Madras

languages in addition to English: French and German, which he learned at Wellington, and now Hindi, Tamil, and Telugu.[26]

In 1870 the entire 102nd Regiment left India for a tour that ended in England—the regiment was permanently reassigned to home service.[27] Hornsby and his brother packed and, in February, set out with 1,664 other soldiers and sailors aboard the troopship *Serapis*. The *Serapis* was a new ship, a massive, three-masted iron screw beast with an iron hull and a gigantic, four-cylinder engine. They first stopped in Alexandria. Despite the stay lasting only a few days, Hornsby quickly formed another rugby team and began teaching local sailors the game.

After a brief stay in Malta, the *Serapis* landed in Portsmouth on March 25. The *Serapis*'s captain was John Stoady, a forty-two-year-old experienced seaman from a long line of naval officers. Stoady had captained the *Serapis* since her launch, but this voyage was his last as captain, and he was eager to finish the trip and return to England, making as much haste as possible.

The regiment's final call, Aldershot, was just a little over thirty miles away from Portsmouth. Aldershot was a major military base southwest of London, and Hornsby spent the next year at the base, stationed in its North Camp. Sprawling through a vast, treeless field, the camp consisted of a few permanent structures: offices, officers' quarters, a hospital, and other buildings. Far more numerous were the soldiers' barracks, seemingly endless rows of tents and simple wood frame housing, all painted stark white. The forest of barracks was bisected by Centre Road, the broad, main thoroughfare through the camp. Aldershot was efficient, clean, and bustling, but aesthetically offered a bland and grim smear on an already-depressing swath of featureless English countryside.

In December, Hornsby learned that England was trying to field a national football team to play Scotland using rugby rules, rather than the common association rules. He applied to join. In March 1871, the teams met at Academical Cricket Club in Edinburgh.[28] The English team wore all-white uniforms and sported the team's red rose for the first time. Over 4,000 people attended the game, the first-ever international rugby match. Scotland won, having scored a goal and a try to England's single try. According to an interview with Hornsby in 1909, he had joined the team in 1870 and participated in the 1871 match,[29] even though his name does not appear in contemporary reports of the game nor in historical lists of the team members. This is not surprising. Hornsby often enjoyed embellishing his accomplishments and historical importance. It is certainly possible that Hornsby did make the twenty-man squad for England and was accidentally left off the surviving lists; however, it is just as likely that Hornsby was at the game as a backup and never took the field.

Whether or not he played in that initial rugby game against Scotland, Hornsby definitely played in a series of rugby matches across England while quartered at Aldershot's North Camp.

In October 1871, Hornsby returned to Wellington and played as an alumnus alongside the current Wellington players.[30] As an O.W. ("Old Wellington"), Hornsby played several games throughout the month. The school divided its players into various teams, including Mathematical and Classical, which accepted aid from Hornsby and a few other O.W.s. In the climactic game on November 10, Hornsby made a fair catch in front of the Mathematical goal but was unsuccessful in the place. The game ended with a goal and three tries by Mathematical to zero by Classical.[31]

• • •

In November 1871, Hornsby journeyed with part of the regiment one last time. The army briefly stationed him in South Africa, coincidentally in the same region where his grandfather had commanded Britain's 55th Regiment nearly a half-century earlier. There Hornsby tried his hand at diamond mining. His search for fortune had become overriding by this time, and Hornsby saw South Africa as a sure bet.

Just five years prior, a teenage boy found a diamond near Hopetown, South Africa. By 1870 miners had found diamonds in several sites, and a series of rushes took off. The De Beers mine began in May 1871,[32] and in July a mine began at New Rush (later called the Big Hole; the Big Hole, it was claimed, was the largest hole on Earth dug by hand[33]), in the center of the country. Hornsby was one of the first miners to stake a claim at New Rush, among a group that swelled to over 50,000 during the following forty years.[34]

Hornsby decided to dive fully into his mining prospect. He asked for, and was granted, a leave of absence from his regiment and became a full-time miner.[35] He didn't have many funds, but he managed to cover the $130 needed to begin his venture: $90 for equipment and $40 required to pay a team of eight Zulus to help him dig.[36]

"Do men make fortunes [in South Africa] now by digging?" Hornsby later wrote.[37] "Yes! Eight months ago the finest stone of 288¼ carats was turned out at Waldeck's Plant for which $125,000 was refused. Shortly after at New Rush, one man found within ten days, three large and handsome stones, which together weighed over 300 carats, and were worth about $100,000. Will such strokes as that satisfy the greedy, or need I tell of men who have in four or five years amassed sums from 100,000 to 500,000 dollars by digging?" The idea of a large sum of money, easily and quickly made, must have been an irresistible lure for Hornsby. It fed into his gambling addiction dangerously, particularly with Hornsby's view of the odds of success in South Africa for those who come to make money: "No failures are heard of except on account of drunkenness, gambling, and laziness—*and for no other reason.*"[38] He was, however, aware of the small likelihood of striking wealth from actual digging. A miner "plays against fortune, who can see his hand and plays herself with a sorted pack, so that he can rely on nothing."[39]

While in South Africa, Hornsby passed the time by organizing more rugby teams and game hunting. For Hornsby, game hunting in Griqua Land West was "paradise" and allowed him an opportunity to—in his words—"go against the mighty elephant, ponderous rhinoceros, and lordly giraffe."[40]

Hornsby's attitude toward hunting was typical for the era, as were his opinions of South African Blacks and his racial views in general. During this early period, he freely and proudly wrote about his racial prejudices and anti–Semitism.[41] However, for all the contempt he held for dark-skinned South Africans, Hornsby kept his deepest vitriol reserved for the White South Africans:

> A Dutch boer is the very skunkiest white man in existence, and it is not difficult to give credence to Darwin's theory of physical improvement by culture, when one sees such an inversement of the theory in the degradation of a once enlightened race; it is perhaps owing to their phlegmatic natures that they have gone on to desiring to be no better than their fathers, and, as is human, falling short of their desires by becoming worse. They are human, and that is the best that can be said of them.
>
> They exist to cheat and lie in a manner almost inconceivable, and with a stolid persistency that would make them subjects of envy to an Arab merchant or Yankee notion seller, and their one idea is to persistently hate the "verdomt Engleeshmon." They live in houses truly, but, as such, monuments of filth, ignorance and brutishness—low-pitched, ill-ventilated, and small…. They may be seen [in the diamond diggings] in families, from the grandma to the crawling child, all scrabbling away at some heap, with a success that cannot be appreciated, for they never show it, nor improve their social state, unless demoralized by contact with society at large, when they make it manifest by wearing finer clothes, and big talking.[42]

Hornsby does not say if his claim near New Rush paid off. The average claim on rich soil at the time that Hornsby was mining was about $20,000. Whether Hornsby's score was better or worse, one thing is certain: Hornsby's gambling habit drained whatever he had managed to find, and by the end of the year, he was in debt, with creditors both in South Africa and in England. On January 5, 1872, Hornsby was forced to declare bankruptcy in England[43] and traveled back to Bristol to reconcile his debts. In Bristol, he managed to settle with his creditors, twenty shillings to the pound.[44]

• • •

At some point during these trips through southern England, Hornsby met a sixteen-year-old girl named Marie Blackmore, and the two began dating. Marie, blond, shy, and tall for her age, had, like Hornsby, come from an initially wealthy family with ties to the officer class and somewhat tenuous connections to the aristocracy, now financially troubled. As a child, she too had met with Queen Victoria and years later described how Victoria had kissed her upon meeting her: a forty-five-year-old queen, her jet hair parted in the center, dressed head to toe in black, and an eight-year-old dressed all in white and cream.[45]

• • •

By August, Hornsby had successfully escaped from his creditors in South Africa and had cleared up his debt in England. He transferred from the 102nd to the 98th Foot, and in November he traveled to Wellington one final time to play as an O.W., this time prevailing. The O.W.s played as a group against the current players, the alumni winning by three goals to the students' one goal and one try. It was unsurprising that the O.W.s won: fifty alumni players had shown up for the matches, so their picked team was an elite crew.[46] The students were overpowered, with one star player suffering an arm injury, another receiving a blow to the head, "which prevented him from playing in his usual form."[47]

In March 1873, Hornsby resigned his commission and left the Royal Army.[48] He decided that he would be unable to make his fortune in either Africa or Europe, and that he would have more luck seeking wealth in America. His move is somewhat unexpected, considering Hornsby's opinion of Americans: corrupt, susceptible to bribery and graft.[49] As he worked to convince Marie to make the move to the United States, Hornsby prepared his affairs with the army.

On the evening of May 14, he attended an instrumental and vocal concert by the 102nd Regiment in the camp's drill hall. The concert was open to the public, and a large crowd from across southern England gathered for the performances, which had been advertised beforehand.[50] For Hornsby, it wasn't only a night of entertainment; it was his farewell to the army and England.

Hornsby's brother Henry, now a captain, also attended and treated the party as a chance to bid his brother goodbye. While Gus tended to be quiet in crowds, shied from public speaking, and was not well-liked among the other officers, Henry was nearly the opposite: enormously popular and outspoken.[51] Henry was also a terrific singer,[52] and his fellow officers called for him to perform during the concert. They gave him sheet music to two of Henry Russell's songs: "The Maniac," about a man driven insane from love, and "The Gambler's Wife," a ballad about the dangers of compulsive gambling. Henry Hornsby likely wondered if the second song had been suggested with an ulterior motive—perhaps viciously—by the group, needling his brother for his recent financial problems.

Henry chose "The Maniac."[53]

> *No, by heaven, no, by heaven I am not mad*

Henry Hornsby sang, full-voice, standing on the small, makeshift stage and leering at the crowd, acting in character[54] as a madman locked in an asylum's cell:

> *Oh, release me, oh, release me,*
> *He quits the grate, he turns the key*
> *He quits the grate, I knelt in vain,*
> *His glimmering lamp still—still I see,*
> *And all—and all—is gloom again.*
>
> *Cold bitter cold—no life, no light;*
> *Life all thy comforts once I had,*
> *But here I am chain'd this freezing night;*
> *No, by heaven, no, by heaven, I am not mad!*
> *Oh, release me, oh, release me,*
> *I see her dancing in the hall,*
> *She heeds me not, she heeds me not;*
> *Come, come—she heeds me not.*
> *For lo! When I speak, mark how yon demons' eyeballs glare;*
> *He sees me now, with dreadful shriek he whirls, he whirls me in the air.*
> *Horror, the reptile strikes his tooth, deep in my heart so crushed and sad;*
> *Aye! Laugh ye fiends, laugh, laugh ye fiends,*
> *Yes, by heavens,*
> *They've driven me mad!*[55]

Delighted and amused, the crowd demanded an encore, which Henry granted.[56] The resulting tumult of applause was eventually swallowed by a round of cornet solos, laughter, and obscenity. By then, Gus Hornsby had slipped unnoticed through the exit.

Game Day

A Glimpse of Evanston, Illinois, at High Noon

Evanston was less than a generation removed from wilderness, but its town center had, by 1876, become an expanding knot of buildings and businesses. The town had over 6,000 residents and had experienced a dizzying 50 percent increase in population in just twenty-four months.[1] Gus Hornsby surveilled Evanston's new storefronts as he walked away from the train depot.

Hornsby was no longer alone. As he was leaving his car, he noticed that one of his teammates, C.J. Williams, had taken the same train. Like Hornsby, and unlike many of the other members of the new Chicago Foot-Ball Club, Williams was a powerful athlete who also had a hand in establishing rugby-style football. Williams came from London, where he had been a member of London's Athletic Club. In 1870 he joined "The Flamingoes" rugby club and played as halfback for the team for two years,[2] during which the Flamingoes helped to form England's Rugby Football Union. After playing on the team in 1871, Williams moved to New York and joined the New York Athletic Club. He was now in Chicago, running a successful grocery business.

The two men meandered through the center of Evanston, looking for a place to have lunch. The only restaurant in town that either knew of was Adam Mares Restaurant, but it was out of the question for lunch: it lay a mile south of Evanston's downtown. And both men had heard of it because it was the most notorious spot north of Chicago.

• • •

For a town celebrated for its sobriety, Evanston harbored a wild outlier in Adam Mares, who had gained a regional reputation for daring to serve liquor, *sub rosa*. By state law, no establishment within four miles of Northwestern's campus could sell alcohol. Mares Restaurant, near the

ADAM MARES,
RESAURANT,

A Full Line of Confectionery, Cigars, &c.

CHICAGO AVE., OPP. CALVARY CEMETERY, SOUTH EVANSTON, ILL.

An 1880 advertisement for Mare's Restaurant, which somehow avoids mentioning its abundant selection of alcoholic beverages (Evanston City Directory, 1880).

town's border with Chicago, began its infamous run the previous year, when it was fined $25 and subject to a flurry of lawsuits, the most prominent of them from the Women's Temperance Alliance of Evanston.[3]

The fines against Mares would multiply in later years, including an 1877 penalty of $200 "for selling whisky on the Sabbath."[4] By 1879, the Chicago *Inter-Ocean* noted that Mares would need "to show cause why he should not have the heavy hand of law placed upon him."[5] Heavy or not, Mares slipped the hand and continued to serve alcohol in temperate Evanston, getting fined or arrested two or three times a year. Finally, in 1884, Mares was arrested in a shootout with police and slapped with a $2,000 bail. His wife physically attacked the arresting officers; they also put her in jail.[6]

• • •

Hornsby and Williams walked past the V-shaped intersection where Sherman and Orrington streets meet. At that moment, Evanstonians were busy planning the future of the intersection, on which they would erect a tall fountain and would christen Fountain Square later that year as a part of the town's extravagant centennial celebration. However, when Hornsby and Williams passed, the intersection was still a mostly frozen morass of choppy mud and ice, and carriages crisscrossed the square, bounding over the holes and ruts.

The men landed at a confectionary on Davis Street, run by Miss Alice Fleming. Fleming's parlor was among Evanston's largest, specializing in pastries and baked goods. It also sold light lunches, as well as "a complete line of fine and domestic cigars, stationery of all descriptions, and hand-made candles," according to its advertising.[7] Miss Fleming ran a domestic employment bureau from the store, offering to "supply female help on short notice."[8] In 1876, a woman who ran a business typically did so because she was desperate—usually widowed—and needed income from a tavern or other, even less respectable, business to survive. Fleming was none of these: she was, instead, a headstrong and successful entrepreneur. Because of its ownership and focus, the store was a favorite of Evanston's women, and Hornsby and Williams were the only men in the parlor at the time. Both would have passed, however, on the masculine cigars: neither man had used tobacco in his life.[9]

• • •

Fleming's ice cream parlor was one of several in town. One of those parlors eventually claimed to have made the first-ever ice cream sundae the previous year, removing the soda that restaurants typically served with ice cream, attempting to skirt Evanston's laws against selling ice cream sodas on the Sabbath. Apocryphal or not, the story contributed to Evanston's reputation for temperate culture.

Several towns in America make the same claim, including Ithaca, New York. There is some evidence, however, to back the story that the sundae began in Evanston in 1875. Simeon Moss, a staff writer for the *Ithaca Journal* compared the competing claims in a 1986 column.[10] He interviewed Patricia Kelly, who was the curator, at the time, of the Evanston Historical Society.

Kelly said, "The first sundae was served in Garwood's Drug Store on Fountain Square.... At the instigation of the W.C.T.U. the sale of seltzer water was banned on Sundays—probably because of the fizzy drink's association with alcohol. That left Garwood's ice cream sodas with nothing in them but ice cream and flavorings—or ice cream sundaes. [It] was first called a Sunday, but was later changed to *Sundae* in order to remove any sacrilegious connotation."[11]

Evanston in the 1870s was so Sabbath-observant that when the first telephones came to the town, a couple of years after the Chicago–NWU game, the town banned telephone service on Sunday.[12]

• • •

Northwestern's students took the rest of the day off. It was a welcome vacation—while Northwestern has a reputation as a challenging academic school, in 1876 it was almost unbearably demanding. Frank Casseday entered NWU (as the school's name was abbreviated at the time) in 1873 as part of a class of eighty-four students, only thirty-one of whom eventually graduated.[13] More students in that class dropped out before their sophomore year than would ultimately earn a degree.

Frank met one of his baseball teammates, Edward Kinman, for lunch and to talk about the afternoon football game. Kinman was one of the school's best athletes and an above-average student and essayist. Tall, with slightly receding brown hair, a neatly trimmed mustache (or, as the

Evanston Index newspaper put it in describing Kinman in 1876, "suffering from a slight attack of mustache"[14]), and large, expressive brown eyes, Kinman appeared as the classic Victorian gentleman every bit as much as any of the social titans in the Chicago Foot-Ball Club.

Kinman was a twenty-year-old sophomore from Jacksonville, Illinois, the youngest of eleven children. He was indeed from a socially respectable family, but he had suffered his share of hardship by the time he arrived in Evanston, having lost his father, an uncle, and a brother in the war. Kinman's father, William, was a lieutenant colonel in the 115th Illinois Volunteers and fell on the final day of the Battle of Chickamauga.[15] He had risen in rank during a twenty-year military career and had seen battle in three wars. In May 1863, Colonel Kinman had lost his brother in the Battle of Vicksburg. That fall, he helped lead the charge at Snodgrass Hill during Chickamauga. Before the battle, he expressed his rather bleak prospects: "We shall have a desperate battle today, many of us will be killed, and I expect to be among the number."[16] He was shot through the chest. Still alert, he told one of his captains that he thought the wound was fatal.[17] As he lay on the ground, he was shot a second time; this bullet was to the head, killing him instantly. One of Ed Kinman's brothers, Cyrus, served as an assistant to his father. Cyrus later wrote, "[My father] had just ridden along the line encouraging the men to stand firm. The last I saw of him alive, he passed into a cloud of smoke."[18]

At its close, the war claimed a third Kinman. Another of Ed's brothers, Newton—a private also serving in the Illinois 115th—fell ill in February 1865. On February 21, he died from chronic diarrhea, a too-common fatality in the war.[19] Ed Kinman would have probably found it difficult not to compare the two deaths. One was romanticized—almost mythologized: the crack

Edward Kinman, seen here as a senior at Northwestern in 1878, played second and third base on NWU's baseball team and eventually became captain of both the football and baseball squads (photograph by Alexander Hesler, courtesy Northwestern University Archives).

of an immediate and explosive spectrum of pain as metal tore into lung and bone, a dizzying fall from the mount, and then, a moment later, unexpected oblivion. The other would have been mentioned only under the breath: vile, unrelenting pain, days swimming in agony, occasionally submerged through drugs and the brain's (and body's) own exhaustion, but more often surfaced and fully aware, a torment.

• • •

Ed sat across from Frank as they ate and talked about the baseball team and the upcoming football game. Like Frank, Ed wore a fraternity pin. Ed's fraternity was Beta Theta Pi, and he also was proud of his association. Fraternities were an increasingly controversial topic at Northwestern—and the rest of the country—in February 1876: the month began with the issue erupting on campus as faculty and students debated the benefits and harm of secret societies.[20] By the 12th, the Evanston city newspaper weighed in against the local fraternities and their sense of self-importance: "When a lot of boys buy a basket of peanuts, take them into a room, lock the door, and resolve that they know something nobody else knows, they form what is known as a 'secret society.'"[21]

Kinman and Casseday were probably somewhat tired after lunch: the previous evening, both had stayed up later than usual for a school night. The baseball team held one of its first practices for the year, and it followed up the practice by hosting a long pep rally at night, partly in anticipation of the Methodists' football game with Chicago the next day.[22]

• • •

The Northwestern Fighting Methodists?

The earliest Northwestern University teams were occasionally called the Methodists, the Evanstonians, the Northwesterners, or—simply—the NWUs. Eventually, a myth began that the school nicknamed its early sports teams "the Fighting Methodists," but this isn't completely accurate. The Fighting Methodist legend likely stems from the nickname of Charles Wilson, one of the campus seminarians and a guard on Northwestern's 1892 team, who was nicknamed "the Fighting Parson." The team nicknamed him this for good reason: he was among the most aggressive players Northwestern had fielded up to that point. According to a teammate: "The harder the game was, the better he played.... Our team was being driven back until the enemy was on our five-yard line. Wilson stood up, waved his arms, and shouted to us in a voice that could be heard on the sidelines, to stop them in the name of the Lord."[23]

Game Day

The team, by the 1890s, was known as the Purple and would only become known as the Wildcats after sportswriter Wallace Abbey called them that in a 1924 *Chicago Tribune* article.[24]

• • •

Although Frank had selected several of the other NWU football players and was the leader of the group, he still felt unsure of the East Coast college football rules. Ed, however, seemed more comfortable with the concept as they talked, and he assured Frank that he could help the team figure it out before kickoff. Frank asked Ed to captain the team, and Ed accepted and agreed to play as halfback. Frank, though he was a little smaller than the average player for NWU, decided to play the forward position.

Several blocks north, students leaving University Hall, the school's main building, stopped to gape at a muscle-packed bearded man walking briskly toward the lake, wearing nothing but what appeared to be bright blue skin-tight underclothes.

Chapter 3

1873: America

In July 1873, Gus Hornsby and Marie Blackmore married in Kensington.[1] Hornsby dressed in uniform, Marie in a dress of heavy white moiré silk.[2] The two immediately left for the United States, paying $80.00 each for berths on a steamer to New York. Marie brought some wealth to the union, but it wasn't limitless, and the two were resigned to living a bit more modestly in America.

During his brief stay in New York, Hornsby sought out local rugby teams. He discovered that eastern colleges had started playing a mutated form of football, combining English rugby, association football, and their own twists on the rules. By this time, Columbia, Yale, and several other schools had joined Rutgers and Princeton in playing a particular brand of American football, with twenty players to a side, similar to English rugby. However, the ball had to be sent over the opponent's goal to score, and there was yet no "try" or touchdown. Later, Harvard devised its own rules for football and stubbornly refused to accept the other schools' version of the game. In Canada, a couple of colleges had begun playing rugby, closer to the English variety, but still with modifications. Hornsby immediately embraced these new versions of the game.

The couple decided to settle in Chicago[3] and traveled by train to Illinois at the end of the summer. At the same time that the Hornsbys made their move to Chicago, an up-and-coming organized criminal named Michael McDonald was convincing one of his political associates, Chicago treasurer Harvey Colvin, to run for mayor of the city. Colvin was in McDonald's pocket, and having him in the mayor's seat would provide McDonald with political muscle to expand his emerging gambling interests throughout the city.[4] By the time Hornsby arrived, McDonald's gambling facilities in Chicago would be ready to provide Gus with a range of temptations.

Hornsby found a set of rooms on 12th Street. He also splurged on a separate office, setting up in a small room on the corner of Madison and Michigan Avenues, overlooking Lake Michigan and just a block from the gargantuan Interstate Exposition Building. Standing in front of his second-floor window, Hornsby looked to his right and saw the Exposition Building's massive glass-covered north dome, resplendent in the sunlight and topped with an enormous American flag. Towering over the horses and carriages dotting Michigan Avenue below, the building would have seemed comically oversized and—to Hornsby—positively American.

Hornsby spent his first few months in Chicago writing a book about his experience in South Africa and trying to find the next scheme to make money. Toward the end of the year, he began work for a directory publishing company, acting as the company's Chicago general agent.[5] Hornsby hired a Chicagoan named Joseph Barrington. The two men brought in additional sales assistants to canvass the city and solicit subscriptions to the directory, paying between $2.50 and $5.00 a day, depending on the assistant's success.[6]

• • •

During his first two years in America, there is no hint that Hornsby's gambling led him into trouble again. The opportunity, however, was certainly there: Chicago's downtown business district was a hotbed for gambling at that point.

Just two blocks west of Hornsby's new office, a gambling house had started the same month he moved to the city, and it would thrive through 1874.[7] Two blocks southwest of that lay Mike McDonald's new "Gambling Palace," named The Store, on the corner of Monroe and Clark Streets.[8] Three blocks northwest of Hornsby's office was a stretch of Randolph Street peppered with gambling houses, called "Hair-Trigger Block" because of the frequent shootings that took place there.[9] And, three blocks southwest of Hornsby's offices, there was a string of four (known) gambling houses lining a two-block section of State Street.[10] The only reason there weren't gambling establishments *east* of Hornsby's office is because they would have had to float in Lake Michigan.

The crown jewel of these illegal gambling hideouts in 1873 was The Store, a four-story complex with its own saloons, restaurant, hotel, and multiple casino rooms. According to author T.J. English, The Store "was furnished with the most expensive oak furniture.... Dealers and croupiers were formally dressed, as were the waiters."[11] The Store's hotel "accommodated hard core sporting men who needed only an afternoon nap to revive themselves, replenish their bankrolls, and return to the tables."[12]

• • •

For the first several months in Chicago, Hornsby seems to have immersed himself in writing his book and selling directories. At the beginning of 1874, Hornsby approached the *Inter-Ocean* newspaper with his manuscript.

The *Inter-Ocean* had launched just two years before, out of the ashes of the Chicago Fire and the old *Chicago Republican* newspaper. William Nixon, the *Inter-Ocean*'s manager, approved Hornsby's manuscript and authorized a first printing of 500 copies. Hornsby's book, *The South African Diamond Fields: A Practical Matter-of-Fact Account*, gave a brief history of diamond mining in South Africa and Hornsby's description of his time in New Rush. Hornsby began his book by assuming the ignorance of the reader:

> Arriving from the South African Diamond "Fields," as they are popularly called, I found my friends and acquaintances more or less ignorant of their existence, locality, size, inhabitants, &c.; judging by them that the large majority of folk must be equally ignorant, I feel constrained to write and publish a brief matter-of-fact account of Griqua-Land West (as the diamondiferous territory is now styled), dedicating it to the ladies, for whose adornment and delightment especially are the precious stones exhumed from Mother Earth, in whose bosom for so many untold ages they have been hid, till chance put one of them, after many vicissitudes, into the hands of a man who knew its value. He at once proclaimed the fact, and that the gem had been brought down from the far-away almost unknown land beyond the Orange River, till then (1867) the bourne of most ordinary travelers.[13]

While the book sold relatively well, there was no second printing. There are only three known surviving copies of Hornsby's book. According to the South African Historical Society of Kimberly (which printed a facsimile), one copy of the original printing is in a private collection in South Africa, the second is at the University of Oregon, and the third rests in the Library of Congress—submitted there by Hornsby himself.[14]

The money the book made was not enough to sufficiently augment the meager income that Hornsby was getting from soliciting directory subscriptions. Just as Hornsby began looking for an additional income source, he noticed a new business setting up next door to his office on Madison Street. A startup publication called *Field & Stream* was preparing its debut issue, and the magazine—"the only sporting journal west of New York"—needed editorial assistants.

The magazine is not to be confused with the modern *Field & Stream* magazine, which started in 1895. The Chicago *Field & Stream* was founded by physician Nicholas Rowe and initially covered all manner of sporting dog, hunting, fishing, and turf activities. It soon changed its name to *Field*, then *Chicago Field* (in 1881, it would change titles yet again to *American Field*, and its content became dedicated solely to sporting dogs. *American Field* is currently the longest continuously printed publication for sporting dogs, and Hornsby was one of its first employees).[15]

Chapter 3. 1873: America

The new journal promised to be devoted to "improvement of the Dog and Gun, and generally to all topics of interest to the Sportsmen of our Times. Among its correspondents and contributors will be found many of the most eminent men and women of the age."[16] Hornsby applied and landed an assistant editor position, covering sporting events and dog shows—relatively new activities in which Hornsby had taken a keen interest (he was one of the earliest members of the new North American Kennel Club). Hornsby worked, off and on, for the journal for the next eight years.

Hornsby's financial position had become stronger with his new post at *Field & Stream*, but his solicitation business was foundering. Hornsby was continuously late paying his salesmen, when he paid them at all. Gradually, he began to suspect that his assistant, Barrington, was skimming money. By April, Hornsby had three additional employees canvassing the city, yet money seemed to be constantly short. In May 1874, Hornsby thought he had proof of Barrington's theft, and he went to the police. On May 23, Hornsby presented his case to a court, arguing that Barrington had robbed the directory company—and Hornsby—and had vanished. The presiding officer, Judge Haines, issued a warrant for Barrington's arrest.[17]

Police quickly found and captured Barrington, and he appeared before Haines on May 30.[18] Barrington did not, however, appear alone. He brought two witnesses, a current and a former canvasser of Hornsby's, to testify that Hornsby had told his employees that if he did not pay them on time for their work, that they could keep the money they collected on the job, at least enough to cover their pay. The court ruled that Barrington had done precisely what Hornsby had instructed him to do.[19]

Humiliated, Hornsby shut down his solicitation business, abandoned his Madison Street office, and focused on editing *Field & Stream*. The family moved to an apartment on North Clark Street in Chicago, but quickly moved again, this time to a house in the suburb of Hyde Park, south of the city.

Hornsby eventually got the chance to write for as well as edit *Field & Stream* and began a regular column called "East Indian Sporting Sketches." At the time, many of the magazine's writers were anonymous, using quirky *noms de plume* (the editor-in-chief, Dr. Rowe, typically used the pen name "Mohawk"). Hornsby also wrote under an assumed name, taking the title "Bengalee." He wrote of his exploits in India during his time in the Royal Army, and he did not shy away from describing his gambling activities, although his accounts were somewhat sanitized:

> Book-making [here, Hornsby is specifically discussing gambling on horses] seems an easy road to fortune, but it requires a clear head, quickness in calculating and some nerve to carry it successfully through. I may safely say that I never did try to make a book: I felt it to be beyond my abilities to do so successfully, and I always have had an objection to trying that which I had no hopes

of succeeding in. But I have betted and betted, sometimes with success, sometimes with ill-success.

Upon one occasion, however, I was on the brink of a terribly nasty fix, and I must now own that I thoroughly deserved it.... Suffice to say, that when I got to my bed, it was with the knowledge that I had pledged my reputation against 1,300 rupees ($650), that a certain pony, Bullfinch, I very much fancied, would win the pony race.

The race had no joy for me on that day ... after a close race Bullfinch came in second. I owed $650 to my name wherewith to meet the inevitable call on the evening of the last day of racing.[20]

• • •

In early 1875 Marie Hornsby gave birth to the couple's first child, a boy they named Henry, after Hornsby's father and older brother. Gus Hornsby settled in with his family for a time, and during this period, while he spent more time at home, he tried his hand at inventing. In March, he developed an armchair and pursued a patent for it. The United States ignored the invention, but Canada granted Hornsby a patent in April.[21]

Interestingly, just one day after Canada granted Hornsby's patent, it issued one for a "quadruplex telegraph," submitted by a twenty-eight-year-old telegraph operator and budding inventor named Thomas Edison.[22]

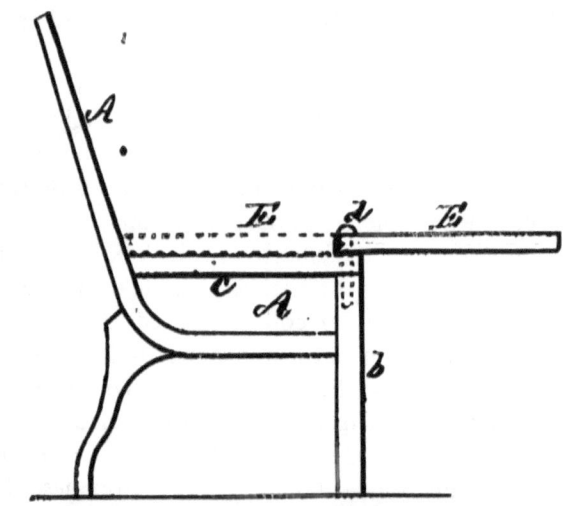

4604   Hornsby's Extension Arm Chair.

Diagram of Hornsby's Canadian patent. "*Claim*—The extra arm rests E, E, in combination with the front leg *b*, and arm rest C, as described" (*Canadian Patent Office Record*, June 1875).

The armchair was a shot at wealth for Hornsby, but the shot missed. Hornsby tried to sell copies of the chair out of his home and his magazine office, but sales did not take off.

• • •

Hornsby broadened his participation in local games and sports, competing again at chess and judging wrestling matches, in addition to covering dog and other sporting events and shows for *Chicago Field*. However, Hornsby could find no football games of interest in Chicago, or, indeed, in the Midwest at all.

People were playing a crude version of football in the American Midwest by this time; in fact, people in Chicago had been playing football, of a sort, for years. At Northwestern, students first began playing football before 1874, pitting classes against each other in the rough, old kicking version of the game.[23] As early as before the Civil War, children and athletic groups throughout the city played the crude full-contact soccer game that would eventually contribute some features to American football. However, the Midwest teams were not specifically football teams but general athletic clubs, playing kicking-style football as part of a set of games during picnics or field day events.

Typical of such events was a game played in Chicago in August 1869.[24] Two state militia groups, the Sheridan Guards and the Zouaves, held a picnic in old Haas Park.[25] During the picnic, the two groups played a game of "football" (in reality, a bare-knuckle brawl during which the players occasionally tried to kick a ball), with the winners getting to keep the ball. The match was part of a series of other field day events. No organized, true game of football had yet been played in the Midwest.

Unknown to Hornsby, the University of Michigan had tried, unsuccessfully, at least three times before to stage a real American football game. In October 1873, students from Michigan challenged Cornell to a trial football game.[26] However, a freshman at Cornell, Mortimer Leggett, had recently died in a fraternity hazing accident. Members of Kappa Alpha Society had led Leggett blindfolded to the gorge at Six Mile Creek, and the group accidentally fell into the gorge. Leggett's is considered the first-ever fraternity hazing death in the United States,[27] and it was a national scandal. Cornell's faculty, gun-shy at participating in a violent sport so soon after the tragedy, turned down the offer. In spring 1874, Michigan tried again to play a game, this time by searching for former Eastern school players living in Chicago.[28] "If there are any [football experts] hereabouts they keep pretty quiet, as no one ever hears of a game of foot-ball in this city," the *Chicago Tribune* wrote, full-snark.[29]

In October 1874, Michigan students tried a third and final time, again with Cornell. Michigan suggested a game in Ann Arbor on November 1, 1874, and offered to pay half of the costs of travel.[30] The Cornell and Michigan students, after further negotiation, agreed to hold the game in neutral Cleveland, Ohio. However, Cornell's president, Andrew White, forbade the Cornell players from traveling for the game and—in doing so—issued one of the great, memorable football criticisms of all time: "I refuse to let 40 of our boys travel 400 miles merely to agitate a bag of wind."[31] Michigan would have to wait until 1879 to play its first football game (staged in Chicago after all); Cornell finally played its first game in 1887.

Hornsby decided to try to organize and train a football team, just as he had in England, India, and South Africa. However, he wanted to forego the old English rugby style he had learned and implement the newer version of the rugby game that the East Coast colleges had started. In October 1875 he described his plan in a column in the *Chicago Field*, arguing for football as a new winter game:

> It is too cold and raw for base-ball.... What are we to do then? Let us answer that question for our readers and propose foot-ball. Not the promiscuous kicking about of an inflated bladder, but the scientific skirmishing of skilled and active men and boys in their attempt to drive the ball through the opposite goal.... The Canadians play the game as it is played by the Rugby Union clubs, and give themselves and hundreds of spectators an intensely exciting hour.
>
> We shall be happy to hear from anyone for the purpose of forming a foot-ball club for Chicago. If there are any who know the game in its delicious vitality, we request them to report themselves at once, and rally to form a nucleus around which a football club may gather. Nor do we wish this for Chicago alone, but for the whole country. Let this noble game be cultivated among us.[32]

On October 23, 1875, he wrote a letter to the *Chicago Tribune*. At the very moment that Hornsby was writing his letter, Harvard kicked off a game in Canada against a group of players from several Canadian colleges. The game used a hybrid of Harvard's unique football rules and the Canadian version, more traditional rugby. The result of the game (Harvard won) is inconsequential compared to the effect that the game had on the evolving rules of American football.

Hornsby's letter (here quoted in full) ran in the *Tribune* the next day:

FOOTBALL.

PROPOSITION FOR A CLUB.

To the Editor of The Chicago Tribune:

CHICAGO, Oct. 23.—Would you accommodate a constant reader with a small portion of your valuable space to ventilate his opinions on a great winter athletic sport that seems somewhat neglected in this part of the country? I allude to the game of football; and not merely to the hurley-burley, rough-and-tumble, village game, but to the game as a science. It is a science such as base-ball, cricket bowls, or any other athletic game that requires the use of brain as well as muscle for its satisfactory result. We all know that a strong team of base-ball players who do not exercise judgment are sure to be beaten by an equally strong team who do use judgment.

What I desire, therefore, is to call the attention of athletes to the scientific practice of football during this promised open winter. It is a game that calls for all the muscular ability of the players, and such moral qualities as pluck, judgment, patience, and decision. Those who have seen the game played in England, in Canada, and in the Eastern schools and universities, must know how intensely exciting it is and how every change and chance is eagerly followed by those most ignorant of football rules and nice points. There are many athletes who desire to keep themselves in condition during the long months of winter; to these the game of football is a big thing. It gives them exercise and amusement combined, and affords them an admirable vent for letting off any feeling of biliousness that might be in the system. I myself am an enthusiastic football player, and am very anxious to find out those of a kindred spirit.

I feel sure that this letter through your columns is the best way to do it. If, then, this meets the eye of any one anxious to form a club, he will confer a pleasure by calling at my office, 14 South Canal Street, or by writing to, sir, yours respectfully.

A.H. Hornsby[33]

The *Tribune*'s readership, with a few exceptions, ignored the letter. However, a handful of people who had played either rugby or American "village" soccer were intrigued and replied.

One of the readers who responded had played in the 1869 field day kicking scrum in Haas Park. He was a member of the Zouaves, having fought with the group during the Civil War. An accomplished athlete, he was a master at track and field, weightlifting, baseball, and rowing. His boating and rowing clubs attracted the social elite in both Chicago and Manhattan. In 1868, he co-founded the New York Athletic Club, and four years later, he founded the Chicago Athletic Club.[34] Of the 400,000 people living in Chicago, Hornsby's letter had found the one man who could craft any sports club and had the resources to make it a success. Sitting in his large, richly appointed office on Chicago's South Clark Street, he reread Hornsby's letter, then quickly wrote his reply, signing it *W.B. Curtis* in oversized flowing script.[35]

Game Day, 1:00 p.m.

As Hornsby and Williams walked up Chicago Street in Evanston,[1] they saw William B. Curtis from several blocks away. He stood at the campus gates, waving vigorously. Legs apart, spine ramrod straight, he looked like a colossus, something carved from stone, except for his blue eyes. Hornsby and Williams, both bundled in coats to brace themselves from the bitter lake wind, were struck by Curtis's appearance: he was already wearing his football uniform and nothing else. He had not brought a coat; in fact, he had no problem with cold and seldom wore any protection from it.[2] His blue knit football cap in hand, he was bare-headed but with a full dark brown beard. He wore the light blue, skin-tight Chicago Foot-Ball Club jersey with a wool "C" sewn onto the chest, white knickerbocker pants, long light blue stockings, and white leather baseball shoes. Curtis was a wall of muscle, standing five feet, nine inches (tall for the time) with a forty-two-inch chest,[3] and he looked nearly superhuman as he stood next to the gathering students at the gates.

William B. Curtis in a photograph taken immediately after the Civil War, upon his return to New England. Curtis was a member of the Union Zouave volunteer units, devoted to light infantry (author's collection, previously unpublished).

. . .

Curtis was from Vermont, but his family moved to Chicago when he was a child. His father eventually became president of Knox College in Galesburg, Illinois. During his youth and into his career, Curtis split time between Chicago and New York. A captain during the Civil War, he returned to Chicago after the war and began to organize amateur athletic clubs.

When the Civil War ended, the wealthy industrialists in the North looked for pursuits that could identify them as members of a leisure class. Athletics provided an answer, and athletic clubs in large cities began to compete with the Masonic secret societies for the attention of the very rich. In Manhattan, Curtis opened a gymnasium less than a year after returning from the war,[4] and in 1868 he co-founded the New York Athletic Club, one of the first amateur athletic organizations in the United States.[5] Curtis had recruited C.J. Williams, among other athletes, in New York. His efforts to do the same in Chicago were hampered by the 1871 Great Fire, in which Curtis lost a significant portion of his fortune and all of the athletic and gymnasium equipment that he had assembled.[6]

Curtis (shirtless, center), posing with the New York Athletic Club's "champions" team in a photo believed to have been taken in 1873. Each team member had won at least one New York or U.S. amateur championship. Curtis was the U.S. amateur tug-of-war champ. Shown from left are M. Elliot Burris, George I. Brown, Curtis, Daniel M. Stern, Charles H. Cone, and Henry E. Buermyer (originally published in *Spalding's Athletic Library*, Group XII, No. 87, 1910).

In the early 1870s, Curtis began several Chicago-area athletic and rowing clubs, including the Chicago Athletic Club and the Lotus Club. When Williams also moved to Chicago, he sought out his friend Curtis and joined Curtis's Chicago athletic clubs as well.

With its headquarters on the Calumet River, the Lotus Club was a unique organization, an all-male club (as all were, during the period) that featured nude swimming, Greco-Roman wrestling, and other athletic pursuits and philosophical studies and readings.[7] Its members were among the Chicago social elite. The Chicago Athletic Club also brought in the area's wealthy males and continued to be a social gold standard well into the twentieth century.

• • •

Hornsby and Williams had strolled down the clean, well-tended sidewalk running down the western side of Chicago Street. They then crossed to the semi-frozen mud of the east side and moved north to the school's gates, flanked by a waist-high picket fence put in place to keep out roving livestock. Past the gates stood the school's most magnificent building, University Hall, still fresh from its construction seven years before. The builders had hauled its beautiful "Athens Marble" white limestone by boat from the same Joliet, Illinois, quarry that provided stone for Chicago's Water Tower.[8] The hall's gothic tower rose over the bare oak trees that dotted the yard. The tower had dark, ornate windows, but housed neither clock nor bell yet.[9]

Curtis greeted the pair at the gate. The group walked across wooden planks through the oak grove to University Hall, then turned east toward the lake. Soon, they stood in front of a new, though somewhat ramshackle, wooden building set in front of a larger and far older structure. The smaller building was the new university gymnasium, funded and built by the students and opened just a week before.

Hornsby was impressed. The gymnasium was a practical two-story structure. The lower floor held bath and changing rooms and a space for bowling alleys, which lay unfinished. The upper level was a large, open room with a hardwood floor and a high, arching roof. Feeble lanterns hung from the rafters. Six windows let the cold light stream in, but the place was still somewhat dark, and the tiny wood stove in the center of the room was barely adequate. The students had already installed some equipment, including gymnastics and trapeze bars and exercise benches.[10] They had hired companies in Chicago to build the custom equipment and had installed it earlier that month. When the students formally opened the building on February 18, several professors attended the ceremony and spoke. The students erected a separate platform for professors and ladies who took part in the festivities. The school's faculty likely approved of

The upper level of the original NWU gymnasium, soon after construction in 1876. Funded and built by students, the gymnasium featured bowling alleys and billiard tables, installed in part as a deterrent to Chicago recreational hubs that could tempt students into drinking. Even so, the features did not last long: the university removed them by the end of the year. "The billiard tables introduced some time ago, and also the bowling alleys, have been removed by advice of the [university] trustees, as being 'deleterious to the moral health of the community'" (Northwestern University *Tripod*, December 28, 1876, courtesy Northwestern University Archives).

the student-run gymnasium because it was seen as a source of alternative activities for students instead of drinking alcohol, again in keeping with the pervasive need in Evanston to maintain temperance.[11]

Several students had arrived at the gym earlier with Curtis, and he now introduced Hornsby to the group, including Frank Casseday, the student leader, and Ed Kinman, NWU's new captain. Hornsby and Williams changed out of their suits and into their uniforms, putting their overcoats back on until it was game time. In the gymnasium, they talked for a while with the arriving students as they waited for the rest of the Chicago team.

One of the students who followed Hornsby and Williams into the building was the person most responsible for the new gymnasium. Senior Fred Manville Taylor was tall, elegant, and well-groomed, with a large Roman nose and a neatly trimmed beard. He wore a new, tailored sack coat on which he proudly wore the pin of the Spade and Serpent Society, the student club that ultimately led to the creation of Northwestern's first football team.

• • •

The Spade and Serpent Society

While college fraternities were controversial in the mid–1870s, more troubling to the Northwestern faculty was the rise of a group called Spade and Serpent the year before. Unlike the typical social fraternities, Spade and Serpent was a true secret society, a seniors-only group modeled on Skull and Bones at Yale and other class groups popular in Eastern colleges. Like Skull and Bones, NWU's new senior society privately selected the fifteen most promising juniors (scholastically and, one assumes, financially) to initiate for the following year.[12] According to one account of the group, its plan "was to select not more than fifteen men from the incoming senior class who were recognized as being more than ordinary students, and to make the society so attractive and select that from the freshman to the senior year the student would prepare himself to become entitled to membership in it."[13] In early 1876 the second batch of fifteen had control of Spade and Serpent, and they were busy looking for the next set of members. The group launched a scholarship, the "Spade and Serpent Prize," as part of their recruitment, offering the prize to the junior—male, of course—who had the highest academic scores. In September 1876, the faculty opted not to award the prize since doing so would provide official recognition to the society, which they hoped to squelch.[14] The faculty succeeded: by 1877, the group appears to have disbanded, although there are vague hints that the society remained, becoming truly secret, a *sub rosa* group within the senior class.

The Spade and Serpent's emblem, according to the *Chicago Tribune*[15] was a "pin of black enamel, coffin shaped, while on the lid is a golden spade with a serpent twined around it, and poking its head through the handle." While the meaning of the society's symbol is now lost, it appears to refer to the adage of *wisdom and virtue through work*. In the early 1600s the artist Gabriel Rollenhagen illustrated the adage in this emblem shown on the next page.[16]

The poet George Wither expanded on the Spade and Serpent emblem several years later, writing:

> ... For, by the *Spade*, is *Labour* here implide;
> The *Snake*, a vertuous *Prudence*, doth expresse;
> And, *Glorie*, by the *Wreath* is Typifide.
> For, where a vertuous *Industry* is found,
> She, shall with Wreaths of *Glory*, thus be crown'd.[17]

While it is not certain that the Northwestern Spade and Serpent society adopted Rollenhagen and Wither's meaning to the symbol, it does fit with Fred Taylor's lifelong interest in the value of labor and explains his attraction to the group.

The society was important to Northwestern's football team because

This emblem, made in the early 1600s by artist Gabriel Rollenhagen, illustrates the adage (Gabriel Rollenhagen's *Nvclevs Emblematvm Selectissimorvm*, Arnhem, 1611).

fully one third of the first NWU football players came from the small senior society, including Taylor, Frank Scott, and Theophilus Hilton (the student who, as will be shown, eventually received the invitation from the Chicago Foot-Ball Club to form a team and took that idea back to his society).

It is probably for the best that the Spade and Serpent members took an interest in the new gym and football. Their previous sporting interest had been "pigeon popping," in which they held contests near the campus lakeshore oak groves, firing rifles at the birds on Friday mornings.[18]

• • •

The Spade and Serpent members had contributed to the gymnasium fund, and Fred Taylor led the fundraising effort. Taylor proved an effective fundraiser: he was on par with Casseday as an adept public speaker, and the Northwestern students considered Taylor a natural leader.

In his junior year, Taylor began to lecture on economic and labor issues. In April 1875, he gave a presentation called "Why We Work." NWU's newspaper called the speech "well-written, a little rambling, however, and was well-delivered, except where he overstepped some of his climaxes with a superabundance of voice. His effort was above the average."[19]

• • •

Students gathered at the campus ball field. The field lay in a clearing of oak trees about 250 yards north of University Hall.[20] Between University Hall and the athletic grounds was Heck Hall, set back a little over 100 yards from Chicago Street. Heck Hall was an imposing five-story building.[21] The first four floors were white stone, and the fifth was gothic, with dark tiles. It was home to the seminary students of Garrett Biblical Institute, which shared portions of the campus with Northwestern. Garrett students, called "Bibs" by their Northwestern colleagues, peered from their windows, beginning to take an interest in the increasing buzz of activity to the north of their building.

Northwestern students would likely have treated the celebration in much the same way that they handled similar occasions. Events like these usually featured music, but the students did not have their own band. Their first attempt at a genuine student band, mysteriously called "The Owls," began in November 1871, but it was short-lived.[22] Since then, NWU students hired local bands to provide entertainment. In the mid-1870s, their favorite go-to band was Chicago's Great Western Light Guard,[23] and the band likely played at Northwestern before the football game.[24]

Northwestern did not yet have a fight song; in fact, the first fight song in the country wouldn't be written for nearly another decade. However, the school did have a march, simply called "The North-Western University March," written by an Evanston music teacher named Eliza Pattiani in 1868.

• • •

One of the earliest American women to have her music published nationally,[25] Pattiani was originally named Elisabeth von Bergen, daughter of the Baltic Baron H. von Bergen.[26] She and her husband fought in the 1848 German revolution,[27] fled Germany,[28] and changed their names to make them sound less German.

She initially settled in Chillicothe, Ohio, where her son, Alfred W. Pattiani, was born. Alfred would become one of the foremost architects on the West Coast. Eliza began publishing music under the name

"Madame Pattiani" and moved to Evanston in the early 1860s.²⁹ During her time in Evanston, Pattiani taught piano to Northwestern students and penned several compositions, including the Civil War song "Grand National Medley."³⁰ In 1880 she founded a music institute near Oakland, California.³¹

Her music, including "The North-Western University March," eventually fell into obscurity. Northwestern stopped using the tune by 1890, although the school's band director made an unsuccessful attempt to rearrange it for the marching band in the 1930s. He never used the new arrangement.³² In the late 1980s, several publishers, delving into works by early American women composers, began to republish some of Pattiani's piano compositions.³³

Cover of the sheet music for Pattiani's march. The cover features a sketch of the planned University Hall, which was still under construction when the sheet music was published in 1868 (published by Lyon & Healy, 1868).

Pattiani's march was likely the first music of any sort crafted specifically for the university. Throughout the early and mid–1870s, the Great Western Light Guard played this march³⁴ at most Northwestern celebrations and ceremonies. The tune—elegant, graceful, and a bit somber—was better suited to a graduation procession than to pre-game festivities. The Great Western's music would have carried in the cold air across the campus as the first few students gradually gathered in the clearing.

• • •

Two more Chicago players made their way to the campus. Younger by far than Curtis, Hornsby, or Williams, the Sullivan brothers could have easily been mistaken for Northwestern students. They also dressed in the specific style of shirts, ties, silk hats, and sack coats common to the student body. Albert Sullivan, twenty-one years old, was the more athletic of the brothers: tall, slightly heavy-set but strong, he was fast and powerful. He carried his football uniform under his arm, and he joked with his younger brother while striding past University Hall. They both played the forward position on the team.

Albert's younger brother was nineteen, not quite as tall, and carried a slighter build. Louis Sullivan was agile, but he was not destined to be a world-class athlete. The boy who would eventually become "the Father of Skyscrapers," arguably the second most important architect in American history, had already begun his trade. He had recently returned from studying in Paris and was earning his way by helping to rebuild Chicago.

CHAPTER 4

1875: Chicago

William Curtis was eager to set Hornsby's idea for a football club into motion, and he began immediately once he responded to Hornsby's *Tribune* letter. He reached out to several members of his Chicago Athletic Club, including William Borner, a 33-year-old railroad executive. Like Curtis, Borner was also a boating club member. He was from Pennsylvania but would stay in Chicago for his entire adult life. He was later involved in the 1893 Chicago World's Fair, and after the fair he and his wife lived permanently in the new Chicago Plaza Hotel.

The other Chicago Athletic Club members who agreed to join up with Curtis were John Flanders, another Chicago architect, and Ralph Cleveland, a close friend of Curtis. Both Borner and Flanders were eventually listed in the who's who of turn of the twentieth-century Chicago residents, *The Book of Chicagoans*.[1]

By the first week of November 1875, Curtis had used his extensive network of contacts to find Hornsby's new football team a home. Hotel executive Charles Hilton managed Chicago's prestigious Sherman House Hotel.[2] Hilton secured a spot not at his hotel, but at the mammoth Tremont House Hotel, on the corner of Lake and Dearborn, by reaching out in turn to Ira Couch, Jr., a colleague of both Hilton and Curtis. Couch was the son of Ira Couch, who had bought the Tremont—one of the oldest hotels in the region—in 1836. Couch's family still owned it.[3] The new club held its first meeting at the Tremont the following week.

Hornsby must have been overwhelmed by the response to Curtis's outreach. The group sat in an opulent parlor at the Tremont House, under chandeliers the size of carriages, in seats made of exotic imported wood, surrounded by walls with black walnut ornamentations. In addition to Curtis, Hornsby, Borner, Cleveland, and Flanders, this initial group included Charles J. "C.J." Williams, a member of the Lotus Club who was one of the few direct respondents to Hornsby's ad; William Day and John Jeffrey, both employed by the *Evening Journal*; businessman G. "Pat" Valentine; and William Hulbert, an official with the Chicago White Stockings ball club (eventually renamed the Chicago Cubs). Just before the meeting, Ira Couch, Jr., also decided to join the club. These were among the first names associated with an American football team in the Midwest.[4]

Attending the meeting, Charles Hilton decided to join the team and serve as an officer of the club. Hilton was a decorated Civil War officer[5] and was eventually appointed adjutant-general of the state of Illinois. He later founded the Hotel Men's Mutual Benefit Association in 1879. The Association, with its secret society feel, regalia, and influence, resembled an early version of the twentieth-century concierge organization called *Les Clefs d'Or*, or The Golden Keys (the inspiration for Wes Anderson's "Society of the Crossed Keys," in his film *The Grand Budapest Hotel*).[6] Hilton's organization ultimately merged with Bankers Life and Casualty. By the twenty-first century, Bankers Life claimed to be the oldest life and health insurance company in Chicago, thanks to its merger with the Hotel Men's Mutual Benefit Association.[7]

The Sullivan brothers arrived at the football club meeting later that evening. Louis Sullivan had been the first of the pair to be drawn to Curtis. Louis had joined Curtis's Lotus Club earlier in the year[8] and took pride in being the club's youngest member.[9] He later recruited his older brother. While Louis enjoyed the Lotus Club's athletic activities, it was Albert who excelled at them. Both were intrigued at the idea of trying a new sport that the Eastern schools were pioneering.

The group decided to call itself the Chicago Foot-Ball Club, and it chose Curtis as

Charles Hilton, Civil War officer (later brigadier general) and fullback on the Chicago Foot-Ball Club. By 1880, Hilton managed the Tremont House and later owned hotels in Chicago and Wisconsin, including the luxury Wellington Hotel. As a hotel manager and owner in the wake of the Great Fire, Hilton was obsessed with making his hotels fire-proof, and he made several innovations standard in his rooms, including hot and cold water and telephone service (originally published in the St. Louis *Post-Dispatch*, February 16, 1896).

the club leader and Hornsby as the football team captain. The initiation fee was $2.00, with $0.50 monthly dues.[10] They agreed that the team would use the modified rugby rules that the Eastern colleges had created and that Hornsby would obtain the most recent version of the rules and forward it to the rest of the club.

A final point on the group's initial agenda was to offer honorary membership in the club to Jimmy Wood, the Chicago White Stockings' manager. Wood was one of the players on the White Stockings' original 1870 team and the man responsible for creating professional baseball spring training (he relocated the White Stockings to New Orleans to prepare for the 1870 season).[11] He had suffered from an infection and lost his leg a year before the meeting.[12] Hornsby later noted that he was "pleased that the young athletes remembered an athletic hero by paying Jimmy Wood the compliment of placing him upon the directorate. But for cruel fate there would have been no more enthusiastic foot ball player than this splendid ex-second baseman."[13]

Hornsby, standing in front of the group and looking them over, struck a dramatic tone as he cheered the formation of the club: "Gentlemen, tonight we have fairly established foot ball as a western sport."[14]

• • •

The club needed to find playing grounds, and William Hulbert had the obvious solution. He arranged for the club to use the White Stockings' ball field, on the corner of State and Twenty-Third streets. Hulbert worked out the arrangements with Thomas Fauntleroy, a White Stockings executive and the man who had designed the Twenty-Third Street athletic grounds.[15] Hulbert's description of the new football club convinced Fauntleroy to join as well.

Fauntleroy came to Chicago during the Civil War and soon began to organize baseball teams in the city, including a predecessor to the White Stockings, with Albert Spalding on the team.[16] In October 1869, Fauntleroy served on the committee that developed the plan for the White Stockings,[17] the first professional sports team of any kind in Chicago, created to compete with the Cincinnati Red Stockings. Among the other members of that organizing group were Potter Palmer (the creator of the Palmer House Hotel and developer of Chicago's State Street) and General Philip Sheridan.[18]

The Great Fire in 1871 wiped out the White Stockings' lakefront ball grounds, and Fauntleroy secured the Twenty-Third Street location in 1872, before the team had even reformed.[19] In fact, Northwestern University's baseball team played at the new ball park (in an 1872 game against an amateur club called the Ætnas) before the White Stockings could.[20] In addition to the baseball diamond, the new facility had a surrounding track, per the request of William Curtis's Chicago Athletic Club.[21]

• • •

The Chicago Foot-Ball Club held its first practice at the field on November 12 and advertised it in the newspapers.[22] This follow-up ad attracted a large crowd of observers, including several more members for the club. At another meeting at the Tremont on November 15, the club decided to practice at the ball grounds every afternoon at 3:00, staging mock games on Mondays, Fridays, and Saturdays. These scrimmage games would use picked teams among the club members. The team's initial goal was to prepare for an eventual visit by an English rugby football team and to play them in Chicago, using the American rules.[23]

On Friday, November 19, the club arranged its first actual football game.[24] The Chicago Barge Club, a boating club of which Curtis was a member, agreed to be the test subject, throwing together a football team despite not fully understanding the rules. The clubs hastily set the match for the following day at the White Stockings' park at 4:00 p.m. This was supposed to be the first American football game held in the Midwest. However, the Barge Club could only muster a few of its members for Saturday, so they could not stage a full match as hoped.[25] Instead, the Chicago Foot-Ball Club split its members, included the handful of Barge Club players, and ran a couple of scrimmages, with Hornsby as captain of one side and C.J. Williams leading the other.

Despite this setback, the Chicago team had already lined up another potential opponent, and they began preparations for the game. Charles Hilton's cousin, Theophilus Hilton, Jr., was a student at Northwestern. Charles had written to him about the club, and Theophilus was trying to organize a football team at the school. Students at the time were only aware of the loose, carry-and-kick variation of the game. The Chicago club quickly arranged to meet the NWU students at the White Stockings' park on Thanksgiving morning, November 25.[26]

Given the resources of the Chicago players, it is no surprise that the club quickly acquired uniforms, including blue caps, jerseys, stockings, and white knee-pants. They began practicing in their new team suits, preparing for the Methodist students from Evanston. The club erected new goal posts and crossbars at the White Stockings' playing field and arranged for a celebration.

By Wednesday morning, it became apparent that the game was not going to happen. Theo Hilton failed to find more than a handful of Spade and Serpent members interested in playing football against Chicago. Although several of the juniors and seniors had played on class squads, there was not enough material to form a team. The Chicago Foot-Ball Club scrambled to find yet another replacement team but again failed. Not wanting to give up the chance to showcase football on Thanksgiving, the club invited several members of the Barge Club[27] back to scrimmage.

As the club ran football scrimmages in Chicago on Thanksgiving and the following weekend, more Northwestern students began to express interest in the prospect of a game. Theo Hilton recruited baseball player Frank Casseday, who in turn got Ed Kinman to join and began to organize the team along the same lines as the baseball team. Theo Hilton sent word to his cousin that the school might be up for the challenge after all. The Chicago club proposed a formal game on Saturday, December 4, 1875, this time at Northwestern in Evanston.[28] It is unknown why this second attempt also failed, but the Chicago Foot-Ball Club found itself drifting into December, still not having played a formal match. It continued to meet at the Tremont Hotel. Hornsby, now working out of the *Chicago Field*'s new office on Canal Street, actively tried to recruit a team to challenge the club.

On Thursday, December 9, the club found another team: a group of students from St. Ignatius College (present-day Loyola University Chicago) agreed to play, with twenty students facing off against fifteen players from Chicago.[29] While the teams did meet and practice the game, the Chicago Foot-Ball Club treated it as another practice scrimmage, still waiting for a true "outside match."[30]

The club continued to stage practice games, including a session on Christmas Day, 1875. Dividing the club into Blue and White squads, Hornsby watched, frustrated and angered, as the two groups bumbled around the White Stockings' field. C.J. Williams led the Blue squad and powered the group to a quick touchdown. "The game became very fast and exciting," Hornsby recalled, but was marred by "utter disregard of the rules and common sense. Firstly, there was too much talk; every man seemed to [think he] was qualified to lay down the law, whereas not two men on the field knew the law, and very few anything about it. Secondly, the picking up in the scrimmage is disgracefully flagrant, which spoiled both the cohesion of the forward and the life of the halfback play."[31] Hornsby worked to correct these issues as 1876 began.

• • •

At the end of 1875, Gus Hornsby had a steady income from the *Chicago Field*, but it wasn't enough to cover the expenses from his house in Hyde Park and his new family. His pay also couldn't support his gambling, which was more frequent and reckless. Hornsby was frequenting the nearby gambling houses throughout the city, and his debt mounted. He looked for additional work, and Curtis set him up as a referee for wrestling matches.[32] Hornsby had acted as a wrestling judge before, but never as a referee.

Hornsby's career as a referee was not an overwhelming success. His first big match took place in Detroit, held—of all places—in the city's splendid opera house. Surrounded by the lush stage and 3,000 screaming wrestling fans, Hornsby was already dangerously out of his depth. His calls during the match were so unpopular that coaches in both corners of the ring began screaming at him, and Hornsby shouted back at them and to the audience, which sent the crowd into hysterics. When one of the wrestlers fell and appeared to lose, Hornsby shouted, "no fall!"[33] The judges looked at him, shocked, and the two wrestlers stood and waited for something to happen.

Standing on the blazingly bright, prickly warm stage, eyed by the two quiet, dumbfounded wrestlers and the furious coaches, Hornsby tried to calm the participants by shouting at the unseen mass of viewers in the black cavern of the auditorium that he knew the rules. According to reporters covering the match, "the uproar became so great that an extra force of policemen were sent for, and Chief Rogers addressed the spectators from the stage, threatening to arrest anyone who created a disturbance."[34]

Rather than back down, Hornsby raced to the footlights of the stage and tried again to explain his position to the audience by shouting out the rules to the mob. The reporters were stunned: "The action of the referee was well-calculated to produce disorder. He ran hither and yon in a great state of perturbation and excitement."[35] Hornsby began to panic. He wasn't sure that he was going to leave the stage alive. His eyes bulging, he screamed at the audience, "Look here! I accepted the position of referee at the request of both parties. Everyone who knows me knows that I am thoroughly impartial! I would have refused to take a wager even for cigars on the result of this match!"[36] Hornsby paused, and the crowd laughed and shouted even louder. "Both coaches have requested that I resign, and so I do, and I'll leave it to them to settle the matter to suit themselves." With that, Hornsby raced from the stage, which filled in his wake with people screaming at each other.

The *Detroit Free Press* called Hornsby "disgracefully incompetent and prejudiced ... a marvel of stupidity. He is more a fool than a knave."[37] The *Chicago Tribune*, seeing an opportunity to take a shot at an employee of a competing publication, cattily added to the *Free Press*'s criticism: "It would have been better for the *Free Press* to have said of Hornsby that he was thoroughly incompetent to judge of any sporting matter, and left the question there. So far as this, the sporting men of Chicago would have gone with the Detroit people."[38]

• • •

Washington's birthday, February 22, 1876, was the next big holiday on the calendar, and cities were treating it as a run-up to the American centennial celebrations. Hornsby and Curtis wanted to stage their first successful "outside match" as part of the holiday. For the third time, they turned to Northwestern University.

Hornsby chose to use his own modification of the Harvard–Yale "Concessionary Rules," which the schools had created for their November 1875 game. Hornsby considered these rules "the essentials, the very best rules that the game of foot-ball can be played under by man."[39] He made copies for each member of the club, and he forwarded a copy to Northwestern.

As mentioned earlier, some schools in the East in the 1850s and 1860s played a crude version of the association football game, but prep schools in Boston, influenced by British rugby, played the carrying game. Schools devised their own rules of the game, with virtually no coordination between them.

The first recognized game of American football was *not* the carrying game, but a modified game of association football between Princeton and Rutgers in 1869. Harvard formed its first football club in 1872, and its members were mostly from the Boston-area prep schools, so Harvard favored the evolving rugby game, rather than the early soccer style. Canadian prep schools and colleges also gravitated to the English rugby style. The other American colleges playing football by then—Yale, Columbia, Dartmouth, and a few others—only played association style, using their own various rules. Some of these schools tried in 1873 to consolidate the rules of American football, but Harvard refused, because the other teams demanded the association style. Tufts College joined Harvard in adopting rugby-style rules, and the first carrying game of American intercollegiate football took place on June 4, 1875, when Tufts defeated Harvard by one goal and a touchdown to one touchdown.[40] It was at this point that Harvard and Yale began to draft the aforementioned Concessionary Rules.

These influential teams provided the framework for the new style of American football play. However, most other eastern colleges still clung to the more chaotic association style, which did not permit carrying the ball. The Concessionary style allowed carrying, favored drop-kicks for scoring, and set up the goal posts in a way that eventually facilitated further changes as the game moved toward a genuinely American variety.[41]

When Northwestern faced the Chicago club, the Evanston school became just the fourth college to play a game using the new, Americanized rugby rules.[42]

The Chicago team immediately began holding scrimmages using the newly revised rules, including a public scrimmage on February 12 that included neighborhood residents.[43]

As the club prepared for its match with Northwestern, it also planned its first large-scale public event, scheduling a cross-country steeplechase through the southern portion of Chicago for Saturday, February 19. Hornsby and Curtis turned to John B. Mayo, one of Chicago's top jewelers, to ensure a draw for the event. Like Hornsby, Mayo was an English immigrant, having come from Wiltshire to Chicago as a child.[44] He and his brother launched their jewelry business before the Civil War, on Wabash Street, but had lost it in the Fire. Mayo restarted his work, crafting a store in the Palmer House and becoming one of the country's foremost watch and clock makers. By 1873, Mayo had created a standard time system, using one of his custom clocks, a telegraph, and his own astronomical observations, that the major railroads adopted throughout the Midwest.[45] In the absence of standardized time zones (which the United States would not implement until 1882), Mayo's station in the Palmer House transmitted a daily pulse that the railways and public buildings used to regulate Chicago time, one of dozens of time localities in the country. Mayo was also an enthusiastic supporter of athletics, and he was an early member of Curtis's Chicago Athletic Club. He later joined the Chicago Athletic Association and stayed active in that organization for the rest of his life.[46] Although he never formally joined the Chicago Foot-Ball Club, Mayo was a staunch supporter and sponsor of the group, frequently socializing with Hornsby, Williams, and the other English members.

For the steeplechase event, Mayo customized a $25 silver cup and presented it as a prize. In return, the club christened the race "The J.B. Mayo & Co. Cup." However, the club overreached: Hornsby and Curtis decided that the team needed to practice for Northwestern the weekend before the game in Evanston. They postponed the race until the following weekend.

That Saturday, three days before Washington's birthday, the third attempt at a football game with Northwestern appeared to be on track. On Sunday, Hornsby and Curtis announced in the *Tribune* that "the Chicago Foot-Ball Club play their first outside match on the 22d against the Northwestern University at Evanston"[47] and gave the list of club players, with Hornsby as captain. The Evanston town newspaper took sides in a terse statement[48]: "Chicago wants to beat NWU at foot-ball."

"Go in, boys."

Game Day, 2:00 p.m.

The teams met at the gymnasium,[1] and the Chicago team finished changing into their uniforms. The players sat and removed their new white football shoes. They passed to each other a special key, which allowed them to release a set of small plates in the soles of each shoe. The Northwestern players then watched, curious and a bit awe-struck, as the Chicago men attached three cleats to the bottom of each of their shoes, tightening the spikes with the key.[2] By this point, football teams on the East Coast were using spiked shoes, and they had William Curtis to thank for them. Curtis had introduced spiked, or cleated, shoes in American athletics, taking them from English sports and using them for the first time in the United States for track and field sports just after the Civil War.[3]

Together, the Chicago players looked imposing, all dressed in the club's blue jerseys. The Northwestern players, however, did not have uniforms. Only Ed Kinman and Frank Casseday came close to dressing for the occasion, wearing their team baseball uniforms, white wool

NWU player Walter Lee Brown, who dressed in blue for the game with Chicago, is shown here in a photograph taken around 1894. Brown served as president of Evanston's gas company but is better remembered as one of the country's foremost metallurgists and a rare book collector (originally published by the Evanston, Illinois, Public Library, *Annual Report: 1904*).

pants and a white flannel baseball shirt with a wide collar and necktie. Their jerseys had a white flannel shield, or bib, buttoned into place on the chest. Frank's shield had "N.W.U." printed in brown in large old English letters; Ed's shield was plain. The rest of the Northwestern team was a motley group. They removed their coats and prepared to play in shirtsleeves. Senior Walter Lee Brown came dressed in blue, and Edwin Munroe wore a tattered shirt "that had once been scarlet."[4] The team dressed in a variety of colors, but apparently no purple. Northwestern did not yet have a school color and would not until 1879. The school first chose black and gold, but quickly switched to purple and gold in October 1879 and has had purple as its color, in some combination, ever since.

While the Chicago team all had matching knit caps, neither team wore a stitch of padding or real protection.

Theo Hilton kept his coat on and decided to play while wearing his silk hat as well. Hilton was a senior, and seniors had the honor of wearing "plug," or top, hats on campus, while other classes did not. Hilton decided to exercise his senior privilege, even during the game itself. A junior named Frank Early had recently defied the top hat rule and later recounted the experience:

> It was a sacred custom that Seniors only should wear 'plug' hats, and woe be it to a lower classman to presume on their prerogatives by appearing in public with such a headgear. At the same time it is "agin human natur" to take a dare; so when one of my Senior fraternity brothers dared me to wear one of my father's hats when I should drive down Davis Street, to meet him at the evening train, down Davis Street I drove—"plug" hat and all. Three Seniors were lying in wait for me at the post office, and the three made for me as we approached, but 'Old Nell' would go through a stone wall at word of command, and when told to keep going, she did, while those fellows walked back to the post office.[5]

• • •

The group made their way from the gymnasium to the field by heading north on campus, through the thick oak grove that skirted the lakefront. Despite the cold, somewhat cloudy day, the lakefront looked dazzling. There was little ice on the shore, and the waves crashed into the surf with the endless calming sound that provided part of the campus background.

The players passed the back of Heck Hall, doomed to burn to the ground in the early twentieth century. The university's Dempster Hall was directly to their north, a wood-framed, three-story dormitory, the oldest building on campus,[6] and another building fated to burn—though much sooner. The freshmen on the Northwestern football team would be seniors when a student's faulty stove led to the dorm's destruction in 1879.[7]

Drawing of Northwestern and Evanston, looking south, 1874. Heck Hall is in the foreground, University Hall behind it. The Davis Street pier is visible in the background. The trees at the bottom edge of the illustration mark the southern end of the school's athletic field (the field is not shown). To the right is Chicago Street (later renamed Sheridan Road), leading to the Evanston business district (originally published by Mason Turner & Co., American Oleograph Co., Milwaukee, Wisconsin).

• • •

As they walked through the oak grove, it's possible that the nineteen-year-old Louis Sullivan would have taken the opportunity to talk about the campus architecture with his teammate, John J. Flanders, who—though still quite young himself—was Sullivan's senior by nearly a decade and had already established himself as one of Chicago's preeminent architects. It is remarkable that, at that very moment in 1876, Chicago was home to the three men who would play the most critical roles in the development of the modern American skyscraper. It is even more remarkable that two of them were on the Chicago football team (the third architect was William LeBaron Jenney, who was not a known member of any of the Chicago athletic clubs).

Flanders was perhaps the most important of the three in terms of his early contributions to the skyscraper. Jenney's Home Insurance Building, which he designed for Chicago, and which was built in 1884 (completed in 1885), is considered by many architects to be the first true skyscraper. Its ten stories were impressive; however, they did not match the twelve stories of Flanders's steel and masonry masterpiece, the Maller's Building. Built on the corner of Chicago's Quincy and LaSalle streets, Maller's was begun in 1883 and completed in 1884, giving it a legitimate claim to be the first skyscraper. Ironically, the style of the Maller's would imitate to a great degree the work that Sullivan was doing in Chicago at the time, with its grouped windows, narrow bays, and vertical accents.[8]

Born in Chicago and raised in nearby Glencoe, Illinois, Flanders had established his independent architecture practice in Chicago the year before joining the Chicago Foot-Ball Club.[9] In 1876, he was busy rebuilding homes and other residences in Chicago's recovering north side. Later, he would design a string of schools throughout the city, some of which are still in use.

• • •

The teams came to a small stream that the NWU students called "The Rubicon." The Rubicon, a thirty-foot-wide drainage ditch that twisted its way to the northern portion of the campus, looked particularly filthy; a trickle of muddy water snaked through it, despite the cold. The group crossed over the Rubicon as they made their way to the field, stepping across a decidedly shaky-looking wooden footbridge. The stream and surrounding field resembled Aldershot: the smell of damp, cold earth, the mud and wooden walkways of the camp, and the rock-hard dirt field on which Hornsby taught other officers to play rugby. He was again in uniform less than five years later, a uniform now devoted solely to sport.

A surprisingly large group of spectators had already gathered at the grounds, including most of the university's women students. The attendees weren't just Northwestern students: Garrett Biblical students also left Heck Hall to watch the festivities. Many Evanston residents made their way to campus since the game was the only holiday event in the town. The Evanston *Index* lamented, "Tuesday was the anniversary of Washington's birthday, and as such was turned into a day of rejoicing everywhere. Evanston was an exception. The foot-ball match was the only thing we know of, that grew out of the fact that Washington once lived and lied not."[10]

Most of the prep students on campus joined in, walking from the larger building next to the gymnasium, which housed Northwestern Preparatory School.[11] One of those prep students was a fourteen-year-old first-year boy named William Dyche, who years later would be elected Evanston's mayor, and who would have a substantial impact on Northwestern's football program for decades. William's father, Dr. David Dyche, served as president of Evanston's Citizen's League, another of the town's prohibition groups.[12] Frances Willard said of David Dyche's temperance efforts, "to this good man and his coadjutors Evanston owes more than can be told."[13]

As the players approached the field, the crowd gaped at the Chicago team and their natty uniforms. Some of the spectators recognized Curtis, and his presence caused a bit of a stir: he was well known by this point as a champion weightlifter and rower. The Northwestern students looked a bit dazed. They had read the new football rules, Kinman had explained them further, they had tried a couple of practice plays, and they had asked Hornsby questions at the gymnasium. Still, the rules bothered them, and most of them would have preferred to play the virtually rules-free kicking football to which they were more accustomed.

Hornsby was discouraged by the condition of the field. It was not a smooth surface, and the students had not prepared it for a football game. The school had not marked boundary lines; there were no goal lines, and—most distressing—no one had erected the goal posts. Fortunately, the students did have proper goal posts, but they lay on the open ground. Hornsby asked if they had a shovel to help ground the posts.[14] After some frantic searching, a student managed to find a small spade, but the ground, still semi-frozen, proved too hard to dig. Hornsby found a novel solution. Employing the help of several of the spectators, he moved each goal post into position flat on the ground just beyond each goal. During the game, he instructed the group, when a goal or drop-kick was about to be attempted, the group responsible for the posts would quickly raise them and hold them in place until the kick attempt finished. This was met with derisive laughter; however, with no better plan offered, the group began to move the posts into position.[15] To one post they tied the Chicago club's banner, a blue silk pennant with "CFBC" sewn onto it in gold, with gold silk fringe. To the other they tied a plain white flag with "NWU" painted on it. Several spectators carried American flags.

Hornsby had brought his own football, which he offered to the Northwestern players to keep, replacing their old, (mostly) round kicking ball. Hornsby wanted to use a true, oval-shaped rugby football, rather than the completely round football that even the East Coast schools were still using.

• • •

Since Hornsby's departure from Wellington, the ball used in rugby games there had changed significantly. Throughout his childhood and during his stint with the regiment, Hornsby had used an inflated pig's bladder as a football, carefully fashioned and molded into a roughly round shape. However, while Hornsby had been away, a man from Rugby had improved the ball significantly. Richard Lindon was a cobbler who lived in a house across the street from the Rugby School. Lindon and his wife made balls for the Rugby students, and, according to one legend, Lindon's wife blew up so many balls made from pig's bladders—some of them diseased— that she became fatally ill from them.[16] Lindon's experience with working leather allowed him to craft a football that had an improved all-leather casing with an inflatable bladder made of rubber. The new football was rounder than the old pig bladder ball, but retained a bit of the eccentricity, giving it a slightly oval shape. Lindon kept the oval shape at the request of the Rugby students, who had become accustomed to the pig bladder shape

A drawing of association and rugby balls of the time, taken from an 1873 sporting goods catalog, *Peck & Snyder's Encyclopedia* (which the Chicago Foot-Ball Club would later use to purchase their uniforms and equipment).

Ball used in the Harvard–Yale football game, November 1876, even though the game used rugby rules (originally published in the November 1876 Harvard–Yale Game Program).

of the ball and wanted the oval shape to distinguish their ball from the perfectly round ball used in the kicking-only version of association football.[17]

For comparison, on top of the facing page is an illustration of both types of balls from an 1873 catalog.[18]

Most of the East Coast schools, even the ones playing the carrying versions of football, still used a round ball. Harvard and Yale would continue to use an association ball even in their 1876 match (see bottom of facing page).

Hornsby wanted a good rugby ball, so he went to the source. He splurged, paying $6 for a first-quality ball made by Richard Lindon in Rugby, featuring an Indian rubber bladder and fine leather.

* * *

The players measured out the playing field and marked out the goals as best as they

Rugby ball creator Richard Lindon in 1880, holding four-panel "buttonless" balls, identical to the one used for the February 1876 NWU game (1880 photograph posted on www.richardlindon.com).

could. With that, the teams were ready to begin. Hornsby allowed Northwestern to use five more players than Chicago, to try to account for the students' lack of experience. It isn't known who refereed the game, but he gave Northwestern the choice of goal to begin. Ed Kinman chose to defend the north goal, moving with the slight wind that was blowing that afternoon. The teams agreed to play two thirty-minute halves, switching goals at halftime. At a few minutes after 3:00 p.m., the twenty NWU players and fifteen Chicago players took the field. Chicago was to kick off.

Hornsby put on his knit cap, took the ball, placed it on the ground, and gave it a swift, violent kick.

Chapter 5

1876: Chicago

After Northwestern played its first American football game, it wasted no time trying to get another game together. Frank Casseday led the school's new football club, which grew to thirty students within a day of the game. Just four days after the game, the new club staged its first intramural game on the NWU grounds.[1] Thomas Fauntleroy, of the Chicago Club, wrote on behalf of Hornsby to Edwin Munroe at Northwestern, noting that the Chicago players enjoyed the game on the 22nd and would be happy to continue the "missionary work" by hosting another game with the university.[2] While the students continued to play football among themselves, they eventually declined the rematch, preferring to keep their further football games within the university group. During the next few years, Northwestern students continued to play football using the modified rugby rules but only staged a couple of games with outsiders, mostly high schools. It was not until 1882 that the university finally played its first intercollegiate game, against nearby Lake Forest College. By then the games of the 1870s had been forgotten.

The new version of football was already in jeopardy by early 1876. Just a day before Chicago visited Northwestern for its first game, a player in England died while playing rugby rules football. He had been thrown backward and had struck the back of his head on the turf. News of the death came to the United States several days later and shook the East Coast teams. Experts thought that the death might "at last lead to some modification of the deadly rules under which [football] is occasionally carried on," according to the *New York Sun*.[3]

• • •

Hornsby and Curtis expanded the Chicago Foot-Ball Club after the Northwestern game, with several more immigrants joining the team, men who had played rugby football back in England. They tried to schedule another game before summer, inviting Cornell[4]—the very same school targeted by the University of Michigan for a football game just two years before—but Hornsby and Curtis were, as expected, rebuffed by the eastern school. Cornell was still reluctant to try the carrying style of the game (although, by 1876, Cornell was playing the older kicking game as an inter-class exercise[5]). Later in the year, Hornsby and Curtis went after the University of Michigan itself, which was still trying to organize a game. The university—somewhat surprisingly—rejected the offer, stating in November 1876 that

> a challenge has been received by the University [of Michigan's] Foot-ball Association from the Chicago Foot-ball Club, to play a game of foot-ball at Chicago on Thanksgiving Day, the Rugby Union rules to govern the game. The association decided not to accept for the date mentioned, but to ask that the matter be allowed to rest till next spring. It is probable that a match will be arranged at that time.[6]

There is no record, for either the Chicago Foot-Ball Club or the University of Michigan, that they joined up the following spring and played. However, Michigan, had begun to think about the carrying game of football again and trying to muster a possible team. The student newspaper went so far as to print the carrying game's rules (slightly different still from the Concessionary Rules of the previous year), mentioning that it offered up the rules "for the benefit of those of our readers who are interested in the game of foot ball. [The rules] will be seen to differ in many respects from the chaotic traditions which have heretofore been the game's guide."[7] As the spring loomed, Michigan's frustration increased, with calls to accept Hornsby and Curtis's challenge and "wax those Chicago fellows at foot-ball."[8] One Michigan student further remarked:

> A good many of us have already taken up the Rugby Union rules as an extra study.... [This spring] we expect to see only professionals in uniform, playing foot-ball on campus, with professional sports staking money on the result, and the whole body of admiring medics, laws, and lits, standing around and watching the fine plays. Then we shall eagerly subscribe money to send our pet crew to Chicago to wipe out the Westerners. O, how glorious that will be![9]

• • •

Hornsby decided that spring was too warm to play football,[10] and the White Stockings needed their grounds to practice for the 1876 season. So the club instead focused on track and field and held its long-delayed steeplechase event, a four-mile cross-country race throughout Chicago. Hornsby practiced by sprinting up and down Chicago's Michigan Avenue on the lakefront. Louis Sullivan, originally slated to run, had to drop out, as did C.J. Williams.[11] The race quickly shaped up to be a fierce match between Hornsby and club member Charles Keith, who was forced to slow due to a cramp in his side. Hornsby took a 400-yard lead in the race. However, an oncoming train threatened his lead, and Hornsby had to sprint to the tracks to head off the train and maintain the lead. Hornsby raced across the tracks moments before the train sailed across, and he won the first—and only—John Mayo Cup.[12]

Soon after the race, the club secured a new field on 34th Street, between Michigan and Wabash Avenues.[13] They proposed a new football

PROGRAMME

Chicago Foot Ball Club

Athletic Sports,

— AT —

BASE BALL GROUNDS,

CORNER 23D AND STATE STREETS,

SATURDAY MAY 27TH, 3 P. M.

JUDGES:

CALVIN COBB, Commander Chicago Barge Club.

F. B. HAMILTON, Secretary Chicago Barge Club.

A. OGDEN DOWNS, Captain Farragut Boat Club.

T. WILY TAYLOR, Judge of Walk.

RULES:

Any one starting or going over his mark with either foot, before the signal, will be put back a yard for the first offence, and disqualified for the second.

A bell will be rung before each heat, when competitors will at once proceed to their marks. Races will be started punctually.

The decision of the Judges will be final.

No Person will be allowed on the Course, except the Competitors and Judges.

TICKETS, admitting Gentleman and Ladies, - - 50 Cents.

The Prizes for these Races are from the well-known Establishment of J. B. MAYO & CO.

Chicago Evening Journal Print.

The CFBC's program for its May 1876 field day, held at the Chicago White Stockings / Chicago Cubs' ball grounds. This program is the only known surviving artifact from the team (originally published by the Chicago *Evening Journal*).

field on the site, as well as a quarter-mile track and a baseball diamond. The group planned to hold its biggest event to date later that spring, a track and field spectacle, participation in which would be open to the public. John Mayo again agreed to use his jewelry business to craft prizes for the event, and club member John Jeffrey committed to supplying programs for it, using his printing house at the *Evening Journal*.

• • •

John B. Jeffrey was another immigrant, having come from Canada to Chicago during the Civil War. Of all the Chicago Foot-Ball Club members, he was probably the best-known in Chicago by the 1870s. Jeffrey had started his career as a printer's assistant and editor, working first in Ontario, then with the *Inter-Ocean* in Chicago. In 1869 he traveled to Indianapolis and began the first-ever mass-produced, tabloid penny newspaper, the *Indianapolis News*.[14] Jeffrey complained later that "the *News* afterward sold for over $900,000, but I didn't get any of that money."[15] Regardless of credit and compensation, he took the idea back with him to Chicago.

Jeffrey spent the next couple of years shuttling between Chicago and New York, where he worked with Charles Dana on the *New York Sun*. During this period, Jeffrey befriended Mark Twain, editing his copy, as well as early works by James Whitcomb Riley.[16]

Jeffrey was in Chicago, working at the *Evening Journal* on October 9, 1871, when the Great Fire hit the paper's offices. As the *Evening Journal* burned, Jeffrey raced through the chaotic city and took over the old Edwards Directory press. In a few hours, he managed to put together an extra edition of the *Evening Journal* using the Edwards's antique

John B. Jeffrey, newspaperman and printer, in a photograph taken in the early 1890s. Jeffrey had experience with rugby and East Coast American football before joining the CFBC. Although his printing empire collapsed in the late 1880s amid allegations of fraud, Jeffrey defended himself successfully against the charges (originally published by the Press Club of Chicago, 1894).

printing works. The *Evening Journal* got to claim that it was the only Chicago newspaper not to have missed releasing a daily issue through the Great Fire and its aftermath. The paper's owner, Charles Wilson, rewarded Jeffrey generously. Wilson later said that the paper's claim of an unbroken line of daily issues was worth thousands of dollars to him.[17]

In the hours and days that followed the Fire, Jeffrey filled the *Evening Journal* with increasingly fantastical tales of the Fire's origin, including the now-legendary details of Mrs. O'Leary and her much-maligned cow.

• • •

Years after the Chicago Fire, Jeffrey recounted the events leading up to the O'Leary legend:

> My cashier's name was Dan Horan. We had taken temporary quarters in [the Edwards printing building] and Gen. Sheridan[18] had given me a company of soldiers and told me to get out a paper if I could.
>
> I didn't have any copy, but I set up the first column and a half of type, with the exception of one tiny paragraph. The first column was composed of a headline.
>
> Well, Dan came in drunk. I asked him where he had been. "Sure, sir," he replied. "I've been saving the files of the *Journal*; they are in your stables on the West Side."
>
> "What do you know about the origin of the fire?" I asked him.
>
> "Sure, I know all about it," he replied. "It started in a stable on DeKoven Street. A woman was milking a cow there, and the cow kicked over the lamp." He added that the woman was a Mrs. O'Leary. I set up the story without any copy, and it made about a stickful. It went all over the country. Mrs. O'Leary denied it up to the day of her death, but nothing could stop the story.[19]

General Sheridan had indeed instructed Jeffrey to try to put out an issue in order to inform the city of the situation, but Horan's story, and whether he and Jeffrey came up with it, are less certain. Toward the end of his life, Jeffrey was circumspect: he admitted that the story was not based on verified fact, "but why spoil one of our few traditions?" he asked.[20] As with several other members of the Chicago Foot-Ball Club, John Jeffrey was not the most reliable narrator. In addition to taking credit for publicizing the story of O'Leary's cow, Jeffrey claimed to have helped establish both the Chicago Press Club and the Order of Elks. While he was a member of both clubs, he had a role in founding neither group.

The origin of the O'Leary legend is not settled, and Jeffrey's is not the strongest claim. The *Chicago Tribune*'s Michael Ahern also wrote about O'Leary while a member of the newspaper's police beat, and he (along with two other reporters on the beat) also took credit for the story.[21] Of course, Ahern and his colleagues had to wait to publish their account: the *Tribune*

EVENING JOURNAL-EXTRA.

CHICAGO, MONDAY, OCTOBER 9, 1871.

THE GREAT CALAMITY OF THE AGE!

Chicago in Ashes!!

evening, being caused by a cow kicking over a lamp in a stable in which a woman was milking. An alarm was immediately given, but, owing to the high southwest wind, the building was speedily consumed, and thence the fire spread rapidly. The firemen could not, with all their efforts, get the mastery of he flames. Building after building was fired by the flying cinders, which, landing on the roofs, which were as dry as tinder, owing to the protracted dry weather, instantly took fire. Northwardly and northeastwardly the flames took their course, lapping up house after house, block after block,

In fact, as stated above, the entire South and North sides, from Harrison street, northwardly, with a few isolated buildings left standing in some remark- able manner, are in hopeless ruins,

HELP COMING.

During the night, telegrams were sent to St. Louis, Cleveland, Milwaukee and nearer cities for aid, and at the time of going to press several trains are on the way to the city, bringing free engines and men to assist us in this dire calamity.

BOARD OF TRADE.

The Board of Trade has leased for present use

Jeffrey's Chicago Fire issue, one of the first newspapers to have large headlines (Chicago *Evening Journal*, October 8, 1871).

only managed to print a rough two-page edition two full days after the Fire.

Jeffrey's splash headline for the *Evening Journal*'s extra issue, "Calamity of the Age," was his first experiment with large headlines, and it was Jeffrey who eventually led newspapers away from small-font page one headlines to large, attention-grabbing banners.[22]

• • •

Four years later, Jeffrey owned a large printing house, and his wife, Emma, was the toast of Chicago society. Having a member with so many publicity and press resources would have been a godsend to Curtis and Hornsby's new football club, and Hornsby went to visit Jeffrey just a couple of days before the team's inaugural meeting on November 15, 1875. Jeffrey's printing company occupied the entire second floor of the *Evening Journal*'s headquarters. Hornsby likely expected to see Jeffrey in a cramped printing office among the presses. He was utterly mistaken and was shocked when he entered Jeffrey's opulent office.[23] The suite was richly appointed, more splendid than any officers' club or fashionable hotel Hornsby had ever seen. Jeffrey's quarter featured plush pile carpet, a maroon and gold-swirled indulgence that seemed to envelop Hornsby as he strode to Jeffrey's titanic mahogany desk. The office smelled of a delightful combination of freshly cut linen paper, ink, orchids, and sandalwood, providing sensations similar to what Hornsby would have encountered in India, in English oases of luxury and overindulgence that, though wrought through cruelty, were nonetheless comforting and exquisite to him.

Jeffrey sat behind his fortress of a desk and listened to Hornsby describe his vision of the new football club. Jeffrey was only thirty years old, and he looked like an athlete—tall, muscular, and energetic. He was known for being good-humored and likable,[24] and he showed that charm to Hornsby as he agreed at once to join the club. Jeffrey explained to Hornsby that he had experience playing football, both in Ontario and New York, and he relished the chance to have another go.

• • •

The Chicago Foot-Ball Club held their field day on May 27, 1876, during which Hornsby, Curtis, and the Sullivan brothers all competed in various races. Hulbert managed to get the White Stockings' field again for the occasion, and several hundred people turned out to watch, paying fifty cents apiece—an expensive ticket at the time.[25] As expected, Curtis, Albert Sullivan, and C.J. Williams won most of the events, with Williams winning the featured one-mile run in five minutes and twelve seconds. Times were not the best, "as the grass was indifferently cut," Hornsby later complained.[26] Hornsby, wearing his standard black and white athletic suit, failed to win an event, as did Louis Sullivan.

Though only thirty, Hornsby was slipping from the top form he had exhibited when he came to America in 1873. By the fall of 1876 Hornsby relinquished the captain position on the Chicago team, and a young Chicago member named William Vernon Booth took over. Hornsby was justifiably proud of his role in introducing football to the Midwest, and he wrote about it in the *Chicago Field* that December:

> For a long time racing and shooting were the only two gentlemanly and honorable sports indulged in by us, but gradually as the wealth of the country has been increasing, the old country pastimes have been taken hold of one by one and with each adoption the country has gained a fresh impulse in the direction of many sport.
>
> Just one year ago the glorious winter recreation of foot ball was almost unknown in this country, except to be indulged in occasionally in a rough and tumble style. Harvard University had a trained and skilled team, and the only foot ball club in the country outside of an educational establishment was the then newly started Chicago Foot Ball Club in this city. This latter was formed by a few energetic athletes, mainly, we believe, owing to articles on the manly sport that appeared in our editorial columns, and by its birth stimulated the formation of a club in the University at Evanston....
>
> From our own locality let us turn East and note there the rapid advances in popularity of the game.... Four games in one week each attracting an average enthusiastic attendance of about one thousand spectators among whom were many ladies! Does not this speak well for the interesting nature of the game and the strong hold it has taken on the public. At present the colleges alone are playing the game scientifically but we hope shortly to hear that New York has a club of its own among its business men, and that they are as ready to do battle with the West, as the West is willing to meet them.[27]

In his last paragraph, Hornsby was hoping that William Curtis would form a sister football club in New York. If Curtis tried, he did not succeed. Curtis did attend one of the eastern football games in November 1876 that Hornsby referenced in his column, a match between Yale and Princeton played in Hoboken. Yale won, 2–0, powered by smart playing by Walter Camp. However, it was a Yale senior, halfback William Hatch, who caught Curtis's eye with his rushing abilities.

• • •

In January 1877 Gus and Marie Hornsby had their second child, a daughter they named Rachel. Rachel, however, was not the only addition to Hornsby's Hyde Park family. Gus's youngest brother, Arthur, had traveled from England and asked to stay with the family in Chicago for a while. Gus and Marie agreed, and Arthur moved in. He would remain with the family for nearly a decade, making money by training hunting dogs to retrieve.

Gus Hornsby also worked with sporting dogs during this period, and in 1877, while still with the *Chicago Field*, Hornsby accepted a well-paying freelance position to write about dog contests for the *Chicago Tribune*. He recalled his sporting dog coverage twenty years later for a special column in *Field & Stream*, despite the fact that—as Hornsby put it—"twenty years leave cobwebs in the halls of memory, which it is not easy to sweep away without the besom of reference to some journal of the day."[28] He also began marketing his second book, *The Sportsmen's Record*, a small volume of hunting and field trivia and memoranda. "It is just the thing every sportsman wants, for at any time he can look back and give the particulars of a day's bag."[29] The book sold for fifty cents.

For the next couple of years, Hornsby continued working for the *Chicago Field*, occasionally refereeing sporting events in Chicago and handicapping horse races (which did not likely help his gambling obsession). In November 1878, he traveled west and then left for Japan, covering his travel for the *Chicago Field*. This allowed Hornsby to teach and play football for the first time in the Far East.

He left Japan aboard the British tramp steamer Malacca in December, bound for Hong Kong.[30] While in Hong Kong, Hornsby socialized with the British Colonial Service members serving on the island, playing rugby football and teaching the officers the American twists on the game. Just a few months after Hornsby's departure, a cadet named James Stewart Lockhart arrived from Scotland.[31] Stewart Lockhart was delighted to see that his fellow officers already knew and enjoyed football; he had played for the University of Edinburgh from 1874 to 1876.[32] Six years after his arrival, Stewart Lockhart founded Hong Kong's Football Club. The club still exists, better known now for playing association football. However, it began by playing the modified rugby football that Hornsby initially taught to the British officers and Stewart Lockhart eventually perfected.

• • •

Hornsby and Marie had their third child in 1879: they named the boy Arthur, after Hornsby's brother, the baby's godfather. By 1881 Gus Hornsby served the magazine (now called the *American Field*) as a traveling correspondent, reporting on hunting and dog breeding. He visited spots throughout the Midwest, as far as Kansas, where he received a better welcome than he had in Detroit. The Kansas journalists who covered Hornsby's visit called him "a most agreeable gentleman who it gave us great pleasure to meet."[33] Hornsby's position at the magazine was paying better, but he was gambling more frequently, and he sought out games as he traveled. Again, Hornsby teetered toward debt.

Hornsby traveled to St. Paul, Minnesota, covering local events for both the *American Field* and the *New York Sportsman*.[34] He planned to continue his trip to Winnipeg and then return to cover the Minneapolis exposition. However, Hornsby made a couple of discoveries. First, while meeting with the representatives of two local papers, the *St. Paul Globe* and the *Pioneer Press*, he learned that the *Pioneer Press* did not have a sporting section. The paper told Hornsby that it would be interested in hiring him as its first-ever sports editor. What neither he nor the newspaper's staff knew was that, at the time, virtually no newspapers outside of the east coast had a dedicated sports editor.

The other discovery that Hornsby made while in St. Paul was that the city was in the early stages of a real estate boom—at least, that was the word from a couple of his contacts there. The city enjoyed an initial boom in the early 1870s when the St. Paul Street Railway began.[35] Streetcar service facilitated a dramatic expansion of the city. Real estate was about to explode, and the prospect was too great a lure for Hornsby to resist. Here, he might be able to find a diamond mine before the masses and become a rich man. His gambling habit was raging, and now he had in his sights the most wonderful gamble of all.

PART TWO

The Fraud

Game Day, 3:05 p.m.

To start the game, Hornsby had kicked the ball deep into Northwestern territory. To his surprise, the NWU players made no effort to get to the ball; instead, the university players stood in place, watching the Chicago players to see what they might do. The CFBC players, on the other hand, did not hesitate. The instant that Hornsby kicked off, the nine Chicago forwards sprinted toward the ball. A forward named Charles Keith got to the ball first, grabbed it, and handed it to Thomas Fauntleroy, who was also playing forward for Chicago. At last, the Northwestern players raced to the ball, but too late to stop Chicago. Fauntleroy took the ball and lobbed it back to Hornsby. Hornsby sprinted to the goal line, getting the game's first touchdown.

While the crowd had no idea of the rules of this new version of football, it had no problem discerning that the Chicago club had just done something good in the game's first ninety seconds. The spectators sent out a loud series of groans.

• • •

Several members of the school's faculty were likely present at the game, including Professor Cumnock, Frank Casseday's elocution teacher, who occasionally attended the school's baseball games.

One professor who was doubtless at the football match was Julius Kellogg, Northwestern's head of mathematics, who was the biggest supporter of athletics at the university. He made a point of attending all NWU's ball games, and football would have been no exception. The Northwestern students called Professor Kellogg "Baldy" because of his smooth, prematurely bald head, but rarely to his face. One student who did call Kellogg Baldy to his face, and got away with it, was the aforementioned Frank Early (who seems to have pressed his luck through much of his time at Northwestern), who recounted the following: "I shall never forget my embarrassment when, one day, absorbed in a blackboard demonstration in geometry, I inadvertently addressed Professor Kellogg as 'Baldy,' his campus nickname. The class roared, and the genial Professor's sides shook with laughter at my expense."[1] Professor Fisk, the principal of NWU's Prep School, once said of Kellogg, "If he could ever forgive stupidity in a scholar, it was because that scholar was a good ball player."[2] However, Kellogg would not have forgiven the stupidity witnessed in the first play of this football game, and he likely joined the crowd in sounding out its displeasure, possibly shouting out a few salty suggestions to the players. "He had an inexhaustible supply of dry humor, and his jokes and stories were always current among the last good things," Frank Casseday recalled of Kellogg years later.[3] "Dear old Baldy would sit on the sidelines, cheer, and enjoy the games to the utmost."

Professor Julius "Baldy" Kellogg, the first Northwestern faculty member to support athletics at the school and a frequent spectator at the NWU athletic grounds. Kellogg died in 1894, suffering an accidental fall under rather mysterious circumstances in Chicago. The accident and its aftermath were shrouded in secrecy (photograph by Alexander Hesler, courtesy Northwestern University Archives).

However, the school's president, the Rev. Charles Fowler, was indifferent to athletics and never attended games. Fowler, Frances Willard's former fiancé,[4] was in his final year as president. He was a supporter of women students at Northwestern, but he eventually clashed with Willard, who wanted more control as dean of women over the women on campus. Fowler, however, took a position rare for the time, arguing for coeducational autonomy, that the same set of rules should apply to all students. This position undermined Willard's authority and helped to drive her from her post at NWU and toward a full-time career with the W.C.T.U. Willard agonized over the decision to resign from Northwestern, but from her standpoint, the women students needed a woman to guide them and required a set of rules separate from the "men's faculty." As Willard put it, she had to be mindful "of the parents asking, 'What safeguards can you offer my daughter in her youth and inexperience?'" She felt a duty to advocate "such care and oversight, as will replace, so far as it can be done, the influence of home."[5] Willard and Fowler's brief relationship was turbulent yet defined by mutual admiration. In her autobiography, Willard admitted, "Dr. Fowler has the will of a Napoleon, and I have the will of a Queen Elizabeth; when an immovable meets an indestructible object, something has to give way."[6]

• • •

Following Chicago's touchdown, Charles Keith took the ball and placed it in front of the goal for Hornsby to try a kick. Using Hornsby's rules, the teams recorded each touchdown, but they did yet count as a score to win the game. They were useful only as a means to secure the best position on the field for a goal after the touchdown. Players could also score goals from elsewhere on the field, either by placing the ball on the ground or through a dropkick. However, these kicks were more challenging than the try after a touchdown. There were no "points" yet in football: all successful goals counted as a score. While teams kept track of the numbers of touchdowns, goals, and safeties that they accomplished, the number of goals usually determined a victor.

On cue, the goal post keepers lifted the northern poles, allowing the white NWU flag to flutter in the air. Hornsby kicked the ball flawlessly, splitting the uprights and sending it soaring over the crossbar.

Chicago led, a goal and a touchdown to nothing, with less than two minutes played.

CHAPTER 6

1882: St. Paul

The Hornsbys moved to St. Paul in early 1882, bringing Gus's brother Arthur with them. The family settled on Dearborn Street in West St. Paul, south of the Mississippi. A reporter with the *St. Paul Globe* later described the Hornsby house as "a snug little home earned by economy and hard work, a beauty spot reclaimed from the natural wilderness of hazel brush and burr oaks, and attractive outlook for visitors ... to halt and look out upon the Father of Waters and the distant panorama of the opposing hills."[1]

Hornsby immediately began work at the *Pioneer Press*.

It was Marie Hornsby, however, who first began to speculate in real estate. With the family settled, Gus working at the newspaper, and Gus's brother Arthur helping watch the children, Marie used the last of her money to buy up undeveloped lots in West St. Paul.[2] Hornsby soon joined his wife. His first purchase was an old St. Paul brewery, and he followed that with properties throughout St. Paul and West St. Paul.[3]

To Hornsby's delight, his lots sold quickly and at dramatic profits. He and Marie had a knack for picking the right lots, and they were ruthless to those who could not fulfill their obligations, hauling dozens of people into court during the mid–1880s. Toward the end of 1886, Hornsby was developing entire city blocks of property, including an extensive new development just a block north of Hornsby's home.[4]

• • •

Hornsby eventually frequented the illegal gambling houses during his time in Chicago, and when he moved to St. Paul, he found plenty of gambling spots awaiting him. In 1882, when Hornsby arrived, Minneapolis and St. Paul were dealing with a proliferation of gambling houses. Minneapolis harbored a strip of secret gambling sites similar to Chicago's "Hair-Trigger Block," only (typically) not as violent. Down the city's Nicollet Avenue, Hornsby found gambling houses crammed onto several blocks. Most luxurious was a saloon called Paul's. When Hornsby first visited, he opened the discreet second-floor entrance and found a richly-appointed chamber that seemed like Chicago's Store, in miniature: plush carpeting, marble fixtures, and formally-dressed servants.[5] Paul's gambling centered on roulette and the card game faro, and would not have appealed much to Hornsby. More to his liking would have been the poker games hosted at a secretive club nicknamed "The Gentlemen's Own," a Minneapolis gambling house that required both a pass key and a password to enter.[6] The Gentlemen's Own, in the words of a local reporter in 1882, catered to "business men, gentlemen of leisure, professional men, capitalists and salaried persons. The laboring man, who has not much to lose, is excluded."[7]

While Hornsby usually frequented these Minneapolis houses, he also had gambling options even closer to home. By the late 1880s, there were roughly a dozen "high-class" gambling houses in downtown St. Paul itself, and ten times that number of lower-class houses, or "hells," as they were called, spread across the city.[8] Hornsby would not have usually gone to a St. Paul gambling house: he had a reputation to uphold in the city. However, if desperate, he might have tried to be discreet and hit one of the closer halls.

Mere blocks from Hornsby's house was an enormous gambling establishment called the "Turf Exchange." Former gambler John Philip Quinn described St. Paul's Turf Exchange and its complex and surprisingly sophisticated operation of the late 1880s:

> The "Turf Exchange" is known as a pooling room. Pools are sold there on horse races, boat races, ball games, prize fights, and elections.... During base ball season this resort is crowded by day and night, and a considerable force of telegraph operators is employed in receiving the reports which come in over the wires, and the services of a large staff of assistants is needed in checking up the results on the boards....
>
> Little more than a year ago the pool room was victimized by some adroit sharpers who tapped the telegraph wires, and by withholding messages for a few minutes were enabled to make bets which proved disastrous to the proprietors of the institution.
>
> It is only the initiated, however, who are aware that immediately above the pool rooms a gambling hell is in full blast. The up-stairs den is well furnished and the games include faro, roulette, poker, the wheel of fortune, dice, etc.[9]

For much of the 1880s, the Minneapolis and St. Paul authorities chose to ignore gambling rather than confront it. However, if the situation began to get out of hand, as it did in late 1886, police were forced to intervene. One newspaper noted that "'Major' Pond, who is still the leader of the largest [gambling] gang, is still in the city, but the ugly mugs of his followers are conspicuous by their absence from their usual haunts."[10] Gamblers took the hint, scaling down their operations and avoiding public spectacles when possible.

• • •

Back in Chicago, the Chicago Foot-Ball Club had disbanded. The team had played its last few significant games in 1877, when Hornsby was still in Chicago. Hornsby, though then still a member, had little to do with them. In addition to giving up the captain position in the fall of 1876, Hornsby transitioned his role as secretary to Louis Sullivan.[11] Thomas Fauntleroy soon took the captain's role from William Vernon Booth, and William Borner had taken over as the club's president earlier from William Curtis.

Curtis spent most of his time in New York, where he was president of the New York Athletic Club. From 1878 to 1887, Curtis was instrumental in founding the National Association of Amateur Athletes of America, the National Amateur Skating Association, and the Amateur Athletic Union.[12] His time in Chicago had tapered to increasingly fleeting visits.

In New York, Curtis did manage to recruit at least one player for Chicago: Yale's star halfback William Hatch, a former member of the famed 1876 Yale football team. Hatch had played alongside Walter Camp, the man who essentially created football's quarterback position along with a host of new rules for the modern game.

Hatch hailed from a prosperous and famous New York family and frequented the same yacht clubs that Curtis did. His father was Alfrederick Smith Hatch, a wealthy stockbroker. The elder Hatch commissioned Eastman Johnson to paint a family portrait of himself, his parents, and his children. *The Hatch Family* from 1871 currently hangs in the New York Metropolitan Museum of Art. William Hatch only played for Yale in 1876, and he did not graduate. He pursued the usual activities of New York's leisure class, including piloting the New York Yacht Club boat *Wayward*.

Getting Hatch as a player (at least while Hatch also split time between Chicago and New York) was a coup—Hornsby mentioned Hatch's contributions to the Chicago Foot-Ball Club in his recollections decades later.[13] However, the benefit was short-lived. The Chicago team failed to arrange any big games, though it tried to host games against Harvard, Yale, and any English rugby teams that elected to visit America. Hatch soon left the team. Sullivan, as the team secretary, tried to set up matches against worthy opponents, but there were not yet many teams in the Midwest that were willing to play the college-style American football, so he switched his efforts to arranging social events for the club.[14]

An attempt to remake the CFBC came in the spring of 1882, but as a traditional English rugby squad, rather than a team that played using the modified East Coast college American football rules. Hornsby was gone by then, and with him left any motivation to continue to play the American college style of football—at least for the rest of the 1880s. C.J. Williams, one of the team's founding members and (next to Curtis) perhaps its greatest athlete, captained the team in 1886 in a rugby match against a team from Windsor, Ontario. Williams would be dead by year's end. Another new group called the Chicago Football Club—this one unaffiliated with Curtis and Hornsby's creation and dedicated to association football—started the following year and continued off and on for over a decade. By then, other American football teams were cropping up in Chicago, including the Chicago Wanderers (a club that fielded teams for cricket, rugby football, association football, and the college-style American football) in the late 1880s and the Morgan Athletic Club (later known as the Chicago Cardinals) in 1898.

• • •

Hornsby's brother Arthur left St. Paul in 1886, heading for California. While Gus's wealth continued to rise in Minnesota, his brother was not nearly as fortunate. Arthur struggled to find work, eventually landing a spot as a brakeman on the Santa Cruz train line. In 1887 Arthur was helping to switch out train cars when he lost his balance and fell under the train. A wheel rolled over his leg at the knee, and Arthur's leg had to be amputated.[15] He lived the rest of his life in difficult circumstances in Pajaro, California.

• • •

Gus Hornsby's real estate speculation was successful, and his business was becoming one of the largest in the Minneapolis-St. Paul area. He quit his job with the *Pioneer Press*; the rival *St. Paul Globe* took particular glee in this: "A.H. Hornsby used to be the turf reporter on a morning contemporary, receiving the princely sum of $5 per column. He was a dandy sporting editor, but as his matter didn't run over a couple of columns a week he shook the job and went into real estate. He caught onto the Sixth ward boom on the ground floor."[16] Hornsby moved his family into one of the largest homes in St. Paul.[17] He celebrated his success by taking his family on an extended tour of Europe, a trip that cost him over $2,500,[18] a tremendous amount for travel in the 1880s. The Hornsbys spent the next three months traveling throughout Europe.[19]

While he was abroad, Hornsby did not stop working on his Minnesota real estate empire. He tried to recruit English investment as well. In June, he posted the following (including the formatting and capitalization as shown) in the *London News*[20]:

Chapter 6. 1882: St. Paul

MILLIONS
are earning next to nothing owing to financial depression,
whereas in the capital of the American North-West,
ST. PAUL, MINNESOTA,
money is earning not less than 7 per cent. Buyers of Real
(landed) Estate for
INVESTMENT
realise and annual profit of from 20 to 50 per cent, according
to the measure of their judgement.
Speculators have made during the past four years, and are
making, 100 to 200 per cent yearly.

THIS IS NO WILD-CAT
speculative craze, as in Winnipeg in 1881–82, but the results of the most
MARVELLOUS GROWTH of the CITY of ST. PAUL in
past years.

Is there any wonder it still grows?
HEAD OF MISSISSIPPI RIVER NAVIGATION
TERMINUS of all RAILWAYS of the NORTH-WEST.
GREAT BUSINESS MART WEST OF CHICAGO.
RAPIDLY INCREASING MANUFACTURING CENTRE.
CATTLE DEPOT of MONTANA and WYOMING.

HEALTHIEST
Large city in the world!

For full Particulars, Statistics, Opportunities of Investment
for Farmers, Capitalists, and Investors, apply to
A.H. Hornsby, late Lieutenant 102nd Regiment.
Temporary office till July 28: National Passenger
And General Agency, 57, Charing-cross
American Address: St. Paul, Minn., U.S.A.

• • •

In August the Hornsbys returned to America as first-class passengers aboard the White Star liner SS *Celtic*. (Of the 1,100 passengers aboard, the *New York Times* only reported on a handful of the arrivals, including Gus and Marie Hornsby.)[21] St. Paul elected Gus as a director of the city's chamber of commerce.[22] He became a notary public and a deacon of Ascension Church.[23]

Hornsby joined social clubs throughout the city, including the new St. George Club. The St. George Club was a social fraternity and athletic club that had several Canadian chapters, including Montreal and Winnipeg.

The club had organized a St. Paul chapter in November 1885.[24] Much like the social clubs of New York and Chicago, St. George also competed in athletic events; however, since this was Minnesota, the events were a little different—races included snowshoe competitions.[25] Hornsby dressed in the club's uniform of a blue tuque, white coat and knickerbockers, trimmed with blue, and a blue sash. He competed in the 200-yard snowshoe dash but didn't take to the winter sports as well as he'd hoped. The club was also similar to the New York groups by providing its members with social and intellectual stimulation and mutual aid; its motto was *Solvitur Ambulantem*, "safe on one's feet."[26]

The same year that Hornsby joined the St. George Snowshoe Club, Englishmen in St. Paul were starting up a local chapter of the Order of Sons of St. George, a relatively new secret society composed of English immigrants.[27] Formed in Pennsylvania in 1871, the Sons of St. George was a product of English and Irish animosity: the order's founders sought to counter the Irish Molly Maguires. English and allied groups accused the Molly Maguires of staging attacks on Pennsylvania mines, and the Sons of St. George worked to expose members of the Molly Maguires and have them arrested.[28] However, within a few years, the Sons of St. George expanded beyond Pennsylvania and mutated into a more standard social and benefits society. When the Sons of St. George spread to St. Paul, several of the St. George's Snowshoe Club's English members joined the other St. George group as well. At the Snowshoe Club's suggestion, the order invited Hornsby to join.

In early 1888 Hornsby walked into the social hall on Seventh Street belonging to the Grand Army of the Republic veteran's club. The new Pioneer Lodge of the Order of the Sons of St. George had rented out the hall for its meetings and initiations. Members escorted Hornsby to a small, unpainted room near the front of the building. They asked him if he believed in God and gave him a blindfold, requesting that he wear it.[29] Hornsby complied, slipping the hoodwink over his eyes. The fabric hung over his nose, and the faint sawdust smell of the room took on a thin reek of ancient sweat and old wool. A couple of men led Hornsby from the smaller chamber and into the hall, escorting him around the room. The members sang, slightly off-key, "Enter stranger, freely enter, none but friends around the stand. Offering thee, with manly frankness, entrance to our noble band." The group had Hornsby swear an oath while still blindfolded, promising to "band together for the promotion of each other's welfare and the mitigation of suffering in times of sickness or distress."

When the group removed Hornsby's blindfold, he found himself standing in the center of the large hall, its chairs having been moved to the sides, filled with nearly one hundred members. In front of him was an altar, cloth-covered, on which rested a bible, a sword, and a shield. Hornsby looked, disoriented, at the shield, then raised his eyes to the Worthy President standing on the other side. The Worthy President wore a navy tunic embroidered with symbols across the chest. To his right, an even more resplendently dressed member stood and addressed Hornsby. This man wore a brilliant scarlet robe, thick plush velvet with gold trim, and an enormous collar that featured gold and navy filigree. His hat was made from the same material, an imperial design that was simultaneously majestic and ridiculous. Hornsby was unsure how to react.

The red-robed man finished his lecture, during which he implored Hornsby to welcome Americanization, to contribute to "this country great in its ideals of democracy, but also in science, in art, in literature, in mechanical ingenuity, and invention."

"But its greatest attribute is its humanitarian principles: offering equal rights and opportunities to all who come under the protection of its flag—the Stars and Stripes." The people to either side of Hornsby—all of them white, all of them Protestant, all of them most assuredly men—cheered and began singing a welcome ode.

• • •

Marie continued to share in Gus's real estate success, controlling several blocks of developing property herself. She also rose in St. Paul society, hosting receptions—always wearing her iconic white—and staging elaborate English lunches.[30] At a glitzy 1888 charity ball thrown to benefit a local hospital, Marie joined several of the city's most prominent women, wearing "white silk *en traine*, combined with blue brocaded velvet, and handsome diamonds."[31]

While Marie was a well-liked and admired real estate developer and social figure in the city, Gus's reputation was beginning to suffer. Through 1887 he continued to sue would-be partners for their share of investments, but now he was receiving lawsuits as well. He was accused of pocketing a co-investor's share of a $1,000 commission earned from a large housing deal. The judge ruled against Hornsby. Hornsby was forced to pay his colleague nearly $500.[32]

Hornsby's wealth, at that time, was estimated to be over $300,000.[33]

• • •

As fall 1887 turned cold, Hornsby stopped wearing the sideburns and drooping mustache that he had sported since his time in the army, and instead grew a heavy beard, which he would wear the rest of his life.[34] (It says something about Hornsby's social status in St. Paul that the *Globe* reported this grooming change. That, or it says something about the rate and urgency of news in St. Paul in the 1880s.)

As his athletic pursuits drew to a close, he continued to play chess at an impressively high level. In October 1887, Hornsby accomplished perhaps his greatest feat. In the nineteenth century, automatons, mechanical devices that resembled robots, caught the interest of Americans and Europeans. Many automatons toured throughout both continents, drawing thousands of spectators. Some were indeed machines; others were complex contraptions that secretly housed a human operator. One example of the latter type was "Ajeeb," a chess-playing automaton, with a life-sized statue that was dressed as a stereotypical Arab, complete with hookah and turban, sitting atop a large box.[35] The automaton moved chess pieces with its right hand; its left hand never left the hookah. The "machine" never made a noise and would indicate check by nodding its head once, nodding twice for checkmate. The box opened to reveal what appeared to be a hopeless tangle of machinery. It concealed a space for an experienced chess player. Ajeeb competed against human competition, winning nearly every time.

For years the chess automaton toured England and then the United States, later taking on opponents including Theodore Roosevelt, author O. Henry, and other celebrities. In 1887 the machine and its entourage toured the Midwest, stopping in Minneapolis. The automaton's owners invited local chess champs in Minneapolis-St. Paul to play Ajeeb "and find how little they know about the game."[36] During this leg of the trip, the automaton secretly employed the services of American chess master Charles Moehle. Moehle was apparently undefeated during the tour, until Hornsby challenged the robot.

On October 28, in front of a capacity crowd of hundreds in Minneapolis, Hornsby faced Ajeeb / Moehle.[37] No one in the group, Hornsby included, knew that a person—let alone a chess champion—lay inside the box, despite being allowed to inspect the machine's inner workings.[38] The group's ignorance of the trick with Ajeeb was ironic: Moehle was the secretary of the St. Paul Chess Club.[39] Moehle's specialty was blindfold chess, and he would succeed in beating Hornsby while blindfolded the following year.[40] Secretly crouched inside Ajeeb, Moehle did not need to see the board; he only needed someone to call out the moves so that he could move his arm inside Ajeeb in order to handle the pieces. Occasionally Ajeeb's handlers would impress the crowd by removing his head mid-game. One chess commentator at the time noted that the head was removed "with no worse consequences than that Ajeeb is unable to indicate check by nodding ... for it would be too much to expect, even of so mysterious a being, that he should be able to nod without having a head to nod with."[41]

Propped on a small wooden stage, with the audience surrounding it, Ajeeb sat cross-legged on his pedestal box, his chess board in his lap, his unlit hookah resting by his left hip. Ajeeb's handlers placed a wooden chair, a small table, and a glass of water nearby for Hornsby, but he stood during the game, hunched over Ajeeb's board. Before the game began, one of Ajeeb's assistants gently parted Ajeeb's burgundy silk robe and removed the light blue silk from the front of Ajeeb's blouse, exposing the clockwork-like gears and springs within his chest. To Hornsby's relief, the assistant refrained from removing the robot's head. Ajeeb's lifeless eyes seemed to glare at the game board.

The event's hosts offered Hornsby the advantage of the white pieces, and he moved his pawn to king four. "Pawn to king four!" Ajeeb's assistant called out in a loud, crisply enunciated voice. Ajeeb did not hesitate, moving his wooden hand to his own king pawn and moving it a space forward, initiating the French Defense. The competitors in turn moved their queen pawns, their knights, then exchanged pawns. On the eleventh move, Hornsby moved his queen a bit prematurely, and inside his hidden compartment, Moehle must have relished an imminent kill.

Hornsby stared at Ajeeb's painted face, his dexterous right hand. Here was the future, Hornsby must have suspected: a scientific marvel, strategy and creation from wheels, paths to higher orders. He was, then, deceived: this future was hollow, a fraud, paths to more false wonders, disappointments, and graft. Nothing ever as it seemed; everything always wearing a mocking mask of progress in perpetual motion.

The white bishops moved into position, and Hornsby rolled out the most brilliant combination he had ever played. Ajeeb, unaware of the danger posed by Hornsby's well-placed clergy, attacked the white king with his knight on the twenty-fifth move. As he brought Hornsby into check, Ajeeb nodded his head. The fixed eyes drew an arc from the board to Hornsby's right shoulder, then returned; Ajeeb's oversized yellow turban bobbed rhythmically. Hornsby sacrificed his queen to capture Ajeeb's checking knight, and—in doing so—exposed his twin bishop and rook assault. Moehle recognized the strategy far too late, and he motioned Ajeeb to resign on move number twenty-eight. The three hundred spectators rose as a single body and cheered until they were hoarse. More than any moment on the football field or at the card table, it was Hornsby's most exquisite memory.

• • •

To the uneducated observer, it would have seemed at the beginning of 1888 that Hornsby's fortunes could not be better: he and his wife had both struck stunning wealth, and he was a respected man throughout the city, even if that respect was starting to show cracks. A few of Hornsby's associates had discovered his secret passion, and Hornsby's gambling was now running rampant. Again, however, his luck held. During the last two years, he had made an additional $50,000 gambling throughout Minneapolis and St. Paul, betting primarily on horses, but also making any other kind of wager he could.[42] He wanted higher stakes, and in March 1888 he found them: rumors of an illicit card game being arranged in Chicago with virtually no limits. For Hornsby, the pull was irresistible.

Game Day, 3:10 p.m.

The custom at the time was for the team that had been scored upon to kick the ball away to the scoring team. Northwestern kicked the ball into Chicago territory, and this time the students raced south to defend, stopping the CFBC ball carrier.

The game produced its first scrimmages, and it was the Chicago backfield's turn to take control. William Booth, serving as the Chicago team's halfback, proved to be an elusive runner, slipping away from the mass of battling players and picking up great swaths of territory, eventually driving the ball back into NWU territory.

Booth was a founding member of the club, but he was not originally supposed to play in the Northwestern game. William Hulbert, the Chicago White Stockings' leader, was initially slated to play halfback, despite his age: Hulbert was forty-three, the oldest member of the club. However, Hulbert was held up in New York that week. Earlier in the month, he had led the effort in New York City to create a new professional baseball organization, the National League. By the week of the Northwestern game, Hulbert remained in New York. Enlisting Albert Spalding's help, he had formed a powerful coalition of baseball teams across the East.[1] Hulbert's motives for establishing the new league were undoubtedly colored by his potential to gain from his ties to the White Stockings. However, Hulbert was earnest in his desire to "clean up" professional baseball. He was also a teetotaler and did not want players (or fans) to indulge in alcohol at games, and he wanted to ban alcoholic beverages from professional baseball parks.[2]

Hulbert publicly decried the rampant gambling within the league's predecessor organization, stressing the need for a new, clean organization. He had become the public face of anti-gambling, a fact that could not have sat well with Hornsby.

Other critics questioned Hulbert's motives, accusing the White Stocking's chief of strongarming the new league into existence in order to make Chicago the center of power for professional baseball, taking resources away from New York, Boston, and the other eastern teams.[3]

Part Two—The Fraud

According to baseball historian Tom Melville, "because eastern baseball teams so thoroughly dominated other clubs throughout the country, baseball supporters in the Midwest abandoned their hopes of developing local talent,"[4] bringing in veteran eastern players instead, a practice Hulbert wanted to stop. Regardless of his motivation, Hulbert rose in wealth and power through the late 1870s, and by his death in 1882 he was among the most influential Americans in sport. Hulbert's grave in Chicago features an enormous baseball-shaped monument, with the date *1876* engraved in numerals eight inches high, commemorating the year he helped form baseball's National League.

• • •

Curtis and Borner also took turns carrying the ball and continued to pound toward the NWU goal again. Curtis, playing as one of the Chicago team's two fullbacks in the game (along with Charles Hilton), proved nearly unstoppable, dragging Northwestern players across the lumpy field. Borner served as the team's lone *three-quarters back*, shouting out directions to the forwards as Curtis lurched ahead.

Chicago White Stockings / Chicago Cubs executive William Hulbert, in an uncredited drawing from about 1880. Hulbert's efforts to form the National League led to Albert Spalding calling him "the man who saved baseball." One of his top priorities as head of the league was to root out and eliminate player gambling (artist unknown, originally published in Albert Spalding's *America's National Game*, New York: American Sports Publishing Co., 1911).

The three-quarters back (or ¾ back) is an old rugby position frequently used during the transition to American football, designating the player literally three-quarters back. (Walter Camp had not yet developed the quarterback position. He would do so at Yale, later in 1876.)

An excellent description of the three-quarters back position, as it existed during the transition from English rugby to American football, can be found in the 1874 book *Football: Our Winter Game*: "If a captain has three good half-backs on in a fifteen, he will generally find it advisable to place one of them three-quarters-back, choosing the best one at dropping, and reducing his [half]backs by one, if the forwards want strength ... he may often have a chance of dropping a goal, and the two half-backs will look to him to back them up and tackle any player who may pass them."[5]

This description of the three-quarters back position makes sense when one compares it to the original football quarterback position as devised by Walter Camp later that year. The initial job of the quarterback was to block for his halfbacks, and the position was even nicknamed the "blocking back" early on.[6]

• • •

Curtis, to his surprise, was stopped dead by one of the Northwestern players, who jarred the ball loose and began running toward the Chicago goal. Edward Esher proved to be the strongest and most adept of the NWU players. He was the son of Bishop John Jacob Esher, who helped to establish the nearby North Central College in Naperville, Illinois.[7] Edward would transfer out of Northwestern in 1879.[8]

The CFBC crew watched, stunned, as Esher bolted to midfield and then, unwisely, tried a drop-kick. The goal crew, seeing Esher stop and stand ramrod straight to prepare his kick, lunged to the posts, frantically hoisting them. The south goal post shot skyward just in time, but the ball dropped, harmlessly, well short of the goal. Chicago recovered the ball and their momentum toward the Northwestern goal. Charles Hilton, carrying the ball, slammed soundly into his cousin, knocking Theo Hilton's top hat into the air and sending the senior crashing to the turf violently. A new player for Chicago, named Brown, provided superb blocking as Chicago retook the ball on the Northwestern side. But there Chicago's progress was momentarily checked. For several minutes the teams were bogged down in repeated scrimmages for little or no gain. Finally, Curtis managed to take the ball laterally, skirting around the group and sprinting untouched past the goal line. Throughout the game, when Curtis managed to make it into open field, his speed was too much for any of the students to run him down.

Again, Hornsby was called to kick the goal from the goal line, and again he delivered. Chicago led with two goals.

Chapter 7

1888: Chicago

Hornsby set out for Chicago just after sunset. The game, he knew, could take days. He packed his case, filling a satchel with $40,000 cash.[1] He left St. Paul on the Minneapolis & Omaha Railway's new *Vestibuled Express*, booking a luxury sleeping car on the 7:30 p.m. train. He had told Marie that he had an opportunity to bring in new investors and would be meeting with potential partners.

He arrived in Chicago just after 9:30 the following morning. As he stepped from the station, a northerly wind struck him. It was a bright, clear, pre-spring morning, but quite cold. He was just a couple of blocks away and across the Chicago River from the old Tremont House, the grand hotel that had played host to his football club—and to his addiction—over a dozen years before. Hornsby had received word from one of his St. George clubmates that the Tremont still hosted illegal poker and faro games, as it did when he lived in Chicago. The men who controlled the Tremont's underground gambling were preparing for a week-long event, one with the highest stakes to date. Hornsby's clubmate asked if he was interested. Hornsby didn't hesitate. There were rumors that the game was controlled by "Big Mike" McDonald, the same man who had been responsible for many of the gambling houses that dotted Chicago when Hornsby first moved to the Midwest, the person who had controlled the city's gambling since the Fire. This also would not have deterred Hornsby.

Now, however, as he stood in front of the bridge that would take him across the river and to the Tremont, he did hesitate. He could see the Tremont's rooftop from where he stood, its gigantic American flags fully unfurled in the northern breeze. He paused at the base of the bridge, his suitcase in his right hand. In his left hand was his satchel, filled with more money than most Americans would make in their lifetimes—no, nearly *double* what many would make in a lifetime. In the last two years he had gone on a wild streak of gambling, and he was deliriously ahead.

He crossed the bridge. He walked into the Tremont.

Chapter 7. 1888: Chicago

The Tremont House Hotel, the former meeting place of the Chicago Foot-Ball Club, as it looked in the 1870s and 1880s. This was the fourth structure called the Tremont House, constructed soon after the Chicago Great Fire (artist unknown, c. 1877).

His teammate Hilton had eventually managed the Tremont, but he had moved from the Tremont to the Revere Hotel long ago. The Tremont looked much the same as it had under Hilton and when the Chicago Foot-Ball Club made it their home. Hornsby walked through the dark, mammoth lobby to sign in. The man at the front desk looked at his name, paused, and then gave him an envelope with "A.H. Hornsby" written on the front in tight copperplate. Hornsby opened the envelope. Inside was a slip of paper, on which was written, in large script, a single number: *177*

• • •

Hornsby washed, dressed, and lunched. If McDonald did, indeed, control the games at the Tremont, that would work in Hornsby's favor. McDonald knew him from the seventies, and he might remember him.

Mike McDonald was the original Chicago gangster, the man who first truly organized Chicago crime, and he had been in business for two decades. He was legendarily credited with the phrase "Never give a sucker an even break."[2] And he took his own advice. His gambling tables were set to cheat the "small fry," while favoring business contacts and— to Hornsby's occasional favor in the 1870s—newspapermen. McDonald knew the advantage of good press, so he usually cut a break for journalists, even if he was merciless to others.[3] He was particularly merciless to law enforcement. A well-known story is that a pair of police officers approached McDonald, asking for a $2 donation to help defray the burial costs of a fellow policeman. "Good," said McDonald. "Here's $10. Bury five of 'em."[4]

Early that afternoon, Hornsby stepped back into the Tremont's lobby, passing the spacious marble staircase, and made for the elevator. Room 177 was, oddly, on the hotel's third floor.[5] Hornsby stepped off the elevator, walked down a long hall, and stood in front of Room 177. Just under the three brass numerals, someone had attached a small, well-made drawing of a tiger. Hornsby knocked softly. No answer. He knocked again. A voice came through the door's keyhole.

"Good afternoon, sir. Looking for a game?"[6] The door opened.

Hornsby stepped into the room. An attendant took his hat at once. The room was large, with the usual hotel furniture. However, in the room's spacious sitting area, the gaming hosts had added three massive tables. There were two poker tables, fully stocked with chips, as well as a faro table, with a complete layout. The hosts introduced themselves: Cy Jaynes and Tom Sheedy. Hornsby was familiar with neither man, which would not have been an auspicious start to the evening. In addition to the attendant, there were a handful of other men in the room, spread across the three tables. The three dealers did not introduce themselves, but Hornsby did recognize one of them. John Ferris was a notorious gambler in Chicago, and Hornsby had encountered him several times while living in the city.

Jaynes and Sheedy had run the gambling operation at the Tremont for a couple of months. Occasionally they switched rooms for discretion, but they need not have bothered. The current owner of the hotel, John Rice, was unconcerned about the prospect of illegal operations at the hotel, and he was possibly paid off by the syndicate running the ring. When police eventually did raid the Tremont two days later (mere hours after Hornsby left the hotel to return to St. Paul), Rice is reported to have said, "Gambling in Room 177! Why, how should I know! Your house is your castle. Neither I nor anyone else may enter it, except on your invitations, without a search warrant. For all I know there may be gambling going on in every other room in the house. I wouldn't be at all surprised if there was." Rice paused as he argued with reporters in the wake of the raid, then added, with a bit of sacrilegious bravado, "I don't play the game, but I am told that wherever there are two or three gathered together there will be poker in the midst of them."[7]

Hornsby was willing to play any game, but he did not trust the faro table. Faro typically had the best odds of any house game, but only when it was played straight: it seldom was. Instead, he bought some chips from Jaynes and sat at one of the poker tables.

For Hornsby, hours blurred into each other when he gambled. Soon the handful of players multiplied; by 10:00 p.m., the room was bursting, each table full. Hornsby was ahead by several hundred dollars. At 4:00 a.m. Hornsby's attention was challenged; his senses were dulling. He left the game room, staggered to an elevator, and sought sleep in his room.

On the second day, Hornsby woke late in the morning and refreshed himself. He counted his money and found that he was ahead by nearly a thousand dollars. He lunched, then returned to Room 177. The attendant and Jaynes were there, along with a fresh set of dealers and one or two players Hornsby recognized from the night before. Hornsby got back to work at once.

This time, however, his luck turned. He lost more hands than he won, and he seemed to lose large-pot hands much more frequently. By mid-afternoon Hornsby didn't need to count his chips to know that he was down from when he arrived. By nightfall Hornsby had lost nearly half of his $40,000 and was making increasingly reckless decisions.

Hornsby moved to the faro table, despite his misgivings—he needed to mix things up. He began making large bets, splitting them seemingly blindly across the table. His luck improved somewhat. The dealer had said nothing during their games, but when a new man entered the room, Hornsby's dealer called a break. The new man, replacing the dealer, introduced himself to Hornsby. He was John Ferguson. Hornsby had not heard of him. Ferguson had made a name for himself in gambling halls across Chicago, but only after Hornsby's departure from the city.

Ferguson dealt at the faro table for the next two hours, and they were hours of pure torment for Hornsby. The house was supposed to have a meager 2 percent edge in faro, but Hornsby was being cleaned out. If he suspected that he was being conned, he was likely right: Ferguson was a skilled cheater, with a specialty for marked cards.[8]

The Tremont operation was actually Ferguson's, who had the hotel—and occasionally even law enforcement—in his pocket.[9] The fact that Hornsby was a former newspaperman with journalist connections would have meant nothing to Ferguson. The Englishman with the seemingly endless pocket would have been Ferguson's central concern that night, and public relations would not have been high on Ferguson's priority list.

Unbeknownst to Hornsby, McDonald had scaled back his involvement in Chicago gambling by 1888. Tainted by scandal, McDonald had even sold his "gambling palace," The Store, the previous year.[10]

• • •

Faro: Chasing the Tiger

Faro was played using a special table with a tableau of all of the playing cards of one suit displayed, usually all of the spades.[11] Players could place chips onto one or more of the displayed cards. The dealer then took a full deck of cards in a card box and turned over, in succession, three of the cards. The first card, called the "soda card," was not used for the bets; instead, it was a discard used to help prevent cheating by the dealer. The second revealed card was called the "banker's card." If a player had chips on the card with the same number or rank as the banker's card, regardless of suit, he lost all those chips to the dealer. The final revealed card was the player's card. A player with chips on that card doubled his bet. If the card on which the player had bet did not turn up as one of the revealed cards, nothing happened, and the player kept his money.

Early games of faro were played with cards that had a tiger design on their backs, leading to the game's reference to tigers and tiger imagery.[12] Playing the game was sometimes called "chasing the tiger's tail," and gambling houses featuring faro often posted an image of a tiger in their windows.

By the end of the nineteenth century faro play had declined in the United States. Today it is virtually unknown, and no casinos still offer the game, due to faro's nearly even odds, which provide a (legitimate) gambling house with minimal income from the game. Because of this, by the 1880s, many faro games were crooked, or—as John Ferguson called it—a "brace game." The term refers to the card box that the faro dealer used. A rigged box was known as a brace box.[13] "Brace game" is one of several terms faro contributed to English, some of which are still in use, even though faro is long gone. A player who did not trust the card keeper was allowed to keep track of the cards used in a series of games by marking them down on a small slip of paper called a "tab." Players could then "*keep tabs*" on the progress of a game.

• • •

Hornsby's instinct likely told him to cut his losses and leave at once. However, like so many people, his reason cowered when confronted by his obsession, which now needed to chase his losses and make up for them. If he could just break even, what a story he would have for the fellows in St. Paul. Another thought had to have swum across his mind: these men might not *let* him leave, not until this game was done, one way or another.

Hornsby carried forward, dragging himself through each successive hand. It was long after midnight, and still Ferguson held court at the faro table, and Hornsby sat and took endless abuse. The satchel lay at his side, nearly empty, its opening split wide, looking like a mouth, gaping at Hornsby in surprise and disgust.

Hornsby placed his remaining chips on a single card.

Ferguson turned over the first card, the soda card, the burned one. It meant nothing.

The next card Ferguson turned over was the banker's card, the winning card for the dealer. Ferguson flicked over the banker's card, which matched the card containing Hornsby's meager remaining chips. As Ferguson probably knew beforehand, the third card, the player's card, did not match.

The spell had broken. Clarity returned. Hornsby was awake, and he was broke.

• • •

The sudden change in luck at cards coincided with a slowdown in Hornsby's real estate business. Throughout spring 1888 he watched his fortune begin to erode. Increasingly concerned, Hornsby reclaimed a job at the *Pioneer Press*, albeit a part-time one, doing some editing. He continued to look for another big business opportunity, briefly trying to break into photography, starting up a photo engraving company, which did not last.[14]

Hornsby also took advantage of his recent appointment as a notary by serving as administrator of the estates of recently deceased St. Paul residents. For this, he hired Uri Lamprey as his real estate attorney.[15] Lamprey was an interesting choice, and he had much in common with Hornsby. A wealthy St. Paul transplant (Lamprey came from New Hampshire), Lamprey had given up most of his law practice in the early 1880s to ride the St. Paul real estate boom.[16] He was an occasional partner and a sporadic rival of Hornsby. He, too, was interested in sport and game, having devoted himself to wildlife conservation.

The additional jobs did not stave Hornsby's losses. Though he still had fragments of his fortune by fall 1888, Hornsby defaulted on a $2,666 mortgage. Marie had been a cosigner.[17]

Hornsby continued to gamble, now visiting some of the most dangerous gambling dens in Minneapolis, places that made Paul's and the Gentlemen's Own seem relatively tame. His fortune, over a third of a million dollars at its peak, was gone by the middle of 1889, and for the first time since his Chicago days, Hornsby faced severe debt. He took another gamble, this time using his real estate reputation, by partnering with Lamprey on a scheme to build a $22,500 public natatorium. The pair planned to sell 150 tickets to potential investors at $150 each. The deal collapsed quickly.[18]

By the beginning of 1890, the Hornsbys were in a grim financial crisis. Gus's real estate holdings were under water, the losses compounded by now-crippling gambling debts. Marie Hornsby's own real estate was not faring much better than Gus's. Her lenders sued her in January, and the court placed liens on several of her properties.[19] Gus faced his own spate of lawsuits for debt payment, including one from the phone company.[20]

As the Hornsbys struggled to keep their real estate business afloat, they soon faced another hardship. Their youngest child, 12-year-old Arthur, had fallen ill. Initially, Hornsby thought his son had influenza; eventually, Arthur was diagnosed with typhoid fever. On February 17, 1891, he died at home. Marie was inconsolable. For years she had volunteered at St. Paul's Christ Episcopal Church. After her son's funeral there, she threw herself into her volunteer service entirely, devoting her time to the church and temporarily abandoning her real estate work.[21]

Gus also retreated, spending most of his time in the coming weeks playing chess and writing. He obsessed over his son's death—it reminded him of his younger brother's passing that he dreamed of in India. Hornsby began to write grim, occasionally maudlin poetry, including this piece, which he called "Sic Transit Gloria Mundi":

> As dies a babe whose sails are scarce unfurl'd
> Unto the winds of life's perturbed sea,
> So brightest glories pass from out the world,
> All level'd down to cold mortality.
>
> No mausoleum grand, can long with-hold
> Dust unto dust from turning back again;
> What e'er the casket, be it pine or gold,
> Naught more that clay may either one contain.
>
> Seek then to nurture love's immortal flower,
> While upon earth our pilgrimage is made;
> That, when the hand of Time points out death's Hour,
> Garlands of love upon our clay be laid.
>
> Such are a treasure knowing no corruption,
> Passing beyond the portals of the grave,
> Giving on yonder shore a sweet reception
> To those who cross in peace the silent wave.[22]

• • •

The couple's financial woes did not take a reprieve, however, and they continued to face lawsuits.[23]

Hornsby became desperate. He needed to revive his real estate work, but his remaining properties either had liens or values a fraction of what he had paid. He sought out homeowners whom he could represent to get a commission for a sale, and he began to focus on elderly property owners.

Hornsby contacted a widow named Antonia Wortmann, an immigrant who lived in a rural community several miles from St. Paul. Wortman had a property worth $10,000, and Hornsby wrote twice to her, offering to sell it for her. She refused both times. In April 1892, Hornsby visited Wortmann and tried again to convince her to sell her property. She only spoke broken English, but she said enough to turn down Hornsby's offer for a third time.[24]

That summer, Hornsby inexplicably tried to reach Wortmann to make a fourth attempt at a sell. This time he learned that she had moved away. The property outside St. Paul, however, remained in her name. Hornsby, incredibly, decided to sell it anyway. He found a potential buyer, another real estate broker named Benjamin Martin, and claimed to be Wortmann's agent, telling Martin that he was offering the land for $600. Martin, astounded at the offer, bought it immediately. On June 1 he paid Hornsby $78 for fees and commission and wrote an initial check to Wortmann for $472, which Hornsby, using his power as notary, transferred to himself. On June 20, Hornsby provided Martin with the deed, apparently signed by Wortmann and notarized by Hornsby.[25] Hornsby had gained some cash and a few weeks of safety.

• • •

The security bought with the money that Hornsby swindled was fleeting. By the fall, the Hornsbys were up to $30,000 in debt,[26] and again Hornsby unsuccessfully tried to find a quick scheme to return to wealth. Marie took a job as a clerk with the Northern Pacific Railway Company to help the family,[27] a shocking prospect for a woman in the 1890s, and a profoundly humiliating position for a woman who had been the toast of society just four years before.

In early December 1892, Benjamin Martin discovered, to his shock, that the deed to his property was fraudulent, and Antonia Wortmann still owned the lot. Wortmann reclaimed the land, and she denied that she had signed the deed.[28] Martin went to the authorities and tracked down Hornsby's notary bond. The bond had been signed, in 1885, by Uri Lamprey as a surety for Hornsby, up to $1,000. Martin moved to sue Lamprey and sought out Hornsby. Lamprey, in turn, also went after Hornsby and contacted the police.

Hornsby's friends in the Sons of St. George heard about Martin's plan for a lawsuit, as well as rumors that a grand jury might indict Hornsby, and they raced to warn him.[29] In a moment of panic, Hornsby decided to flee. His fraternity members escorted him to the St. Paul cable cars and got him a train ticket to Duluth. He told Marie and his children nothing.[30] As he ran to board the train, one of his Sons of St. George colleagues pressed a few dollars into his hand and whispered the motto—not of the Order of the Sons of St. George, but the old St. George Snowshoe Club: "*Solvitur Ambulatem.*"

On December 16, St. Paul police issued a warrant for his arrest upon his indictment on charges of forgery and fraud.[31] Hornsby, however, had skipped town and had nearly a week's head start.

Game Day, 3:25 p.m.

Appearing as if from nowhere, Hornsby ran and scooped up Northwestern's next kick and bounded to his left, toward the throng of standing spectators separating the field from Chicago Street. As he turned up to make ground, he met Frank Casseday on the field for the first time. Hornsby's larger frame and speed sent Frank off his feet with a percussive force. Frank felt the wind leave his lungs; his eyes watered as he slammed into the cold turf. He was smaller than Hornsby and less skilled, but Frank was tough. He had proven this on the field the previous spring, when Northwestern faced a west-side baseball club in Chicago. The club, according to Frank's recollection, "turned out to be a gang of toughs from the packing house district.... They started a rough house. Our lads rushed in and rallied around. Our lads from N.U. were ready to fight at the drop of a hat."[1] Crumpling to the ground, Frank nevertheless managed to reach out and grab Hornsby's ankle, bringing him down.

After twenty-five minutes of play, the Northwestern students, at last, had become acclimated to the game's tempo, and their play picked up noticeably. The Methodist players regained possession of the ball and drove into Chicago territory for the first time. Ed Kinman led the charge, setting up positions and getting the ball to Esher and Hilton. Theo Hilton was proving to be a scrapper, looking for someone to hit and staying at the front line, even if his top hat didn't always stick with him. A pair of seniors, Frank Scott and William Arnold, also stepped up, blocking and making room for Esher and Kinman. Scott received the immediate attention of the Chicago players, and several wondered if they might be able to persuade Scott to switch sides, or at least consider joining the Chicago team after the game.

Frank Scott did not end up joining the Chicago Foot-Ball Club. After his graduation in 1876, he became one of the most influential lawyers in Chicago.[2] When he died in 1931, his estate was estimated to be worth over $1.5 million.[3]

Senior Will Arnold was a budding songwriter and was, along with

114 Part Two—The Fraud

Frank Casseday (center, with arm on trophy table) poses with the members of the 1875 NWU champion baseball team, who were "ready to fight at the drop of a hat." The silver ball on the trophy table is one of the earliest college athletic trophies in the American Midwest. Frances Willard helped to purchase the trophy as part of her efforts to support athletics as an alternative to alcohol use (courtesy Northwestern University Archives).

William Curtis and Charles Hilton, one of the Civil War veterans in the game—the only one playing for Northwestern up to this point. Arnold was a thirty-three-year-old senior, originally from Virginia, but he fought for the North, initially serving in the 68th Indiana and later in the 116th Indiana.[4] By an unsettling coincidence, while serving in the 68th's Company K, Arnold fought at the battle of Chickamauga and was present when Ed Kinman's father was killed.[5] Whether or not Arnold or Ed Kinman was ever made aware of their fuller connection is unknown.

Arnold eventually became a history and English professor, but in February 1876 he was a human powder keg, and he was the first NWU player to give Hornsby a solid belt, landing him on the grass and hard-packed mud, allowing Kinman to slash past them.

Although the Northwestern players were getting more comfortable with the new game, it remained mystifying to most of the spectators. Most had never seen a football game of any kind, and only one or two had witnessed American football as eastern schools were playing it. The reporter on hand for the Evanston newspaper was baffled, later calling the game "novel and ridiculous."[6]

Northwestern's twenty players began to stymie the fifteen Chicago men on the field, and NWU drove the ball further into Chicago territory than at any point before. However, C.J. Williams and Albert Sullivan, who combined for a fearsome defensive tandem, managed to stop the students and reclaim the ball.

Louis Sullivan had watched his older brother's athletic exploits somewhat enviously during their time in Chicago.[7] Albert routinely won contests with the Lotus Club, and he had taken well to the new football club, showing flashes of skill that were in keeping with the more experienced English players on the team. Now, however, the ball came for the first time to Louis, and he took off with more speed than he had ever shown with the Lotus group, bounding past the NWU defenders and streaking in for one of the longest runs of the afternoon, getting his first—and apparently only—touchdown with Chicago. However, the position of the touchdown wasn't ideal for the try after. The spectators dutifully hoisted the goalposts, Hornsby lined up and kicked, but the ball sailed just wide of the mark. With only a couple of minutes before halftime, Chicago had three touchdowns, but only two goals.

Frank H. Scott, co-founder of the Chicago firm Scott, Bancroft, and Stephens, in a photograph from around 1880. Scott was a native of Iowa; his family moved to the Chicago area in 1864. Scott served a chief legal counsel for the Chicago Stock Exchange and continued to practice law in Chicago until his death in 1931 (photographer unknown).

CHAPTER 8

1892: St. Paul

John C. McGinn's career as a detective had been a series of successes throughout the late 1870s and into the 1880s, and in 1892 the City of St. Paul named him its chief detective. His reputation, however, was founded on his work in Chicago. It began in 1876, just a couple of weeks after the Chicago—NWU football game, and a few blocks west of Gus Hornsby's old office on Madison Street, in a poorly lit, seedy tavern called "The Hub." Men gathered there in March 1876 to discuss a plot to steal President Lincoln's remains from his tomb in Springfield, Illinois. The men were counterfeiters—skilled, though incredibly unwise. They concocted a plan to rob Lincoln's grave and hold his remains for ransom, in an effort to secure the release of one of their leaders from the jail at Joliet.[1] They eventually chose to delay carrying out their plan until later in the year.

The police informant within the gang promptly relayed that decision to authorities.

Conspiring with the informant who remained embedded in the counterfeiting gang, detectives decided to follow the group and let it break into Lincoln's tomb, so that the evidence would be strong enough to prosecute them. The U.S. Secret Service and a pair of Pinkerton detectives secretly boarded a train with the criminals, bound for Springfield. They informed Robert Todd Lincoln, the late president's son, of the situation and their plans to apprehend the would-be grave robbers. Before moonrise on November 7—election day—the criminals entered the Lincoln mausoleum's catacombs, walked past the chambers holding three of the president's sons, and removed the marble lid to Lincoln's sarcophagus.[2]

Outside, members of the Secret Service gathered with the two Pinkerton Agency reinforcements. One of the Pinkerton agents was twenty-seven-year-old John McGinn, who raced through the darkness to try to head off the grave robbers. McGinn had fought with the 15th Infantry in the Civil War before joining Pinkerton. He was young, brash, and remarkably successful as a private investigator and guard, but his luck did not hold this night. McGinn and his group were too late. The counterfeiters, caught in the act and before they could remove Lincoln's coffin, managed to escape the grounds. McGinn and his partner searched desperately in the dark for the gang, and at once came under fire. McGinn drew his gun and returned fire, only to realize that the other group was the Secret Service detail, who had shot at the Pinkerton men by mistake. The two groups, frustrated but unharmed, rejoined and resumed the search for the counterfeiters.[3]

Ten days later, Agent McGinn's luck rebounded. Based on another tip from the informant within the gang, McGinn and other officers discovered that the grave robbers had returned to The Hub, their previous hangout in Chicago. McGinn and the Chicago police raided the tavern and arrested President Lincoln's tomb raiders.[4]

• • •

In October 1887, still working for Pinkerton and still renowned for his part in foiling the Lincoln's tomb caper, McGinn tracked down and captured notorious British forger William Markham, a Royal Navy veteran and paymaster of HMS *Espoir*, who had hidden out in Kansas City.[5] Just a few weeks later, McGinn captured the Southern Express train robbers, who staged a series of hold-ups in Arkansas and Texas. When local police failed to capture the robbers, the sheriffs contacted the Pinkerton Agency. William Pinkerton himself assigned McGinn. McGinn found a coat worn by one of the robbers, tracked the coat to its manufacturer, then to the store that sold it. From there, he discovered who bought it and managed to stake out one of the gang's ringleaders.[6] The successful capture brought more acclaim to McGinn and Pinkerton.

The following summer, McGinn made news again when he arrested a group of anarchists who plotted to place dynamite on railroad tracks in Chicago. Another Pinkerton agent had joined the terrorist ring undercover; together, the undercover agent and McGinn captured the bombers as they carried dynamite onto a train bound from Aurora, Illinois, to Chicago.[7]

Within a year, William Pinkerton promoted McGinn to superintendent and moved him from Chicago to St. Paul, putting him in charge of the St. Paul office in the city's Germania Bank Building.[8] From there, McGinn continued his spectacular career, gaining a reputation among St. Paul police. When the city's chief detective, John Mason, was ousted in November 1892, the mayor named McGinn as Mason's replacement. The *St. Paul Globe* announced the move, while demolishing the previous chief detective:

Robberies occur nightly, hold-ups occur daily, and the entire city is at the mercy of these vampires almost every hour of the twenty-four. The detective force is powerless and the police stand by paralyzed with stupidity.

After the 1st day of December John C. McGinn, superintendent of the National Pinkerton Detective agency in St. Paul, will step into the shoes of the present chief of the detective force, who has been unable for the past several months to even partially check the career of the hordes of criminals that have infested the city....[9]

McGinn immediately used his new position to attack St. Paul's illegal gambling, shutting down the same houses that Augustus Hornsby was so desperately frequenting that year.[10]

Less than three weeks after the city installed him as chief detective, McGinn faced another mystery, eerily similar to the William Markham case he had solved in 1887: a powerful veteran of the English military, accused of fraud and forgery, had taken flight and was believed to be hiding out in the West.

• • •

Gus Hornsby's flight from arrest shocked St. Paul, and it made national headlines. The *New York Times* put the story on its front page: "HORNSBY FLEES FROM ST. PAUL: He Forged a Deed and Deserted His Wife and Children."[11] Other newspaper accounts and surviving correspondence about Hornsby's disappearance provide a detailed account of the reaction from the community, but not from his own family. There is no known account of Marie Hornsby's reaction, nor do we know what she did while Hornsby was missing.

Stories began to spread that the Antonia Wortmann forgery was only one of several frauds Hornsby committed within the last few years.[12] The police knew that Hornsby had a train ticket to Duluth, and soon rumors sprouted that people had seen Hornsby in that town. Other stories had Hornsby fleeing west to California, trying to head back to Europe, or even to Australia. One report came that he had been spotted in Ontario.

As the news of Hornsby's fugitive status continued to break, some accounts of his wealth—and crimes—took on legendary proportions. The $50,000 that Hornsby had made in St. Paul gambling in 1887 and 1888 was multiplied by ten in some newspaper accounts; others soon claimed that he was $300,000 in debt (confusing the amount that his estate was worth before he began to lose it).[13] Some accounts claimed that Hornsby swindled as much as $20,000 from Benjamin Martin, punching up the actual amount to make the case look more dramatic. And several days later, one truly unscrupulous newspaperman decided to throw out all the facts in the case and make up his own, madcap version of Hornsby's story, in which Hornsby is an entitled lord and Marie Hornsby is not only aware of her husband's gambling, but she is also an accomplice:

CHICAGO, Dec. 20—Augustus H. Hornsby, the scion of a titled English family and whose record while in Chicago astonished the natives, has fled from St. Paul, leaving behind him a dismantled home, forged checks, and debts galore. As a "high roller" Hornsby has no superiors in this city, and his name and $40,000 which he lost are still revered by sundry "gentlemen" whose vocation was and is that of sitting on the other side of the green cloth.

When Hornsby first arrived in Chicago, in 1888, he at once went in search of the tiger with the long claws. He found him, of course, and for a time trimmed the animal's nails in a style that would make forever the reputation of a manicure artist. His wife was with him on his arrival, and they lived for a while at the Palmer and again at the Richelieu. Not liking the accommodations, or perhaps, the figures, Hornsby quit the Richelieu and journeyed to the suburb of Kenwood, where he enjoyed the ease and luxury which come to a titled English gentleman with a large bank account. His family connections were of the first class, and on the quiet, it is said, Hornsby made use of them in more ways than one. On his arrival he was well supplied with funds, and his check on the First National bank was good for $30,000. Carriages and dog carts were his modes of conveyance, and the idea of being cooped up in an 'ansom was especially mortifying.

At the Palmer the employees would break their necks to answer any summons that his lordship might make; he was munificent in his tips, and consequently he owned for a while a large portion of Potter Palmer's hostelry. Midnight "suppers" with white labels on the side cost money, and these A.H. paid for while his funds lasted.

He would make trips into the country—Minneapolis and St. Paul—and while there would inveigle the hard dollars of "the syndicate" to his side of the table. When he had succeeded in accumulating a goodly sized "roll" he would board a train and the following day would blossom forth at the Palmer in all the finery that money could procure. His cigarettes were of the Turkish brand and his brandy was of the "Three Star" order. "Lun'non" soda was used to soften the stings caused by the "Three Star" goods when it began its ramifications in regions known to physicians alone, and in this way he would kill time until evening came. His wife was seldom seen. Often her meals were served in her room, and Hornsby seldom entered the dining room of the Palmer.

One evening he entered a lair where everything was prepared for him. He was well prepared with funds and when he departed in the early morning hours he was compelled to ask for a loan from the dealer. He was in hard lines and it was the beginning of the end. He lost about $8,000 in less than six hours' play. Apartments at the Richelieu were next taken and then he cut a wide swath.

... He was next heard of in Kenwood and had dog arts at his command. How long he remained there is not known; he visited the city every day and always paid the Clark Street "bank" a visit. In his short but meteoric career he dropped $40,000.... Then he went to St. Paul, made money in the real estate market, and again came to Chicago, where he became impoverished by trying to break the faro banks. For a short time he worked on the *American Field*, but, tiring of the work, again went north to recoup his shattered fortune....[14]

The author of this garbled and over-the-top fictional version of Hornsby's life is unknown, but it is possible that he was a journalistic rival of Hornsby's who delighted in a little risk-free libel against him, including throwing in references to fancy cigarettes (when Hornsby was aggressively and vocally anti-tobacco: "I for my part never smoke and cannot imagine how others can"[15]), drunkenness (he rarely drank), and making veiled hints at philandering (there is no evidence that Hornsby was unfaithful). Placing Hornsby in residential stays at hotels and in Kenwood with his wife during the period when he lived and worked in St. Paul (with three children) is provably false. The tone of the anonymous column, however, is not surprising: according to Rutgers University historian Ann Fabian, "Popular writers [of the nineteenth century] depicted gamblers as men whose tastes ran toward the aristocratic, useless, and frequently imported luxuries that threatened to upset the delicate balance of self-interests that maintained the middle-class republic."[16]

Of the rumors and different versions of Hornsby's crimes that swirled around St. Paul in the wake of Hornsby's disappearance, one did end up being true: Hornsby had swindled at least one other person out of money. He had forged a document that claimed he had paid off one of the mortgages that he owed, a property in Hastings, Minnesota, that belonged to a man named William Smith.[17]

Weeks passed. There remained no sign of Augustus Hornsby.

In March 1893, Benjamin Martin's lawsuit against Uri Lamprey and another lawyer proceeded without Hornsby. Martin demanded that Lamprey and his associate pay what Hornsby had stolen from him since they were sureties on Hornsby's notary contract. However, the defense argued that Lamprey was not liable because Hornsby *never became an American citizen*. How could Hornsby be a proper notary if he was not a legitimate Minnesota elector? The case was unprecedented and went to the Minnesota Supreme Court, with Hornsby *in absentia*.[18]

• • •

John McGinn followed all the leads and stories about Hornsby, no matter how ridiculous, but initially found no break in the case. Soon after his installation, McGinn brought in several additional Pinkerton agents and made them St. Paul detectives.[19] They, too, worked the Hornsby case, and they found evidence that Hornsby had indeed made it to Duluth.[20] From Duluth, the detectives tracked Hornsby to Winnipeg and then to the West Coast, where, they assumed, he sought refuge with his brother.

Chapter 8. 1892: St. Paul

There is no evidence, however, that Gus Hornsby reached his brother, Arthur, in California. By spring 1893, Arthur had his own trouble with the law, leading to serious allegations later that summer. Prosecutors charged that Arthur and another man held up a railway office in August. The charges against Arthur were eventually dropped.[21]

Despite the failure to find Hornsby, McGinn's first few months as chief of detectives were a triumph. In March 1893, his former employers, the Pinkerton brothers, presented McGinn with a cherry "rogues gallery" cabinet that could hold 1,000 criminal photographs. The Pinkertons had the cabinet inscribed "JOHN C. McGINN, Chief of Detectives, from William A. Pinkerton and Robert A. Pinkerton."[22] William Pinkerton poured out admiration for McGinn, calling him one of the agency's ablest and brightest men. "Whenever the city wants him no longer, we are ready to take him back."[23]

The St. Paul police were not about to be outdone by the Pinkertons in showing McGinn their admiration. In April, for McGinn's fifty-third birthday, the police threw a party, and the St. Paul chief of police, Albert Garvin, lauded McGinn and his skill. Garvin, the former warden of Minnesota's Stillwater Prison, was a behemoth of a man with a round face and a wide, snow-white walrus mustache. He stood with McGinn for a photograph and then presented him with a custom revolver, hand-made, silver-plated, and with a mother-of-pearl handle. The police force had had it made by special order and had it inscribed[24]

> **John C. McGinn**
> **Chief of Detectives, St. Paul, Minn.**
> **April 18, 1893**

The St. Paul newspaper *Daily News*[25] gave its coverage of this event the headline "Chief of Detectives McGinn Is Handsomely Pistoled," and the reader is not likely to find a better headline in an American newspaper from any era.

• • •

Just one week later, John McGinn received his long-awaited break in the Hornsby case, and it came from a friend of McGinn's in Chicago.

With detectives pursuing him into California, Hornsby had decided early in the year to double back, traveling to Chicago. He took a small apartment in Chicago, under an alias, and started work as a day laborer.[26] There was plenty of work in Chicago as the city geared up for the Columbian Exhibition World's Fair—the titanic White City event that had consumed the region for months. While he was in hiding, Hornsby made no known attempt to contact his wife or children. By April, no one had noticed him in Chicago, and he felt confident—and foolish—enough to use his real name again. He decided to start up an advertising business, and on the morning of Friday, April 28, he went to see a potential client. As the meeting ended, Hornsby offered him one of the business cards he had just had printed. As Hornsby left, the man looked at the card: "A.H. Hornsby, advertising agent." The name finally clicked, evoking the conversations that he had had with McGinn some weeks earlier.[27] The man telegraphed his friend in St. Paul with the story and Hornsby's description.

McGinn wasted no time. Knowing that Hornsby might slip away before he could get to Chicago, McGinn wired the Thiel Detective Service, a competing agency to the Pinkertons.[28] McGinn then made plans to set out for Chicago the following day on the overnight train. By the time McGinn joined the search in Chicago on the morning of April 30, he had learned that two Thiel detectives, Baily and Carney, had found Hornsby and apprehended him on the evening of the 29th.[29] The pair had managed to track Hornsby despite the chaos in the city at the start of the World's Fair.

Here McGinn made his first serious mistake. Rather than crediting the Thiel agents for tracking down and nabbing Hornsby, McGinn sent a telegram back to St. Paul that made it appear as if Hornsby were still at large, and he followed up that telegram with one that claimed that he, McGinn, had made the capture.[30]

The arrest in Chicago sparked pandemonium, both in that city and in Minneapolis–St. Paul. A confounding series of different versions of the arrest sprang up, aggravated by McGinn's intentionally misleading telegrams. The *Chicago Tribune* had the strangest and weirdly erroneous version of the arrest, stating that it took place in Windsor, Ontario (even though all the key figures were still right in Chicago), and that Hornsby was wanted for "cooking the books of a dry goods store."[31]

St. Paul Chief of Detectives John C. McGinn in an undated photograph. McGinn was a teenager when he fought in the Civil War, first joining the navy and later enlisting in the army. His family's home was one of thousands obliterated by the 1871 Great Fire (Pinkerton employee files, Library of Congress).

McGinn was shocked by Hornsby's physical appearance. He looked to be in very poor health and was in a despondent mood.[32] McGinn charged him with second-degree larceny. Hornsby at once denied the charges[33] but said that he was "perfectly willing to return to St. Paul."[34]

• • •

On the evening of April 30, McGinn booked a double berth in a Burlington Rail sleeping car.[35] The train was relatively unoccupied; most travelers were moving in the opposite direction that Sunday, streaming into Chicago for the World's Fair. President Grover Cleveland was in Chicago, and on Monday at noon he would declare the opening of the Columbian Exposition in an address to the city.[36]

McGinn handcuffed himself to Hornsby, who made no effort whatsoever to resist. The private sleeping car was beautiful: dark jet wood surrounding the windows, plush double-wide seats the color of blood and wine, and a string of polished brass chandeliers. The bed was a wide pull-out that occupied the space of three of the seats. Despite a couchette-style upper bunk available via a drop chain from the luggage racks, the two men slept side by side on the lower bed, still chained together.[37]

Early the following morning, May 1, the pair rose and left the sleeping car for one of the day coaches. McGinn no longer shackled himself to his prisoner, but Hornsby remained handcuffed. Hornsby was relieved: the car had no fellow travelers who would witness this shame, and it had comfortable cushioned seats. Despite having slept, Hornsby was still exhausted and in bad shape physically. According to McGinn, Hornsby's spirits rose noticeably as the train neared St. Paul.[38] The two began conversing casually. Hornsby asked McGinn to remove his handcuffs so that he could get a glass of water.[39] McGinn agreed and, rather than follow him, simply watched as Hornsby walked to the end of the car to get a drink.

Hornsby returned, and McGinn decided not to put the handcuffs back on.[40]

In Chicago at that very moment, President Cleveland stood in front of the fair's Administration Building before a crowd of thousands in Jackson Park and began his speech. At the end of his speech, just after noon, he was to push a special electric button that would activate a massive steam engine in the Machinery Hall. As Cleveland took his place to speak, the crowd's cheer boomed across the plaza. Women on the platform took out their white handkerchiefs and waved them.[41] *"We stand today in the presence of the oldest nations of the world and point to the great achievements we here exhibit, asking no allowance on the score of youth.... We have made and here gathered together objects of use and beauty, the product of American skill and invention. We have also made men who rule themselves."*[42]

• • •

Hornsby looked out the window as the countryside streamed past. The Burlington was traveling between thirty and forty miles per hour.[43] The spring day was overcast and rather cold, just over forty degrees Fahrenheit. It started to rain lightly. The train sped toward a tiny station in Prescott, Wisconsin, on the banks of the Mississippi, near the spot where the Mississippi meets the St. Croix. It was five minutes after noon.

Hornsby turned to McGinn and asked to go to the water closet. Hornsby wanted to get a washcloth to bathe his eyes. McGinn agreed and followed Hornsby down the corridor of the day coach toward the small closet that contained a toilet and washbasin. McGinn intended to hold the door open for Hornsby, but Hornsby startled him, suddenly lunging forward into the closet. Hornsby violently pivoted and slammed the door, quickly latching it. McGinn stared at the door, momentarily confused. Hornsby, mustering his lifetime of athletic prowess, leaped onto the toilet and grabbed the wooden sash of the window, jerking it open.[44]

McGinn collected himself and aimed a savage blow at the door with his shoulder. The water closet's door proved surprisingly sturdy. Hornsby looked out the window. The train was still cruising along, going at least 35 miles per hour. Hornsby lifted himself halfway out the window, and a blast of cold, wet air slammed into his face. Hornsby smiled, almost involuntarily from the force of the wind.

In that instant, Cleveland finished his speech. His finger touched the ivory button, affixed to a solid gold telegraph key that closed the electric circuit to a vast engine. Twenty-one guns fired.[45]

"A cup to the dead already, and hurrah, for the next that dies," Hornsby shouted and propelled himself from the window headfirst.[46]

Game Day, 3:30 p.m.

Hornsby's body slammed into the hard-packed earth shoulder-first. As he rolled over, pain shot through his back, and he looked up, disoriented, his head momentarily spinning. A blur like a train car streaked past him: boys in ragged shirtsleeves; men in blue uniforms ran across the field and then suddenly stopped with a dull sound of the ground being thumped hard.

Hornsby slowly stood and shook himself. He had been hit in the back by Theo Hilton, who did not know the rule against such a move, and it did not seem that he would have cared even if he were made aware.

The teams had stalemated on the Northwestern side near midfield when the referee called time: the first half was over. The Chicago team had a comfortable lead, but the Northwestern boys had become more competitive as the half had progressed. Despite this, Hornsby called out to the spectators that any of them were welcome to join the Northwestern team if they were so inclined.[1]

This bit of arrogance was a mistake. Several people in the crowd stepped forward, some students, a few others Evanston townies. The NWU team swelled from twenty to almost thirty. Hornsby realized his error at once and was nearly horrified when Simon Douthart joined the students. Hornsby later described the enormous NWU junior as a "brawny, sandy-haired giant." Not only was Douthart fresh off his weekend wrestling win in the new student gym, but the previous month he had also helped to capture a bear on campus.

• • •

Northwestern and the Bear

In January 1876, Northwestern's campus played host to a runaway 200-pound cinnamon bear.[2] An Evanston resident named J.P. Pierson is believed to have trapped the bear on a hunting trip in nearby Wisconsin.

Pierson chained the bear outside his house to a post. According to one version of what happened next, "one day the bear broke its chain and attacked a passing woman.... This so excited the students of Northwestern University that they felt that for this offense the Pierson family should be deprived of its anticipated juicy bear steaks, and that they, the students, should have the biggest bear barbeque steak dinner ever given in Evanston."

"Therefore with the assistance of ... Simon Peter Douthart, the bear was followed by hundreds of yelling students."[3] Douthart led the bear into the nearby woods, where the students allegedly killed and ate it.

Several versions of the story appeared in the years that followed the bear escapade (each included Douthart in some capacity). Perhaps the strangest is the version that claims that the students first kidnapped the bear, briefly holding it in the basement of University Hall, before barbequing it.[4] After seizing the bear, the imposing Douthart browbeat his fellow students into chipping in money to buy apple cider for their bear feast: "Now, boys, shell out! Bear won't taste good anyhow unless you put in a good foundation of cider and apples."[5]

• • •

Kinman, Casseday, and the rest of the original university team welcomed the newcomers to the game immediately and began to discuss their tactics.

Halftime only lasted a few minutes. There was no entertainment as there had been at the start of the game. Instead, a couple of the goal post handlers swapped the team flags, tying the NWU flag to the southern posts. The players rested a moment and grabbed a cup of tepid coffee or tea. This was almost certainly a better refreshment option than what was *en vogue* with some of the football teams at eastern colleges: devouring lemons between halves.[6]

Theophilus Hilton, who insisted on wearing his top hat during the game with Chicago, was originally from Minneapolis–St. Paul. After graduating, Hilton briefly led the Methodist congregation in Utah and founded the news magazine *The Utah Review* before returning to Chicago. His son would go on to play high school football in the Chicago area (photograph by Alexander Hesler, courtesy Northwestern University Archives).

• • •

During the break, Fred Taylor and Theo Hilton sat and rested next to one of the spectators, a twenty-two-year-old senior named Jessie Brown. The three were close friends, and Jessie often accompanied Fred and Theo to Sigma Chi and Spade and Serpent banquets. Jessie, Theo's classmate and girlfriend, was the one person in the crowd even more devoted to Frances Willard than Frank Casseday was. Jessie's father, Andrew Brown, was a prominent Chicago attorney and one of the co-founders of Northwestern. According to the *Inter-Ocean* newspaper, "Mr. Brown has been called one of the fathers of Evanston.... It was Mr. Brown who, with Orrington Lunt, rode on horseback over parts of Wisconsin, Indiana, and Illinois and finally selected the present site at Evanston. He built the first railway station in Evanston, naming it 'Ridgeville.'"[7]

Jessie Brown's mother, Abbie, was an early "first wave" American feminist and a charter member of the Women's Temperance Alliance (the predecessor to the Woman's Christian Temperance Union, or W.C.T.U., which Willard eventually led). The Alliance had offered Jessie's mother the opportunity to serve as its first president, but Abbie declined.[8]

Jessie was the first woman ever admitted to Northwestern's Academy and the first to graduate from the university's classical course.[9] She was quick to brandish her classical training: clever and expressive, she would casually quote from Phædrus and liked to sign her name in Greek.[10]

She supported Theo Hilton's participation with the new football team and sports in general for the same reason that the Temperance Alliance supported the school's new gymnasium: athletics offered activities that served as deterrents to alcohol. For this reason, Jessie had no problem cheering along as the violence escalated on the field.

• • •

Willard, the Temperance Movement, and Athletics

For Frances Willard and other members of the early U.S. feminist movement, athletics provided a means for women to escape at least some of the cultural restrictions that Western society imposed on them. Willard's personal mode of sport was the bicycle, and she came to it late in life, learning to ride at age fifty-three. She documented this in detail, in her wonderful book *How I Learned to Ride the Bicycle*. She described how she had "always felt a strong attraction to the bicycle, because it is the vehicle of so much harmless pleasure, and because the skill required in handling it obliges those who want to mount to keep clear heads and steady hands."[11]

According to authors Maury Levy and Barbara Jane Walder, Willard's support of bicycle riding for women gave her an opportunity to implore women to engage in activities that did not require—in fact, could not be done properly with—a corset, "those physically restricting straightjackets without sleeves that were supposed to make women look more like women."[12] Willard took the freedom from constraint further than corsets, of course, stating that she wrote her book about bicycling in order "to help women to a wider world, for I hold that the more interests women and men can have in common, in thought, word, and deed, the happier will it be for the home."[13]

Willard and other temperance movement leaders also promoted bicycling and other sports for men, because they considered such activities directly in opposition to recreational alcohol use. Willard clarified this view:

> I had often mentioned in my temperance writings that the bicycle was perhaps our strongest ally in winning young men away from public-houses, because it afforded them a pleasure far more enduring, and an exhilaration as much more delightful as the natural is than the unnatural.
>
> From my observation of my own brother and hundreds of young men who have been my pupils, I have always held that a boy's heart is not set in him to do evil any more than a girl's, and that the reason our young men fall into evil ways is largely because we have not had the wit and wisdom to provide them with amusements suited to their joyous youth, by means of which they could invest their superabundant animal spirits in ways that should harm no one and help themselves to the best development and cleanest ways of living.[14]

Temperance leaders viewed sports not only as a diversion from drinking, but also as a way to counteract a potential backlash toward alcohol abstinence among boys and men who saw temperance as "unmanly."[15] In particular, church groups and Catholic temperance leaders used baseball and, later, football to convince their followers that temperance was also "a masculine movement."[16]

Willard and the other temperance leaders of the late nineteenth century and early twentieth century seemed to be proven right eventually about the use of athletics to support abstinence. There was a spike in sports equipment sales just as prohibition was taking effect in early 1920. According to one East Coast newspaper at the time,

> Sporting goods manufacturers are having the time of their lives at present, trying to increase their production of all kinds of sporting goods. They do not remember such a demand for athletic supplies since they have been in business. Two things, probably, are at the bottom of this unprecedented revival of athletics: prohibition and the war. The men who found their pleasure and recreation in the places where liquor could be obtained now are looking for another form of recreation and find it in athletics.[17]

• • •

Jessie—Jessie Brown *Hilton* after her 1878 marriage to Theo—followed Frances Willard into the W.C.T.U. and rose in the organization's ranks, becoming one of its most important national leaders. She began her career as a student, with Willard as her mentor. Willard saw the promise in Brown and, just a week before her death in 1898, wrote fondly of her mentorship of Brown:

> Neary thirty years ago, when I was president of the Woman's College in Evanston, Miss Jessie Brown was the leading and favorite student whose ability, high character, tactful manners and good looks served to smooth the path of innovation by which the gentler sex was admitted to our University. When the [temperance] Crusade came, the first young person I sought was Jessie Brown.... The first one to "stand by" and help was her schoolmate, Mr. T.B. Hilton, whom she afterward married.[18]

Brown Hilton responded to Willard's comments, providing this insight into her time as a student in 1876:

> As you know, I was the first girl to enter the preparatory school when the doors of the university were thrown open to girls.... I went because my mother said I must, and it was no easy task to stand alone on one side of the hall, the only girl, waiting for the chapel door to open, with 250 young men looking and talking. But I say with gratitude and intense appreciation, that never in my seven years at Northwestern did I receive a rudeness from any student.
>
> Through six years of college life Mr. Hilton and I were classmates, and I always felt that he helped to mold and fashion the college pride and chivalry toward girls for which our university has been so justly admired. He was president of the [Literary] Society and always advocated woman's rights and privileges in every department of life. He helped me to study woman's responsibilities and privileges and the needs of mothers and children so that, as he said, "when you are fifty and gray-headed you will be fitted to teach others."[19]

Jessie took on greater responsibility in the organization. When Theo Hilton died in 1894, Jessie traveled across the country, becoming the W.C.T.U.'s national lecturer, a speaker seen at the time as "an inspiring and instructive leader."[20] Jessie would lead, among other things, an effort to have ship christening ceremonies conducted with bottles of water rather than champagne. Her nationally publicized attempt to do this with the 1898 christening of the battleship USS *Illinois* eventually failed.[21]

While not a drinker, Gus Hornsby had a somewhat less inspired view of the temperance movement and its religious roots, sardonically referring to the women behind the organization in the 1870s as "lady pray-ists."[22]

Jessie and many of the other women in the W.C.T.U. viewed temperance as a path to safety for women and greater women's rights. A later member of the American feminists' first wave, her influence went beyond temperance and Christian goodwill. In a famous essay titled "The Father's Responsibility," Brown Hilton argued that men were accountable for their own behavior and values, and they were obligated to make sure that their sons also idealized strong morals and recognized their responsibility:

> At a convention recently ... a clergyman said, "The women are responsible for the low standard of morals among men. If you would teach your young girls not to associate with young men who smoke or chew; if girls would not marry men of bad habits, and it was understood that such men were tabooed from society, the young men would consider before contracting such habits. Raise the standard of morals for women, increase the demand for young men of good habits, and men of the future will be better fitted for husbands and fathers."
>
> The good brother is partly right and very much in the wrong.... Who is responsible for the belief that man is an animal and must live by preying upon the vital life of another? Who teaches the boys on the street that it is manly to drink and smoke and swear? It is the men of the nation. Every father is directly responsible for the habits of his son. We have some men who live and believe that it requires two to bring up a family properly, but the vast majority relegate this entirely to the women and by example teach object lessons more powerful than the mother's prayers, for boys want to be manly and do as men do.... Children very soon discover if the teaching of the mother is applicable to the life of the father.[23]

Jessie Brown Hilton, shown here wearing the white ribbon of the temperance movement in a photograph from the early 1890s. Throughout the 1890s, Brown Hilton addressed large audiences across the Midwest, discussing the role and responsibilities of mothers and the proper raising of boys. Brown Hilton's father, Northwestern University co-founder Andrew Brown, survived the Great Fire, though trapped at the time in the massive structure that would eventually become Chicago's Newberry Library, surrounded by flames (originally published in *The Prohibition Leaders of America*, 1895).

This was a somewhat radical view in the nineteenth century, and it remains an important one. Jessie Brown Hilton's work following Willard in the W.C.T.U. proved to have an impact on feminism and suffrage even greater than the early suffrage-specific organizations. When Brown Hilton wrote the essay quoted above, Willard and the W.C.T.U. were enrolling approximately 168,000 women in the suffrage movement. The largest suffrage-specific group at the time had enrolled just 13,000.[24]

• • •

As halftime concluded, the NWU students, their shirtsleeves in tatters, blood oozing from the fresh holes in the knees of their trousers, gathered around Casseday and Kinman as they hurriedly explained more of the team's tactics to the newcomers. Speaking more softly, Kinman directed the group's attention across the field, pointing out Curtis. The gesture was unnecessary—no one had any difficulty identifying Curtis's terrifying frame among the blue-uniformed men. Casseday muttered a few more instructions to the group and carefully pointed to Hornsby. From the corner of his eye, Hornsby noticed the students' gaze turn to him. He smiled at the Evanston crew, nodded curtly, but then tried to blend in among the knot of men in blue.

Chapter 9

1893: Hastings

John McGinn launched himself against the closet door a second time. This time he succeeded, and the wood around the bolt latch splintered. The water closet was empty, the window was wide open, and Hornsby was gone. McGinn drew his new silver gift revolver for the first time and shoved his head out the window. He saw Hornsby sprinting past the trees, making for the Mississippi River.[1]

McGinn did not attempt Hornsby's feat. He raced into the train corridor and pulled the train's bell cord. The train immediately began to slow. McGinn bolted out of the car door and onto the car's platform, faced the riverside, and waited for the train to slow to the point where he, too, could safely jump off. He could no longer see Hornsby.

• • •

Hornsby had not planned to escape. As he and McGinn were walking to the water closet, Hornsby recounted the bathroom and its window, easily opened, and decided at once. He landed headfirst into the dirt, rolled, and leaped up, running. He then paused, astonished that he seemed uninjured from the jump. He made for the river, which was less than fifty yards away. As he sprinted, Hornsby couldn't believe his luck: in front of him was a man tying a ferry boat to a pier. Hornsby raced toward the ferryman and shouted that he needed to cross; his wife was dying on the other side.[2] The man at once undid the boat as Hornsby boarded. Here, Hornsby was again fortunate: he had no money with him, but the Mississippi ferry north of Hastings, Minnesota, was toll-free in 1893.[3] They set out for the other side of the river, a spot just north of the town.

After a few more agonizing seconds, McGinn finally leaped off the car's platform and also ran toward the Mississippi. To his left, he spotted the boat—and Hornsby. McGinn ran along the river's edge, waving his arms and screaming at the boat pilot, who thought that McGinn was just another potential passenger (and, apparently, a crazed, manic one).[4] The ferryman did not turn back; instead, he looked quizzingly at Hornsby.

Chapter 9. 1893: Hastings 133

Panting, slightly bloodied, Hornsby stared wide-eyed at McGinn, then at the ferryman, and shrugged his shoulders. McGinn later said that if the ferry boat had not happened to have been moored at that exact spot, "I could easily have overtaken Hornsby after his wild plunge from the car window."[5] Instead, McGinn stood by the pier, fuming, having to wait on the Wisconsin side of the river until the boat returned.[6] After a few minutes, the boatman lurched back, and McGinn boarded and also disembarked on the shore just northeast of Hastings.[7]

Hornsby was gone.

• • •

Hornsby's ferry escape sounds like the product of an unimaginative newspaper reporter throwing a *deus ex machina* into the account of Hornsby's flight. However, the unlikely position of the ferry and Hornsby's last-second escape on it were confirmed by multiple accounts, including Hornsby's and poor Detective McGinn's.[8]

The small Minneapolis newspaper *The Irish Standard* later provided one of the more colorful accounts of Hornsby's escape on the ferry: "[Detective McGinn] pulled the bell cord and stopped the train, but the bird had already reached the river where Dame Fortune had kindly provided a ferry which was just breaking moorings. On this Hornsby set foot and was soon waving his bandana from the middle of the Father of Waters to the exasperated ex-Pinkerton."[9]

As it had with its account of Hornsby's arrest, the *Chicago Tribune* botched the coverage of his escape, speculating incorrectly that Hornsby simply opened the car door and jumped, and that after his jump from the train Hornsby hid in some nearby underbrush.[10]

• • •

Hornsby had run toward the nearby town, still not quite sure where he was. He came across a livery stable on the outskirts of town. Hornsby asked the livery hands where he was, trying to avoid raising any suspicion. He was relieved to find out that he was near Hastings: he knew the layout somewhat. Hornsby should have—in a remarkable coincidence, Hastings was the site of the property for which he had recently swindled William Smith out of over $3,500 with a fraudulently signed mortgage.[11]

Hornsby considered hiring a rig at the stable, but he knew that McGinn would catch him before the liveryman could harness the horses.[12] In an attempt to throw McGinn off his trail, Hornsby told the men that he was trying to make for the Hastings fairgrounds[13] on the town's west side; he actually wanted to bolt a little farther south. An old man with a carriage was about to depart the stable. Hornsby waved him down and told him a story similar to what he told the ferryman: a relative was dying and he needed to get to her bedside.[14] The old man urged Hornsby to get aboard. He was a physician and would take him immediately. Hornsby boarded and looked at the man—*of course* he was a doctor. Hornsby chuckled ruefully at the ridiculous bad luck of this. The doctor drove the carriage south with breakneck speed. Hornsby panicked several minutes later and again leaped from a speeding vehicle, this time lurching from the carriage.[15] Hornsby struck the muddy ground, rolled, and ran. Astonished, the old man stopped his carriage and watched, slack-jawed, as Hornsby sprinted away.

Once he reached the Minnesota riverbank, McGinn searched for a place with a telephone or telegraph rather than continue the pursuit of Hornsby by himself.[16] Finding one, he telegraphed St. Paul police chief Garvin, who responded with fury. Garvin wanted to stave off any embarrassment to the city's police, and he wanted Hornsby caught, no matter what resources were needed. He sent five agents—Ryan, Heeney, McFetridge, Miller, and Werrick—to Hastings to back up McGinn and support the search. Ryan and Heeney were former Pinkerton colleagues whom McGinn had recently hired.

At the St. Paul train station, several more of McGinn's detectives waited for the arrival of the Burlington train carrying the chief detective and Hornsby.[17] They had already left the police station when Garvin received McGinn's telegram. The train arrived just a couple of minutes behind schedule. Rather than their boss, the train's conductor met them and informed them of what happened. The men raced back to their station.

The five agents dispatched by Garvin did not have time to wait for the next train to Hastings, and carriages would also lose them valuable time. Instead, Garvin suggested they race to the river and track down a friend of his named Bronson, a depot supervisor who owned a fast boat. A steam launch would make the fifteen-mile trek faster than any other means. The men agreed and made for the river.

The launch, piloted by Bronson, left within minutes and steamed hard for Hastings. As the detectives departed, McGinn received word of a man spotted near a local farm, and some Hastings residents were in pursuit. McGinn found a telephone and used it to call Garvin, telling him that he'd located Hornsby; he just needed resources for the capture.[18]

Just after 2:00 p.m., the steam launch arrived in Hastings, and the agents split up for the search. Detective James Heeney had the best plan of the bunch. He immediately sought one of the Hastings residents who was most familiar with the area. He found a local named Arthur Fisher.[19] Heeney explained to Fisher that he suspected Hornsby might look for another set of train tracks and try to hop a freight train to get out of the area. The rail on which Hornsby had come, the Chicago Burlington &

Northern Railroad, lay on the other side of the Mississippi. Fisher knew that the Chicago & Milwaukee line's tracks lay just to their south, near the Vermillion River. The pair hopped into a hired carriage and sped toward the tracks. They spent several hours scouring the farms around the Chicago & Milwaukee line.

About six miles south of Hastings, Heeney and Fisher found a witness—Hornsby had passed his farm just an hour before.[20] They continued and met several farm boys who also claimed to have seen a stranger some minutes before. The boys said that the stranger appeared sick.

• • •

While he initially had felt uninjured from both of his high-speed jumps, Hornsby began to feel stabs of fire from his legs. He had sprinted at top speed for what seemed like half a mile, and now his body throbbed with pain—his legs were giving out. Hornsby's mind spun dizzily. He looked about him for any pursuers, and the field around him lifted and tilted. He vomited and collapsed to his knees, which caused jets of hot pain to work through his legs. Hornsby's thoughts moved through delirium, from paper chases to pigstickings. His nausea abated, but the exhaustion did not. Hornsby rose and looked about him again. A house beckoned from a clearing a few hundred yards away.

• • •

Within an hour of their encounter with the Hastings boys, as dusk smoldered into nightfall, Heeney and Fisher found Augustus Hornsby. He was leaning against the side of a farmhouse, drinking from a glass. Hornsby had begged a meal at the house, and the owner had given him some milk. Heeney had the carriage stop and told Fisher to stay put. Heeney then walked stealthily around the house, to its rear. Heeney crept up, put his hand on Hornsby's shoulder, and told him to walk down to the road and get into his carriage. Hornsby complied.[21]

At 8:45 p.m., Heeney arrived in the center of Hastings with Hornsby. Heeney took Hornsby to the Gardner House hotel, walked him into the parlor, and asked for a private room and dinner for Hornsby. The Gardner House complied, but the manager also sent word out that the fugitive for which everyone was looking was at their inn.[22] Heeney asked Hornsby where he was running, and Hornsby confirmed his hunch: Hornsby had indeed been skirting along the Chicago & Milwaukee tracks, trying to catch a freight train, but was too tired to make it.[23]

As Hornsby sat in the Gardner's dining room to eat, a reporter for the St. Paul *Pioneer Press*, the same newspaper that used to employ Hornsby, entered. He had been searching with everyone else for the fugitive late that afternoon, and he had just received the news that Hornsby was at the hotel, in custody. The reporter reacted to Hornsby's appearance in much the same way that McGinn did the previous day. Hornsby was haggard, dejected. "Great black rings encircled his eyes."[24] The reporter asked to sit with Hornsby. He agreed.

"I beg you," Hornsby said, "to say as little about this matter as you can. I do not ask it of myself, but for my wife and children."[25] The reporter was not impressed; Hornsby had already inflicted enormous harm on his family, and his wife and children had the community's sympathy.[26] Hornsby looked at the reporter and then began to sob. He put his head in his hands and cried loudly. After a minute, Hornsby stopped, collected himself, and quietly gave his account of the train ride and his attempted escape. When he finished, he stared straight ahead. "Well, the thing is done, and there is no making any more fuss over it."[27] Hornsby was beyond exhausted, and he could not comprehend why so many people took an interest in what he saw as a private matter—a personal issue. Why must there be such an enormous, boisterous crowd in the lobby of this place? What could they hope to gain by coming here and seeing him?

McGinn did not get word of Hornsby's capture until well after the last train to St. Paul left at 10:00 p.m., so the agents decided to wait until morning to take Hornsby back, and they put him up at the Gardner. The search had caused a sensation in Hastings. When McGinn arrived at the hotel late that night, there was still a throng of people under the great awning around the building, curious townspeople eager to get a glimpse of the fallen real estate magnate.

• • •

Hornsby was arranged in St. Paul the following day and waived examination, saying that he understood the matter entirely. The judge set bail at $3,000, which Hornsby could not pay, so he was sent to the county jail.[28] His family immediately began to try to raise the funds.

St. Paul celebrated James Heeney, and fellow detectives called for his promotion. The manhunt in Hastings, however, was a deep embarrassment for John McGinn. "McGinn is out with a red fire story* as to the manner in which Hornsby was located and arrested by him, which at this particular stage sounds quite thrilling," the *St. Paul Globe* sarcastically wrote after Hornsby's arraignment, viciously recounting McGinn's misleading telegrams from Chicago on Sunday.[29] Rumors circulated as to how Hornsby managed to escape from McGinn, including suspicions that McGinn might have been drinking during the trip from Chicago.

---

* Here, "red fire story" is slang for an action-packed, unbelievable tall tale.

The same *Pioneer Press* reporter who interviewed Hornsby in Hastings went to the St. Paul jail to visit him. Hornsby had barely been able to appear in court, he was so ill. The reporter found Hornsby lying on a cot, "looking miserable."[30] Hornsby made a few terse remarks and then went silent, still ill from the previous day. He ended the brief interview by simply saying, "I have a fearful headache."[31] The jailer walked past the cell, and Hornsby asked him if anyone else had come to see him.

"No."

Hornsby silently rolled toward the wall and waved for the reporter to leave.

• • •

A week later, a grand jury formally indicted Hornsby for larceny and forgery, including the $472 check that Benjamin Martin had intended for Antonia Wortmann. Not only had Hornsby forged the deed, but he had also endorsed Martin's check: "Pay to the order of A.H. Hornsby. Antonia Wortmann, A.H. Hornsby."[32] Hornsby was also accused of forging a satisfaction of the mortgage for $3,517 that he owed William Smith.[33]

Hornsby initially pled not guilty, but a few days later he stood before Judge James J. Egan and changed his plea to guilty.[34] Hornsby's attorney, General John B. Sanborn, asked for a light sentence.[35] The county's attorney recommended three years with hard labor. When Egan asked Hornsby to make a statement and explain why he should not go to prison, Hornsby replied in the same way that he did with the reporter in the Gardner House: he should be spared "not for myself, but for my wife I ask the mercy of the court."

"I want to come back to St. Paul and show her that I can be a man."[36]

The judge was as unmoved as the reporter had been. Egan sentenced Hornsby to two and a half years in prison with hard labor.[37]

Game Day, 3:45 p.m.

As the second half began, the game's spectators became more excited, cheering each play loudly. With its additional players pulled from the crowd, Northwestern's team now resembled a mob, and it was nearly as coordinated.

Hornsby tried to keep the Chicago team focused on its strategy, but the game was devolving into a patchwork of loose scrimmages across midfield. Some of these battles were many yards away from the ball, one with three or four of the NWU players battling a Chicago forward for no apparent possible reward. The forwards on both sides excitedly sought each other out, slamming against each other.

Simon Douthart battered a Chicago player, relieving him of the ball, then turned to his former wrestling opponent, senior Walter Lee Brown, and handed Brown the ball. Brown made a sprint into Chicago territory. Brown's speed impressed Hornsby: "He ran like a wild deer," Hornsby recalled in his *Chicago Field* account of the game.[1]

• • •

Both teams included players who later became foremost experts in their professions, and Walter Brown was no exception. Brown's specialty was metallurgy, and he would write one of the best works on the subject produced up to that time. However, it was Brown's hobby for which he became best known: Brown collected books, including some of the rarest books about ancient Rome. Although best-known for his metallurgical book, Brown also edited a highly-regarded selection of the works of Marcus Aurelius.[2] When Brown died in 1904, Evanston's library—to which Brown had contributed substantial effort and volumes—noted that "as a discriminating and indefatigable collector of certain lines of rarities, Mr. Brown was well known throughout the literary world. His death at the early age of fifty-one is a great loss to science and literature."[3]

Joining Brown and the team in the game in the second half was another Northwestern senior who would go on to have literary success.

Alanson Appleton was watching the game on the sidelines and, along with Simon Douthart, joined the team after Hornsby's ill-advised invitation. Appleton was a small man[4] and had no effect on the game—at least, none that made it into the surviving accounts. By the end of the 1880s, Appleton had served as a reporter for the *Chicago Herald*, was president of Chicago's Authors' and Travelers' Club, had written *The New Awakening, or the Social Movement of the Nineteenth Century*, and was considered one of the leaders of "the literary movement of Chicago."[5]

At the height of Appleton's career, the Chicago World's Fair organizers asked him to write a commissioned address for syndicated publication in advance of the fair. Appleton demanded $10,000, an astronomical amount at the time. The cost, he explained, was justified:

> You would think nothing of paying $10,000 to a railroad for transporting a few tons of woodwork or machinery to your exposition, and what comparative estimate do you place on the value of an address which is expected to inspire enthusiasm in the breasts of some sixty million of people, and have a direct influence upon transporting to Chicago hundreds of thousands of dollars' worth of property, as well as the sympathy and cooperation of a large part of the civilized world? Does inspiration count for nothing?[6]

The World's Fair committee reportedly paid the fee.

CHAPTER 10

1893: Stillwater

Judge Egan sentenced Hornsby on May 19, 1893. Five days later, officials took Hornsby to the old Minnesota State Prison at Stillwater, a few miles east of St. Paul on the banks of the St. Croix River. When he arrived at the prison, it housed 342 inmates. Within a few weeks, the prison's population would plateau at just under 400 as Stillwater welcomed an influx of southern White and American Indian prisoners.[1]

Hornsby was still recovering from his escape attempt and the exhaustion from his trial and sentencing when he arrived at the complex of buildings at Stillwater. He looked many years older than he had just six months ago, before his desperate forgery and his cross-country flight from the police. His hair, which had been thinning, was nearly gone, and his beard had become entirely white. As the cab pulled to the outskirts of the prison complex, Hornsby was startled: for a facility with less than 400 inmates, Stillwater was enormous. The complex sprawled down the riverbank, a mazework of modern buildings set against a vast outcropping of shoreline rock. It sat on a depressed pocket of land about an eighth of a mile square, appearing at first glance to be a miniature quarry. The surrounding grounds and buildings stood about twenty feet above the prison, and the boundaries of the complex were a brickwork wall that was flush with the ground around it, providing an effective deterrent to escape. Stone guard towers marked the corners of the outer walls leading down into the prison.

Although Hornsby was not violent, he was—justifiably—considered a flight risk, and because of this, he would have entered the prison grounds handcuffed to a sheriff or a deputy.[2]

The guards led Hornsby through a courtyard, the admittance office, and then to an office where he was inspected and fingerprinted. The deputy taking in Hornsby asked him his birthday and nationality. Hornsby relayed a brief version of his history, noting that he could speak multiple languages, to which the deputy is reported to have replied, "Humph, we talk English here—and damned little of *that*."[3]

Prison officials gave Hornsby a standard set of essentials, including—according to author John Koblas—"a Bible, two cups, one small mirror, a spoon, a face towel, dish towel, a comb, blanket, sheets, pillowcases, mattress, bedstead and springs, and a small bar of soap."[4] Hornsby would have also been given a ration of tobacco, which he likely would have used as an unapproved trading resource.

Hornsby was issued the uniform of a second-class prisoner: first-class status belonged to Stillwater prisoners who earned it; third-class was punitive. This prisoner grading system had been instituted by the prison's previous warden, Albert Garvin, the same man who was now St. Paul's chief of police.[5] The second-class dress was a black and grey-checked suit with a cap,[6] and Hornsby would have worn this after the guards cut his remaining hair short and shaved off his beard.

After processing, the guards led Hornsby to his cell. While most of Stillwater's cells in the 1890s were whitewashed, with stark white walls and bars, the prison had recently painted Hornsby's new cell dark red, the smell of the umber in the paint still overwhelming: a dark smell, a dead, decaying odor in strange contrast to the fresh, clean walls. A metal table to the side of his room, fixed to the wall, would have invoked an old memory of Hornsby's tiny room at Wellington. That jarring connection certainly awaited him: his joy at being a boy in a room of his own, and now, looking at another room all to himself. He ate tapioca and milk with a square of cornbread and thought of Charles Kingsley, the old rector, his friend and teacher at Wellington.[7]

"Give me a back," the old man had said and had leaped over Hornsby's young frame.

Alone in his cell at Stillwater, Hornsby mimicked Kingsley, hands forward, crouching, then taking a quick, light jump. He sent his dinner crashing to the stone floor. "A too rapid gyration," he later wrote, "and down came supper. There was an aching void in my interior, but not so on the floor."[8]

Yet, even as the guards had helped Hornsby from the carriage and to the prison's front walkway upon his arrival, his mood had begun to improve. The courtyard, an attractive patch of grass lined with healthy young black ash trees, featured a tiny gazebo where a couple of inmates were sitting in the shade, escaping the late spring heat. As Hornsby passed, the inmates looked up, smiled, and waved. Hornsby, for so long having felt like an outcast, having been respected but seldom *liked*, immediately found in Stillwater an unlikely home among friends, despite the miserable conditions of the prison itself. The effect of Hornsby's acceptance by the inmates was noticeable and swift. He became more congenial within days, and he grew self-effacing and witty. "Some of the stairways in the prison were not constructed for six-footers," Hornsby wrote a few days after his incarceration. "My cranium got that knowledge, though we fall two inches short of the fathom."⁹ Hornsby referred a lot to his bald "cranium" in his writing in prison, also noting that "thanks to the state tailor, the flies no longer make a summer skating rink of the bald spot on our pate. He has our thanks for the neat skull cap that now protects the barren waste on our cranium."¹⁰

The inmates, most of whom were younger than Hornsby, began calling him "Uncle," a nickname that one of the new southern prisoners started. Using the *royal we*, Hornsby later wrote, "We are not sufficiently acquainted with the customs of the south to know if this be a title of distinction or affection."¹¹ Hornsby, in turn, began affectionately calling the inmates "the Four Hundred," a comic mockery of the famous New York City Four Hundred, the list of high society in the 1890s.¹² Hornsby used this joke in print several times.

(Hornsby might have been the first newspaper writer to wind up in prison and joke about the New York Four Hundred, but he is not the most famous: the writer O. Henry, a former journalist for the *Houston Post*, spent 1898 to 1901 in prison for bank embezzlement. The title of his 1906 book, *The Four Million*—most of the stories in which centered on the lives of everyday New Yorkers—was a critical play on the Four Hundred.)

The grounds of Stillwater Prison, in a photograph taken about one year after Hornsby's time at the facility. The steep walls leading to the elevated surrounding land are visible, as is the river in the background. The entrance courtyard, with its gazebo, can be seen in the foreground (digital image courtesy Minnesota Historical Society).

Even the appalling condition of the prison—teeming with cockroaches and other vermin—did not dampen Hornsby's improved demeanor: "There seems to be a sort of spider peculiar to the prison; active and vigilant, he is skilled in catching bed-bugs. We are taking lessons of him."[13] Hornsby was likely only half joking: bedbugs were plentiful throughout the cell house.

Hard labor at Stillwater usually meant that the convict was to work in the prison's new twine factory. Stillwater produced 7,000 pounds of twine a day in 1893, "exclusively for the benefit of the farmers of Minnesota,"[14] selling it to the state's farmers for eight cents a pound. Hornsby, however, avoided the twine plant and found a different and far more beneficial path in prison: Stillwater had a newspaper, *The Prison Mirror*.

Cole Younger, of the infamous James-Younger gang, co-founded *The Prison Mirror* at Stillwater in 1887. It was the first paper in the country entirely prisoner-run. The prisoners at Stillwater still publish the paper, making it the oldest prisoner-run paper in the country.[15]

• • •

Cole Younger and his two brothers arrived at Stillwater on November 20, 1876, following their disastrous attempt, alongside Frank and Jesse James, to rob the First National Bank of Northfield, Minnesota. Cole had been shot and wounded eleven times during the raid and the ensuing escape attempt, and both of his brothers had also taken bullets during the fiasco.

According to Cole, most of his injuries came a couple of days after the bank raid, when a party of lawmen discovered the brothers and opened fire. "All of us but [Cole's brother] Bob had gone down at the first fire. [Charles] Pitts, shot through the heart, lay dead. [Cole's other brother] Jim had been shot five times, the most serious being the shot which shattered his upper jaw and lay imbedded beneath the brain, and a shot which buried itself underneath his spine.... Including those received in and on the way from Northfield I had eleven wounds."[16] Incredibly, all three brothers survived the barrage.

Stillwater had initially placed the brothers in special confinement with additional guards, worried that the James Gang might try to break in and free the Coles.[17] By Jesse James's death in 1882, concerns of a jailbreak had subsided, and the brothers had incarcerations similar to the rest of the prison population.

The brothers' incarceration occurred, coincidentally, the same week that John McGinn apprehended the Lincoln grave robbers in 1876, providing the nation with two headlining crime stories at the same time.

Cole Younger viewed starting a newspaper at Stillwater as a valuable financial investment, though he worked on it only briefly. He and his brother Jim were still inmates when Hornsby arrived. By then, Cole was head nurse in the prison's hospital, and Jim was the prison's librarian,[18] having taken that spot from Cole. The third Younger brother, Bob, had died at Stillwater in 1889.

• • •

In May 1893, the paper's editor, whose identity is unknown—all prisoner editors and contributors were anonymous and used *noms de plume*[19]— was ready to step down. He had worked on *The Prison Mirror* for several years and was nearing his release. The middle-aged, well-educated former magazine and newspaper editor who just dropped into the prison was a perfect replacement, and Hornsby welcomed the challenge. "By our own request [we are ending] our editorship of *The Prison Mirror*," the outgoing editor wrote. "The one who succeeds us is a writer of ability and has had experience in the newspaper business, so our paper, under his management, will be better than ever before."[20] With his ascension to editor of *The Prison Mirror*, Hornsby gained control of the prison's entire printing department, including supervising its pressman, compositors, and an assistant, and he had full say on what the paper printed (with the warden's approval; he rarely stepped in).[21] Hornsby also had use of the new editor's room, a comfortable chamber with a small wood desk, bookshelves, a double-paned window overlooking the prison courtyard, and an impressive birdcage for keeping a pet.

Hornsby's improvements were to a newspaper already displaying a higher quality of journalism than the major newspapers of many surrounding cities. *The Prison Mirror*'s inmate writers had kept to an exacting standard, with well-crafted commentary and a breadth of news coverage that was stunning, considering that it came from a literally captive staff. One could expect some piety and moralizing with the paper's commentary since it was coming from convicts attempting to reform (the paper's motto was "It Is Never Too Late to Mend"). The outgoing staff, for example, in one of its last issues, published a lengthy rebuke of gambling, offering that

> robbers of time are more dangerous than robbers of money, because they take away that which no money can purchase or replace; and one of the most notorious robbers of time is gambling, for it tends to no improvement either of body or mind.... Besides being a waste of time, gaming has, in a manifold view, a very pernicious tendency, and, accordingly, in every civilized and well-regulated state, it is either totally prohibited, or limited and restrained by law.... Gambling for money, in large bets, is the highway to every kind of knavery and villainy.
>
> I see by the papers that the late Rufus Hatch of New York, who leaves most of his property to his children, warns them, in his will, not to use tobacco in any shape or form; not to touch, taste, or use wine or liquor in any way, and to

especially refrain from gambling. Shun gambling; avoid it as you would the mansion of death.²²

Hornsby would have definitely taken note of this commentary in the first issue of *The Prison Mirror* that he read at Stillwater, particularly because Rufus Hatch, a stock baron who had died the previous month, was the well-known cousin of his former Chicago Foot-Ball Club teammate, William Hatch.

What Hornsby did not (yet) read was that a couple of weeks before his arrival at Stillwater, *The Prison Mirror* had reported on his train escape from Detective McGinn, covering the event more accurately than the *Chicago Tribune*'s professional—and free—staff.²³

Ironic for a man serving time for forgery and fraud, one of Hornsby's initial concerns was with his staff plagiarizing material for their columns. "There is no reason to be assigned for such petty larceny than innate depravity," he stated, warning—only partially tongue-in-cheek—that the next reporter caught plagiarizing would be "promptly gibbeted."²⁴

The first thing that Hornsby did as editor was to try to find a copy of Kingsley's *Westward Ho!*, his favorite book. Stillwater's library was impressive, a 6,000-volume resource that the prisoners used extensively, and Hornsby—like the other inmates—was allowed to check out two books a week.²⁵ Hornsby checked with the prison's librarian, a forty-five-year-old man with light blue eyes and a full, dark mustache, which only partially obscured the bullet scar running across his upper lip. Jim Younger, the former outlaw and murderer, suffering from acute depression, apologized earnestly to Hornsby that he could not find a copy.²⁶ "Anyone having a spare copy," Hornsby subsequently implored the other inmates, "and donating it to the prison library would confer a great benefit; there is no such pugnacious, brave, simple, thoroughly manly Christian in all fiction as Amyas Leigh."²⁷

Hornsby's opening commentary as editor was a column he titled, "Let Daylight In," which argued for society to increase its effort at crime prevention, rather than at its correction:

> While so much is being said and written on the redemption of convicts, would it not be appropriate to say a word on the means of reducing criminal tendencies? The old saying, "Prevention by protection, rather than cure after destruction," should, most assuredly, have some weight on this subject.... By insensible degrees the youthful votary becomes familiarized with vice and callous to its approach. Later we see our young man, the companion of gamblers, and the more open publicity of the saloon ordinary is forsaken for the well-furnished box-stalls of the rear.
> Our municipal governments are certainly not doing their best for the community when they allow saloon keepers to hold out to youth, as yet innocent, the seductions of pool, billiards, and dice.²⁸

At nearly the same time that Hornsby wrote this, his former football competitor, Frank Casseday, wrote an essay published in the *Wisconsin Medical Recorder* that also argued against the emphasis on crime correction and reliance on prisons:

> We say that the whole scheme of court judgement is based upon the necessity for society as expressed in concrete form in the community to protect itself. To protect itself from what?
>
> The moment a person is convicted of crime he or she becomes a pariah and outcast, and the officers of the law treat him or her very much as they would treat a tiger, or wolf met in the road. They are obsessed by the *force* idea, and that idea assumes the form of force by arms.
>
> On the other hand, whoever heard of an officer taking a convicted man by the hand and telling him he was sorry for him, or encouraging him to lead a better life. Why? Simply because the idea of force has its birth and existence in fear. Society ... is saturated with fear of being crushed by some force which they do not understand....
>
> The day of force and fear is passing. All over the world prison reform is being inaugurated. We find to our utter astonishment that our convicts are human beings, and that they can be placed upon their honor, and will make good.[29]

In that same inaugural issue of Hornsby's *Prison Mirror*, another inmate wrote about immigration, arguing against America becoming "the dumping ground of the world," but maintaining that all are indeed welcome, as long as they have first "become acquainted with the language and institutions, and they understand that limited liberty is true liberty."[30] The paper's editorials were moralistic and cautious, yet surprisingly progressive.

Hornsby, by the 1890s, was changing. His views on women and other races gradually shifted, also becoming more progressive. In his first months at Stillwater, as his friendships with other inmates—including the prison's Black inmates—deepened, his positions shifted even more dramatically.

Hornsby offered one of the prison's eighteen Black prisoners a chance to discuss racial issues directly on the paper's front page. The prisoner, whose *nom de plume* was "HTW," did just that, writing an article called "The Race Problem."[31] It was groundbreaking stuff for a nineteenth-century newspaper that circulated amongst nearby White communities. HTW despaired at the situation of southern African Americans and thought that they would be better to have broken off from the rest of the United States. "It would have been to the advantage of both races. The Afro-American will soon, if just left to his own individual resources, elevate himself out of the slough of ignorance in which he now wallows in the South."[32] Hornsby himself responded, decrying the violence and oppression waged against the Black communities of the South in the 1890s: "Is *this* the last decade of the nineteenth century? Did the North spend a billion of treasure and a million of lives to break the material shackles of slavery from off the negroes to surrender them to the ungoverned, unlawful brutality of worse than savages?"[33]

• • •

For Hornsby, the social turning point seems to have come that summer, when several members of the St. Paul W.C.T.U., taking previous instruction directly from Frances Willard, visited Stillwater and met with some of the inmates (Willard herself was in London at the time and had been ill for several months[34]). The women distributed white flowers to the convicts and listened as the men shared their stories. For the rest of the day, the men wore the flowers in the buttonholes of their uniforms. They took them back to their cells and tried to keep them alive in little cups of water for as long as possible.[35] Hornsby was particularly careful, placing his petunia in a small tin cup and setting it on his cell table, admiring its bright white petals, lightly speckled with violet, against the deep brick-red paint of his cell walls. The inmate nicknamed HTW gave his flower—a sprig of coleus—to Hornsby several days later, hoping that he would have a better shot of keeping it alive. HTW had meticulously kept it in a bottle "until it developed fine roots about two inches long. The editor is now its guardian. In a pot it will doubtless flourish."[36]

The visit from Willard's colleagues had a profound effect on the prison. One prisoner commented that

> from all appearances and different expressions one would judge that the true words of a kind woman can find their way to the heart of us, uncouth as we may appear to others.
>
> The W.C.T.U. uses methods of reformation alone, superior to the government rules regulating the reformatory system. Could the cheerful words and manifest interest of this worthy body reach the ears of all the downfallen, many a man would retain his manhood and perhaps rise to take his place in the ranks of his kind helpers.[37]

Hornsby agreed, writing, "The W.C.T.U., in our midst, ought to help some of us to understand the magic of a wide and comprehensive society. Theirs is no lip service, but an earnest sacrifice of self. And they have their reward. Love begets love."[38] It was a far cry from Hornsby's position nearly twenty years before, when he derisively called the same women "lady pray-ists."[39]

It speaks to the conditions of Stillwater in the 1890s and to the inmates' state of mind that the W.C.T.U.'s visit was so universally admired by the prisoners. Many commented in *The Prison Mirror* about the importance of the visit, with one prisoner noting that "the true, kind, and encouraging words addressed to us by them have caused me deeper reflection than I ever before experienced as a prisoner." Another inmate said simply: "Most of us will remember the visit on August 13 for some little time, some of us may carry it treasured as a life-long memory."[40]

In 1893 Willard and the W.C.T.U. were working with a special Senate committee pursuing women's suffrage, and Hornsby decided to devote all the editorials in one issue of the paper to the suffrage question. At the time, fourteen inmates contributed editorial material to *The Prison Mirror*. Hornsby had each of them vote whether they were for or against women's suffrage and write a column defending their position. Thirteen supported the idea; only one opposed—far more lopsided support for the proposal than shown by the outside public in the 1890s (particularly among men).[41] The group concluded, "society would gain, crime decrease, and Elysium hang low should women vote." Of the thirteen writers in favor, a couple wrote bitterly sarcastic "opposition" pieces, including the following, which Hornsby edited carefully, keeping the original writer's sardonic and intentional misspellings:

> Yer see a woman aint no recount in politicks. She don't drink, so yer can't set 'em up and set 'em up till she don't know a Remocrat from a Depublican, nor a dollar bill from a ballot. She's got convicshuns, she has, and convicshuns aint no good at a ward primary because ther boss furnishes sech with cigyars.... A woman—shaw! She'd want ter know what was did with a 'lection fund, an' why ther school-board kanidate was 'nifed to get Barney O'Toole in fer alderman. A woman's too durn inquisitive to be let vote.[42]

Another prisoner expressed his views tersely: "I believe in human rights, woman's rights, or anything else that is right."[43]

Hornsby voted to support, and wrote a poem for the occasion, which ended:

> Oh, woman's love! Oh, type of love divine,
> Forgetting, all forgiving. Yet decline
> We, sotted with conceit, to let her vote
> For fear the gentle mate control the boat.[44]

• • •

All surviving evidence indicates that Hornsby was a model prisoner and stayed a first-class inmate once he earned that status. This was a good thing, because disciplinary measures at Stillwater in the 1890s were outrageously harsh. The ultimate punishment was solitary confinement in one of the specially-made (usually filthy) chambers in the cell house. According to a contemporary description, solitary confinement at Stillwater:

consists of standing the prisoner on the inside of the cell door, putting his hands through the bars, and handcuffed on the outside. He is kept standing in that position ten hours during the day, and then let down during the night; is allowed only a single slice of bread and a cup of water each day while undergoing punishment. There are no beds in these cells, nothing but a plank on which to sleep.[45]

This description fails to mention that there was a solid iron door just in front of the barred cell door, and the iron door was kept shut, so the prisoner was forced to stand facing the door, inches away, in nearly total darkness.

In the summer of 1894, it became clear that Hornsby might be granted parole. Parole was actually a new concept, and Stillwater had just begun releasing prisoners under Minnesota's new parole law—Hornsby would be among the first prisoners to receive parole.[46] Facing the possible end of his sentence, he was allowed to re-grow his beard, and a tailor re-fitted the suit he wore when he arrived.[47]

Just as it had featured an anti-gambling article in the first issue that Hornsby saw upon his arrival at Stillwater, *The Prison Mirror* printed another as Hornsby was nearing the end of his time at the prison. However, Hornsby himself was responsible for publishing this 1894 commentary:

> Anyone who has ever gambled, whether at cards, dice, or even at marbles, can remember the personal degradation he felt on pocketing his winnings for the first time. Anything obtained without an equivalent return in money or labor has a debasing effect, and this gambling vice has grown to such enormous magnitude in our country that thousands of young men are led to moral ruin by it every year.
>
> Games which combine the elements of chance and skill have a fascination which it is difficult for some natures to resist, and thus many young men of respectable parentage, who occupy positions of trust are corrupted and led to filch money from their employers to indulge their passion for gambling. This evil is more prevalent than is generally supposed....
>
> Gambling, drunkenness, and greater crimes will be rampant so long as the better element of society sit idle and sigh over evils they make no effort to abate.[48]

When he was eventually granted parole in August, the warden gave him twenty-five dollars and a lecture about staying straight.[49] Hornsby immediately returned to his family in St. Paul.[50]

• • •

The Hornsbys' house on Dearborn Street was gone, foreclosed at the beginning of the year.[51] Marie, Henry, and Rachel had moved to a large boarding house that the Hornsbys still owned on 10th Street, and Marie had taken in boarders to supplement the income she received from the Northern Pacific.[52] Living in the house with the family were Mary McKinnon, a seamstress; Abner Dalrymple, a brakeman for the Northern Pacific; a dressmaker named Kathline Young and her sister Eva, a maid; and Will Watson, a reporter. When Hornsby moved in, he reopened his office on Fourth Street and started working real estate, though on a much-reduced level. He made no effort to hide his recent history, not that he could—his scandal was well-known. "I am a marked man," Hornsby admitted just before his release. "I cannot hide the brand. I must wear it out. I must live down the past." With intentional irony, he invoked "the gambler's rule: let me go win back my character where I lost it."[53]

Abner Dalrymple managed to get young Henry Hornsby a job as a brakeman at the railway. However, the income from the three working family members, combined with the revenue from their five boarders, just wasn't enough. Gus Hornsby might have been free, but he was still the subject of multiple lawsuits, including the remaining suits from his former business partner, and his debt was monumental. The family was together, but its problems continued.

Game Day, 3:55 p.m.

The Northwestern mob eventually relinquished the ball, but Chicago could not make further progress. C.J. Williams was stymied, and the team's other halfback, William Vernon Booth, could only manage about ten yards before being swarmed by the students.

• • •

Nineteen-year-old Booth, along with Louis Sullivan, was one of the youngest Chicago players, and he would become the Chicago Foot-Ball Club's captain later that fall. He was another member of Chicago's social elite and an aspiring polo player.[1] Although he was a member of Hornsby and Curtis's club primarily because of his social ties, Booth was a fantastic athlete, having run a hundred-yard dash in ten and a half seconds, "one of the best times on record for an amateur until then."[2] He was a gold medal-winning boxer and horse racer, but polo would eventually be his claim to (social) fame.

Booth's father, Alfred, owned Booth & Co., the largest fishing and fish packing business in the United States, and his company controlled a worldwide fleet of steamship lines. William Booth's future brother-in-law was Philip Armour, Jr., son of the founder of Armour Packing in Chicago, which set William in a position eventually to control food packing and transportation throughout the country.[3]

By the early twentieth century, William Booth led the largest packing operation of meat, fruits, and vegetables in the world.[4] Competitors and newspapers began to accuse the Booth—Armour alliance of forming a monopoly on food packing. Booth pushed back, telling his associates to avoid saying anything to journalists: "Beware of newspaper reporters. When approached by them, do as I do: keep your mouth closed."[5] The states of Michigan and Ohio brought lawsuits against Booth, trying to stop the stranglehold on fishing and food packing in the Great Lakes region.

While the state lawsuits failed, Booth's troubles were just beginning. In 1909, a grand jury indicted him for fraud, alleging that he falsified documents to secure $300,000 from a Chicago bank.[6] The grand jury acted on evidence that Booth had misstated his company's worth by over $2 million. Newspapers at the time, perhaps seeking a bit of payback for being iced out of any information for years by Booth, reacted to the indictment with pure schadenfreude: "[Alfred] Booth of the failed fish firm knew the business, from cleaning a fish, all the way up. His son, William Vernon Booth, was a fine polo player, and bright and shining social light. This will explain much."[7]

• • •

With Booth restrained on the field, the Northwestern students regained the ball. This time, with the crowd of nearly thirty players blocking for him, Esher pounded his way deep into Chicago territory. Esher pitched the ball to Edwin Munroe, who managed to take the ball farther than NWU had until then. With the ball just a couple of yards from the Chicago goal, the teams struggled for several minutes, but the students came out of the battle empty-handed.

Loose scrimmages again sprouted across the field. Because the players' focus was so diffused, Chicago was able to drive the ball back into NWU territory. With only a few minutes left to play, it appeared that the game would end with no further scoring, the teams increasingly deadlocked near midfield.

Chicago's William Borner, taking the ball in what might have been the final scrimmage, made a long, rather desperate lateral pass to C.J. Williams. The pass was off, but Williams leaped and made the most acrobatic catch of the afternoon, electrifying the crowd. No NWU player was near him, and Williams took off, sprinting south toward the university goal. With the students closing in, Williams abruptly squared up toward the goal posts—which the post handlers were hurriedly raising—and drop-kicked the ball. Hornsby might have been the team's official kicker, but Williams was the most skillful kicker on the Chicago squad. Williams's kick was spectacular. The ball struck the icy turf a split second before Williams sent it soaring between the uprights, even as the spectators were still frantically hoisting them skyward. With the successful drop-kick, Chicago led by three goals and three touchdowns.

CHAPTER 11

1895: St. Paul

Despite the Hornsby family's debt in the mid–1890s, there is no evidence that Gus Hornsby returned to gambling to try to make it up. It appears that Hornsby stopped gambling for good upon his release from prison. Marie continued her job as a clerk for the Northern Pacific. While Gus was in prison, Marie worked double-duty by keeping a few of her real estate holdings and developing what she could. When Gus was paroled, he began to rebuild his disgraced business, but for the first three years after Gus's release it was Marie who held the most properties and had what meager success they could find in the market.[1]

The Northern Pacific Railroad's baseball team recruited the Hornsbys' son, Henry, to play second base, and for the next couple of years, Henry tried to break out in professional sports.[2] In the fall of 1897, Henry played right guard for the Northern Pacific football team. Rachel, who had stayed out of public notice during her father's scandal, began to host dances and rejoin St. Paul society.

By 1897, Hornsby continued with his real estate business and landed a job as a proofreader with the *St. Paul Globe* newspaper. He returned, successfully, to the local chess clubs, where he was still known and admired as "being very familiar especially with endgames."[3] Marie felt comfortable enough to retire from her job with the railroad. However, the family kept the boarders in their house, picking up several new tenants, including a twenty-three-year-old Northern Pacific stenographer named Bertha Stackpole, who settled in with the Hornsby family. Stackpole was a member of a St. Paul social group known as the "Fizzle Club," which met to stage music recitals and play cards.[4] She proved to be a far more skilled card player than Hornsby, winning several St. Paul euchre tournaments. Stackpole was a rather outspoken literary critic in her spare time: on the title page of her copy of John Brougham's *A Basket of Chips*, she scrawled, "Poor trash—not worth reading."[5]

His time at Stillwater had transformed Hornsby, making him a kinder, more compassionate and empathetic person, but it didn't change his eye for making money. Hornsby continued to look for a way to make quick money with schemes that bordered on cons. In 1898 he advertised a way to "make money fast selling the greatest curiosity of the day. Sells [on] sight. Big profits; a war relic. Send 50 cents for sample and terms."[6] Just what "war relic" was being sampled and sold by Hornsby is not known. It might have been facsimile copies of an 1805 *London Times* article describing the Battle of Trafalgar and the death of Lord Nelson, which the *St. Paul Globe* mentioned that Hornsby was printing at the time and preparing to sell.[7] It isn't clear how a reproduction of a *London Times* newspaper page would inspire a sell on sight, but Hornsby's marketing prowess was sometimes a wonder.

• • •

In 1898 the Hornsbys briefly had competition in the St. Paul real estate market from an unlikely source. Dr. Frank Casseday, the Northwestern alumnus and co-founder of the school's football club, was having a rocky period as a physician in the late 1890s and joined his brother David in testing the St. Paul land game. Frank Casseday was unsuccessful, and he cut his losses quickly.

David Casseday had moved from Illinois to Minneapolis just a year before Hornsby moved to St. Paul. The parallels between Hornsby and Casseday's moves were uncanny: both moved into the area to take advantage of the real estate boom. Like Hornsby, David Casseday brought a relative to live with him: his wife's father, Thomas Willard. And, like Hornsby, David Casseday was initially employed by a local newspaper; in Casseday's case, he briefly published the *Minneapolis Daily Herald* in 1881.[8] David Casseday and his father-in-law formed a real estate company called Willard & Casseday, and they had enormous success in Minneapolis, while Hornsby became wealthy just a few miles to the east. And, just like Marie Hornsby, Clara Willard Casseday, David's wife, also invested in properties in 1883 and tried her hand in development, though only for a short time.[9]

David Casseday's success lured Frank to the area in late 1881. After leaving Evanston soon after graduation from Northwestern, Frank had been living in Steven's Point, Wisconsin, with his mother, Ellen, and her teenage servant. After moving to Minneapolis, Frank set up a medical practice and moved into the house next door to his brother on Hawthorne Avenue.[10]

Throughout the 1880s Clara also had meteoric success in the area, as a soprano who performed at venues throughout the city. Her appearances were critically acclaimed from the start. At her debut, the *Minneapolis Star Tribune* reported that she "displayed a soprano voice of excellent quality and much warmth and expression, and she is gifted with a pleasing manner. Mrs. Casseday is certainly an accession to our musical circles."[11] Years later, the same paper noted, "To say that Mrs. Casseday's song was well-performed is quite unnecessary. One never tires of hearing her clear, pure, bird-like notes, which seem to flow forth without effort. Her voice appears to improve with every hearing," after one particularly well-received performance.[12]

Frank Casseday occasionally traveled with his sister-in-law back to the Chicago area when Clara went to visit her relative, Frances Willard.[13] The trips allowed Frank to see his old friend and mentor. By the early 1880s, Willard was serving as president of the National Woman's Christian Temperance Union, traveling throughout the United States at an exhausting pace.

When Thomas Willard died in August 1882, David Casseday turned to another local relative, Sam Findley, to form Casseday & Findley, a property agency that prospered during the continued real estate bonanza. For the rest of the 1880s, the Casseday brothers became nearly as wealthy as Augustus Hornsby. Like Hornsby, their success would end near the close of the decade. In 1889, Clara contracted diphtheria and died after a five-day illness.[14] The Panic of 1893 terminated the real estate boom, just as Hornsby was taking flight from his accusers. David Casseday and Sam Findley briefly turned to selling insurance to stave off the depression, but Frank Casseday could not stem his losses. He had briefly moved to Kansas City, then returned to Minneapolis, working as a physician and editing the journal *Medical Argus*, charging subscribers a dollar per year. But his medical practice foundered, and, as the real estate market slowly regained some of its allure in the late 1890s, Frank Casseday tried unsuccessfully to develop Minneapolis and St. Paul properties. He declared bankruptcy in 1899.[15]

• • •

Frank Casseday in the mid–1920s, after he left the Midwest for Oregon, where he set up a successful medical practice, specializing in ear, nose, and throat issues (originally published by United Press International).

During the spring of 1899, the Hornsbys became grandparents when Henry's wife gave birth to a girl, and they prepared for the wedding of their daughter Rachel.[16] Rachel's fiancé was Thaddeus Ferguson Jameson, whose family came from Virginia. They were related to the family that founded the Gordon & Ferguson clothes manufacturing company in St. Paul, where Thaddeus worked as a stenographer.[17] Marie decorated her Tenth Street home for the wedding, placing fresh-cut flowers throughout the house and making up the dining room in pink and green. At her wedding Rachel wore the same heavy white moiré dress that Marie had during her marriage ceremony to Gus.[18]

• • •

Throughout the decade during which the Hornsbys and the Cassedays made money in Minneapolis-St. Paul land deals, there is no evidence that they knew each other or, indeed, even ran into each other; this despite all of them going to many of the same charity and social events, traveling within the relatively small set of Twin Cities society.

In the fall of 1899, Augustus Hornsby's path crossed one final time with Frank Casseday's. Both attended a football game hosted by the University of Minnesota against Northwestern on November 4. While Hornsby had gone to many football games since his time with the Chicago Foot-Ball Club, this was the first time that he had watched the team from Evanston since he played them in 1876. He arrived at the school's new field in a carriage and parked on the east side. The game started at 3:15 p.m., almost to the minute when Hornsby had kicked off that first game in 1876.

Three thousand spectators piled into Minnesota's new stadium for Northrop Field's dedication game,[19] and Hornsby had to have marveled at the difference wrought in less than twenty-five years: a pristine football field, a huge venue, and Northwestern's team, dressed head to toe in purple uniforms with leather padding. Casseday, too, must have thought back to wearing his baseball shirt and battling Hornsby just yards from Sheridan Road in Evanston.

Northwestern was an underdog, but, as the *Chicago Tribune* described, "it was evident that they had come to Minnesota to do business. It was as heavy lot of men as the local players had ever run up against. They were in proper form, and were not long in finding out they had struck an easy proposition. They had one play and only one. They had learned it well, and it was enough to win the game. It was, in short, a V rush, in which every man on the team had a place. The formation was good for a sufficient gain at all times, and there seemed to be no skill on the part of the Minnesota men to break it up."[20]

Northwestern defeated the Gophers, 11 to 5, the first victory ever for

Northwestern over Minnesota. NU students (by 1899, the school used NU instead of the NWU abbreviation) back in Evanston went wild when they received the telegraph wires of the score. Messengers rushed to the school's fraternities and the old Garrett Biblical Institute, and students flooded Evanston's Davis Street and Fountain Square, building an enormous bonfire on the spot and calling for speeches.[21] For Frank Casseday, it was the last time he would see Northwestern in action. In a couple of years, both he and his brother would move to the West Coast. His financial woes were coming to an end. For Gus Hornsby, they were beginning once again.

Game Day, 4:05 p.m.

Almost immediately after C.J. Williams drop-kicked Chicago's third goal, the referee called time and ended the game. Hornsby, however, had other ideas. He found Kinman and Casseday and asked them if they would like to play for a few more minutes. Despite feeling exhausted and bruised, Kinman agreed at once. Hornsby requested that the referee add fifteen more minutes to the game.

Most of the spectators stayed, even though the wind began to pick up, bringing an added chill from the lake.

Even with their superior conditioning, the Chicago players started to feel the effects of the past hour. Fingers numb from cold and throbbing from pain, legs beginning to give out, their play was sluggish, and the teams seemed evenly matched. The scrimmages moved gradually toward the Chicago goal. About twenty yards from the goal, Chicago regained possession, and the CFBC player named Brown raced past one group of students. He encountered the other knot of NWU players at midfield, who grabbed him and tried to bring him down. As the students tackled him, Brown passed back to C.J. Williams, who was sprinting toward the group. Williams had caught the ball most reliably throughout the afternoon, and he again made a circus catch as he ran past the players tackling Brown.

Williams should have had a clear shot to make a fourth touchdown for Chicago, but the sheer number of Northwestern players on the field prevented it. Instead, Williams passed the ball back to William Vernon Booth, and the play became a wild hook and ladder that extended nearly to Northwestern's goal, moving diagonally across the field. Fred Taylor stepped up to stop Chicago's momentum. Until then, Taylor had played a relatively uneventful game.

Williams eventually got the ball back. Knowing that the extra time was about to end, he tried for a last-minute drop-kick. However, his position on the field was not as centered as the last time he kicked, and the wind took the ball, hooking it several yards from the uprights.

Moments after Williams's attempt, the referee called time, again, and the game ended. Both teams met at midfield and congratulated each other.

• • •

The rest of the spectators dispersed at once, except for Jessie Brown and two men. John Jeffrey did not suit up with the rest of the Chicago team, nor did he play in the game, but he did make the trip to Evanston, and he joined the team afterward.[1] The second straggler in the crowd was named Jesse Cox, who arrived late to the game. He was a passenger boat captain and an acquaintance of William Curtis, whose boat club occasionally hired Cox to tow yachts.[2] Curtis had arranged for Cox to take some of the players back to Chicago by boat that evening. Cox's passenger steamer and tug, the *Ben Drake*, was ideal for the job: Cox ran the *Ben Drake* seasonally three times a day, round trip, from Chicago to Evanston.[3] The boat was well-known for having been used in rescue operations during the Chicago Fire.[4] Cox had recently reduced its capacity, but it could still carry eighty people comfortably.[5] He had docked it for the winter in Chicago Harbor. However, there was no ice currently blocking the route, the pier in Evanston was accessible, and Cox had agreed to take out the boat and meet the Chicago players in Evanston. The *Ben Drake* afforded the men the chance to dine in Evanston without worrying about missing the last train to Chicago.

• • •

The players walked back to the gymnasium, and several began to sing, as was the custom at the time after a game. As the group returned to the Rubicon, some of the students sang the school's tongue-in-cheek song about the drainage ditch[6]:

> *Flow on foul Rubicon to the lake,*
> *Thy tribute wave deliver,*
> *No more by thee my steps I'll take*
> *Forever and forever.*
>
> *But here will sigh thy basswood tree,*
> *And here thy willows shiver.*
> *And here in thee the ducks will sport,*
> *Forever and forever.*[7]

William Arnold, the oldest of the Northwestern players, had not contributed much during the game; frequently he stood by, baffled and mostly amused by the scene. As the group reached the gymnasium, Arnold provided perhaps his most substantive contribution, leading the students in singing a song he had written earlier in the school year, "It's a Way We Have at Northwestern":

A view of Dempster Hall on Northwestern's campus in winter, early 1877. The northernmost portion of "The Rubicon" and its bridge are visible in the foreground. Rampaging students would burn that bridge down the following Halloween. By 1905, the university had eliminated the stream, having made significant changes to the campus's landscape (photograph by Alexander Hesler, courtesy Northwestern University Archives).

> ... *For we think it is not sin, sir,*
> *To take our teachers in, sir,*
> *And cheat them like all sin, sir,*
> *It's a way we have at Northwestern,*
> *To drive dull care away.*[8]

The younger Chicago players, notably the Sullivan Brothers and Booth, were the most amused by the song. The students, in honor of the English players on the Chicago team, sang "Rule Britannia,"[9] and the club players quickly joined, loudly belting out the chorus.

Hornsby would have certainly remembered his brother's performance at Aldershot and the embarrassment that it caused him. Despite his reluctance to perform, Hornsby was caught up in the moment as the Chicago players stood around the gymnasium, singing and laughing together. Hornsby took up the next song, singing "Revelry of the Dying" in an overly dramatic voice, a comedic bit that surely would have amused his brother. Henry had, after all, taught him the song, supposedly written by another English officer in India.

• • •

Revelry of the Dying

This song is more commonly known now as "Stand to Your Glasses." According to a paper written by Jonathan Lighter,[10] William Thompson (who was, indeed, a British officer serving in India in the 1830s) wrote the lyrics. The song, commonly misattributed to Bartholomew Dowling, originated as an uncredited poem called "Indian Revelry," published in England in 1837,[11] but created by Thompson some years before.

"Revelry of the Dying" lamented the victims of a plague that swept through the English army in India. As one later account related:

> Many years ago when the plague was ravaging India and sweeping hundreds away daily ... many a strong man and rugged in the morning would at sundown be a corpse. In one garrison were twenty officers that were bound by duty to remain at their posts. Knowing as certainly as the knowledge of existence that they would never again see old England and that death by the plague was absolutely certain ... they formed a sort of society when every evening they assembled and continued to meet until but a single man stood at the table, raised his filled glass and to empty chairs about him, broke the utter silence [with the song's toast].[12]

Stoic, yet cynical, the song was an immediate hit with British soldiers, and—considering how their father succumbed to fever in India—must have had a significant effect on Gus and Henry Hornsby.

Beginning in the 1860s it was a popular song at British and American colleges, including Northwestern. It became a well-known song among airmen during World War I, and since then it has been most associated with military music.

• • •

Hornsby sang:

> We meet 'neath the sounding rafter, and the walls around
> [here Hornsby waved toward the naked wood
> of the gymnasium walls[13]] are bare,
> As they shout to our peals of laughter,
> It seems that the dead are there.
> But stand to your glasses, steady!
> We drink to our comrades' eyes,
> Quaff a cup to the dead already,
> And hurrah! for the next that dies.[14]

Hornsby was only mildly surprised when C.J. Williams joined in singing after the first few lines; however, he was outright stunned when several of the Northwestern students, including Arnold and Casseday, also joined in. The song happened to be one that the students knew and sang as well.

Part Two—The Fraud

Cut off from the land that bore us,
Betrayed by the land that we find,
Where the brightest have gone before us,
And the dullest remain behind.
Stand! Stand to your glasses steady!
The world is a world of lies;
A cup to the dead already;
And hurrah! for the next that dies.

Chapter 12

The Precipice of the American Century

"Alea iacta est"

By 1900 the name Louis Sullivan was known to all—but not because of Sullivan's skill on the gridiron. The man responsible for the final touchdown in the Northwestern–Chicago football game was instead world-famous as the most influential architect alive in America. With his former partner, Dankmar Adler, Sullivan helped revolutionize American architecture. However, the 1893 economic panic had hurt Sullivan, and his wealth and influence waned by the end of the century.

In June 1900, Sullivan addressed the Architectural League of America in Chicago. Sullivan and his occasional competitor Daniel Burnham hosted a banquet for the league at the Auditorium Hotel,[1] a building that Sullivan had designed and in which he and Adler once had their offices. Built in the late 1880s, the Auditorium was the largest building in the United States. It was renowned for its 4,000-seat auditorium, featuring four breathtaking overhead arches. Among Sullivan's young assistants on the project was Frank Lloyd Wright, who helped to plan the interior decoration for the building.[2] The Auditorium Hotel's banquet hall was a spectacle that rivaled the auditorium, a beautiful, cavernous space enclosed by an incandescently lit arch. The vault featured illuminated stained glass at its top, giving the diners in the hall the feeling of being in a cathedral.

Sullivan, now fully bearded and forty-three years old, took his place at the head of the banquet dais and gave a bold, poetic, and freewheeling speech that laid out his view of art, architecture, independence of thought, and American culture at the turn of the century[3]:

> There is a holiness in so-called "pure art,"
>   which the hand of the Modern may not profane.
> So be it.
> Let us be the Cat.

> And let the pure art be the King.
> We will look at him.
> And we will also look at the good king's good
> children, the great styles,
> And at his retinue of bastards, the so-called "other styles."

Sullivan called on American architects and artists (and, indeed, Americans) to be above all creative, to use their imagination:

> The logic of the books is, at best, dry reading: and, moreover, it is nearly or quite nearly dead, because it comes at second hand. The human mind, in operation, is the original document.
> Try to read it.... [Only] when you begin to feel the glow and stimulation of mind which are the first fruits of wholesome exercise of faculties, you may begin to read the books.[4]

His view of twentieth-century America was one of individualism, expressed through originality. Through individualism and creativity, America would strengthen its democracy:

> You will remember that it was held that a national style must be generations in forming, and that the inference you were to draw from this was that the individual should take no thought for his own natural development because if would be futile so to do—because, as it were, it would be an impertinent presumption.
> I tell you exactly the contrary: Give all your thought to individual development, which it is entirely within your province and power to control. Let the nationality come in due time as a consequence of the inevitable convergence of thought.
> If anyone tells you that it is impossible within a lifetime to develop and perfect a complete individuality of expression, a well-ripened and perfected personal style, tell him that you know better and that you will prove it by your lives. Tell him with little ceremony, whoever he may be, that he is greatly ignorant of first principles—that he lives in the dark....
> We live under a form of government called Democracy. And we, the people of the United States of America constitute the most colossal instance known in history of a people seeking to verify the fundamental truth that self-government is Nature's law for Man.... It is the ideal of Democracy that the individual man should stand self-centered, self-governing—an individual sovereign, and individual god.[5]

Sullivan, however, saw America as "too young" to realize that intellectually it was on a course for potential despotism. He warned that our cultural instructions took us on an increasingly dangerous path:

> We are to revere authority.
> We are to take everything at second hand.
> We are advised not to think.

Chapter 12. The Precipice of the American Century

We are cautioned that by no possibility can we think as well as our predecessors.

We are to regard ourselves as the elect, because, forsooth, we have been instructed by the elect.

We must conform.

We are taught hero worship,

We are not taught what that hero worshipped.[6]

• • •

Sullivan's speech in 1900 could have easily been applied to the ongoing fight for suffrage and the later civil rights struggle. However, it was unironically intended only for the period's "elect": the speech was even titled "The Young *Man* in Architecture." While prescient in his description of the threats to democracy and laudable for his call to nonconformity, Sullivan limited his audience and vision to those already in power. He believed that architecture was the province of men, and he did not support "feminine" qualities in art or culture.[7]

As a young man, Sullivan had embraced a narrow view of gender

Architect Louis Sullivan, age twenty, in a photograph taken a few months after the 1876 game in Evanston. Sullivan's architectural work would take off in 1882, when he combined his business with Dankmar Adler's, the start of a fifteen-year partnership (Sullivaniana Collection, Ryerson and Burnham Archives, the Art Institute of Chicago. Digital file #193101.LHS_Portrait_1876).

roles and culture. The members of William Curtis's Lotus Club discussed the advantages of bachelorhood during their meetings,[8] and Sullivan wrote in the club's record, "That holy state in which they will have the legal right to hate each other as much as they please: Matrimony."[9] Sullivan would only wed late in life (the year before his speech to the League), to Margaret Hattabaugh, but their marriage ended in separation.

• • •

By the end of the century, the legacy of Frances Willard and her work had already brought profound cultural change to America and a national spotlight onto Evanston. Willard had been the most famous woman in the United States,[10] and women's rights were taking a public stage that they had never before acquired. Back in Evanston, Jessie Brown Hilton survived her husband, fellow W.C.T.U. supporter Theophilus Hilton, by nearly six years, and she had mourned the death of Willard in 1898.

Brown Hilton, in fact, was among the chief mourners at Willard's funeral, standing by her casket during the funeral ceremony held at Willard Hall in the W.C.T.U. headquarters in Chicago. One of the mourners, the Royal Norwegian Commercial Commissioner, handed Brown Hilton a card as he passed Willard's casket. The card (addressed to Willard) read, "Your great work in the cause of temperance has inspired Norway's women. They have profited greatly by your example.... The entire nation blesses your memory."[11]

A few months after Willard's death, Brown Hilton addressed the national W.C.T.U. convention in—of all places—St. Paul, serving as the secretary of the Illinois delegation.[12] By then, Brown Hilton was a leader of temperance and women's rights herself. She was, however, facing serious health issues, and an accident in 1899 sidelined her. "Because of an accident last winter the year has been full of pain and weakness, and the work so dear to my heart has not been pushed as I could have wished. It grieves me that just at this important time, the commencement of a new department [the Mothers' Meetings], my plans could not be carried out as I had hoped," she wrote to the W.C.T.U. membership in late 1899.[13] Brown Hilton's death at age forty-five in June 1900, after the prolonged illness that kept her in the hospital for much of the year, sent shockwaves through the movement. She was survived by her father, the last remaining founder of Northwestern University.

• • •

William Buckingham Curtis had founded several amateur athletic associations that survive to this day. He devoted his remaining years to evangelizing physical fitness, forming the "Fresh Air Club" as part of that goal. He lived to see his Amateur Athletic Association help organize the United States' first Olympic team, which competed in Athens in 1896. By then, however, Curtis had become estranged from the organization, angered by its decision to forbid unregistered amateur athletes from competing in some of the events.[14]

While Curtis's relationship with the Sullivan brothers continued through correspondence,[15] his friendship with Augustus Hornsby seems not to have lasted past their time in the Chicago Foot-Ball Club. By 1891, when Hornsby was well on his way to destroying his remaining wealth by betting on horses and cards, Curtis was leading a crusade in New York against gambling, defining it as "the desire to get something for nothing."[16] Curtis argued that gambling was on the rise, and not just through traditional games of luck:

Chapter 12. The Precipice of the American Century

That the men of today have a stronger tendency to gamble than their ancestors had is shown, too, by the character of their favorite games. When our forefathers bet on whist, roulette, hazard, or écarté, they had before their eyes a fascinating game, interesting in itself, and attractive independently of its financial results. But, when the modern gambler speculates in stocks or wheat, the game on which he wagers is out of sight, intangible, and of no possible interest save as a means of winning or losing money.... Eliminate from the business of the stock exchange all gambling transactions, and grass would soon grow in Wall Street.[17]

As noted earlier, Curtis's view of financial speculation as just another form of gambling was common in the nineteenth century. That opinion only increased in popularity as America transitioned in the twentieth century. Back in St. Paul, one columnist noted that "we have laws against gambling, and yet [stock speculator] Jim Keene won $1,500,000 on the deal that resulted in the downfall of the cordage trust, and no arrests have been made. Newsboys are jailed for risking a nickel at craps, and the majesty of the law is apparently satisfied."[18]

Curtis believed that Americans, in particular, were leading the gambling wave of the turn of the century, for reasons specific to the nature of the nation itself:

We [Americans] gamble more universally, more persistently, and for higher stakes, than the people of any other country; and the reason for this pre-eminence is easily found. In older countries social and business life runs in deeper grooves. The rich are richer, the poor poorer. A man is a shoemaker or a carpenter because his father or his grandfather was. Men are born, live, and die in the same grade of society. Money is scarcer, wages are lower, expenses are less, and a man's earning capacity is less. Men have less money to speculate with and the established routine of their lives offers little chance for outside ventures. In the United States the conditions are different. The barriers between the different classes of society are so low that anyone can step over them.... The tone of business is speculative.[19]

Curtis guessed, correctly, that Americans' urge to gamble would eventually carry over to betting on amateur athletic events, a practice that was illegal and nearly unheard of at the time. He saw gambling in any form as "reprehensible, but the spirit that underlies it is noble.... Gambling is a misdirection of courage and energy."[20] Curtis, however, was a gambler in his own way, taking risks, sometimes carelessly, for the excitement and the ability to boast about them.

On June 30, 1900, just a couple of weeks after Jessie Brown Hilton's death, Curtis attempted to scale Mount Washington in New Hampshire, along with fellow Fresh Air Club member Allan Ormsbee. Curtis was sixty-three years old at the time; Ormsbee was thirty. Just as he refused to wear an overcoat when he had traveled to Evanston in February 1876, Curtis did not wear proper protection during his Mount Washington expedition, despite warnings of an ice storm near the summit, preferring to wear a medium jacket instead.[21]

That morning, Curtis and Ormsbee climbed Mount Willard, then set out for Pleasant Dome. When they arrived in the afternoon, a storm had started, a driving thunderstorm that was unleashing the promised powerful ice storm atop Mount Washington. The pair signed their names into a log book at the top of Pleasant Dome, writing, "Rain clouds and wind sixty miles—Cold,"[22] and then began the trek to Mount Washington. There was a base with a small hotel near the summit of Mount Washington. A telephone line connected the hotel and base to offices below. A group of members of the Appalachian Mountain Club planned to meet at the summit's hotel and hold a meeting that evening. The other members arrived before the storm and began the meeting without Curtis and Ormsbee, during which one member gave a lecture on "simple rules by which will ensure safety to all on any mountain walk."[23]

The summit soon sent word that hiking paths were unusable, and workers tried to get the warning to Curtis and Ormsbee but failed. The storm raged on Mount Washington for two days.

When the weather cleared, a hiking mapmaker found the body of William Curtis, wearing his medium-weight jacket and a light cap, face down. He had apparently fallen from a ledge.[24] Curtis had suffered a blow to the head that knocked him unconscious, and he likely died of exposure within a few hours of falling. Curtis's friend Allen Ormsbee also died, having almost reached the base. By Independence Day 1900, nearly every newspaper in the country had splashed the news that "the Father of American Athletics" was gone. Hundreds attended his funeral, conducted by members of the New York Athletic Club, the Intercollegiate American Amateurs' Athletic Association, and the Fresh Air Club.[25] True to his Lotus Club tenets, Curtis had never married.

Whether or not Curtis had maintained his friendship with Augustus Hornsby, the news of Curtis's death struck Hornsby deeply. Hornsby later claimed that Curtis was the greatest athlete he had ever met, in Europe or America: "Curtis, to my mind, was the greatest all-around sportsman and athlete the world has ever known."[26]

• • •

After his stint with the Chicago Foot-Ball Club, John B. Jeffrey ran into financial and legal trouble that ultimately cost him his printing business.[27] He made a run at returning to prominence in Chicago, but the 1893 panic ended his efforts. Soon after, Jeffrey and his family left

Chapter 12. The Precipice of the American Century

for California, to join his daughter and son-in-law, who had moved to Oakland.

When the United States declared war on Spain, Jeffrey accepted a commission as a captain and assistant quartermaster. He fought in Manila in 1898 and helped to capture the Philippine province of Iloilo, earning a promotion to major.[28] In Iloilo, American troops had set fire to several buildings, including the house of the commanding Spanish general, who had recently surrendered. Jeffrey decided to save the residence and sprinted into the burning house,[29] in a moment that had to seem to Jeffrey similar to his dramatic race through Chicago as it burned, in search of a functioning printing press. Jeffrey managed to extinguish the fire, and the United States eventually used the mansion as its base in Iloilo. In the still-smoking manor, Jeffrey collected the wardrobe of the former commander, General Rios, and began to wear Rios's general's uniforms as his own distinctive dress.

Jeffrey was wearing one of Rios's uniforms at an Elks Lodge party in San Jose in 1908 when an Oakland businessman named James Nelson offered to take Jeffrey and several other partygoers for a ride in his new Mitchell touring automobile. Nelson eventually managed to cram eight people into his open-topped car before speeding toward Hayward, California. As Nelson raced down a steep hill, the weight of the car's passengers caused one of the tires to blow out, sending the Mitchell careening from the road.[30] Nelson successfully steered the car back onto the pavement and then, incredibly, resumed his speed, over the protests of Jeffrey and several other passengers. Jeffrey screamed at Nelson to stop. Within seconds a second tire exploded. Nelson steered violently to keep control, and as he tugged against the wheel, the rear axle snapped, sending the car into a complete summersault. The car spun end over end, killing Nelson and one other person, and injuring the other five people. As he had in Chicago and the Philippines, Jeffrey somehow escaped death, landing with just a few bruises away from the spectacular crash. Though he survived, Jeffrey retired, withdrawing from public life for several years.

Later, still hearty and athletic, Major Jeffrey resumed wearing the general's uniforms as he campaigned for colleagues running for political office in San Francisco and Oakland in the 1910s.[31] Jeffrey appeared at events, sporting his distinctive gray beard and a still-crisp blue Spanish uniform, with polished silver buttons and gold brocade.

• • •

By the beginning of the new century, former Chicago Foot-Ball Club captain Thomas Fauntleroy owned the Moline Malleable Iron Company[32] and had become as wealthy as most of the other club members. No longer associated with the Chicago White Stockings / Chicago Cubs, Fauntleroy devoted himself to manufacturing, and with the dawn of the American Century, he ventured into the most twentieth-century American product possible, the automobile. Along with partners H.R. Averill and E.H. Lowe, Fauntleroy launched a new automotive factory in Chicago in 1909. Fauntleroy's company initially called its car "A Car Without a Name"—its actual brand name.[33] Its advertising boasted that a name "was all the car was lacking."[34]

Quickly realizing their unfortunate marketing move, the partners decided to name their autos in 1910, choosing "FAL," the first letters of their last names.[35] Apparently oblivious that their new name was most easily pronounced "fail," Fauntleroy and his colleagues slumped out of the auto business in 1914.

• • •

Fred Taylor, the Northwestern student who spearheaded the student-run gymnasium and who led Spade and Serpent's participation on the school's football team, had a unique view of America at the turn of the twentieth century. By 1900 Taylor had become one of the nation's foremost experts on market socialism. He had returned to his native Michigan and joined the faculty at the University of Michigan, writing influential treatises on the nature of the state, currency, and economic reform.[36] From his post in Ann Arbor, Taylor asked, "By what right does any human organization coercively control the will of individuals?"[37] He railed against the theories that gained ground after the French Revolution, "all of them reactionary, tending toward the exaltation of the state and the belittling of the individual." However, Taylor defended the state as necessary against the greater problems that anarchy presented, and he

Professor Fred M. Taylor in 1902, while serving at the University of Michigan. He is perhaps most well-known for crafting Say's Law, which states that increased demand will follow increased production (originally published in the *Michiganensian*).

Chapter 12. The Precipice of the American Century

argued—prematurely, as it turned out—that the time of revolutions and the toppling of states was waning as the new century dawned: "Revolution, as a method of [trying to improve] matters, has largely given place to reform. So, also, among the Western nations there are no longer any considerable conflicts between rival claimants for authority; and there is no general interest in the various efforts to extend political power to new classes of citizens."[38] It would not be long before Dr. Taylor was forced to rethink this perspective.

• • •

St. Paul Chief Detective John C. McGinn emerged from Hornsby's 1893 escape and recapture embarrassed and stalked by suspicions that he was not "fully alert" when Hornsby had made his break. McGinn's career, which had been stellar until his meeting with Hornsby, began a slow and agonizing descent after the incident in Hastings, Minnesota.

The St. Paul press, which had initially fawned over its chief detective, turned on McGinn, questioning his effectiveness and his use of agency funds while on duty. The St. Paul *Daily News* offered up this savage and sarcastic account of McGinn's dining expenses:

> It is easy to see why my friend McGinn, chief of detectives, is plump as a partridge. He lives well. Particularly does he live well when he goes out of town in search of a prisoner. His itemized bill of expenses demonstrates it, and the public may rest assured that quail on toast and my friend McGinn are not strangers. Epicurus would have liked my friend McGinn, who has such a thorough appreciation of the good things in life; the French gourmets are not in it with him. In fact, one would like to be a thief and be caught by my friend McGinn. The transgressor would be well fed, at least, and return to this city looking like a young missionary prepared for the table of the king of Masai-land.[39]

In November 1893, the issue of McGinn's expenses moved from snide comments to full-blown scandal. He and William McFetridge, one of the detectives whom McGinn had brought with him from Pinkerton, were accused of lavish overspending on a recent trip to New York to pick up a prisoner.[40] Each had an expense account of $30 for the twelve-day assignment. McFetridge spent $148, McGinn $267, and he later stood before the board of county commissioners to explain. The detectives kept their positions, but the commissioners reduced their expense allowances.

McGinn no longer had the trust of the St. Paul police chief, so he moved his family to Chicago. When McGinn was accused of failing to monitor gambling pools on horse races in 1896, the Chicago police chief demoted him to a routine police patrolman.[41]

Even if the speculation of McGinn's drinking in the 1893 Hornsby fiasco had been untrue, McGinn was definitely having problems with alcohol by the end of 1899. In December, he and another police officer were socializing in downtown Chicago on a Saturday night. Before boarding a car, they stopped to confront the owner of a newsstand inside the Palmer House Hotel, intimidating him and shouting abuse.[42] The Chicago police immediately suspended McGinn. McGinn's wife, Maggie, despondent over his ouster, gave him a W.C.T.U. pamphlet. It included passages from an old speech by Frances Willard, "Home Protection."

Back in St. Paul that same month, the detective who had replaced McGinn—and who had succeeded in recapturing Augustus Hornsby—was also drinking himself into a career-ending spectacle. Detective James Heeney, visibly drunk, began to bang on the door of a grocery store at five o'clock in the morning.[43] The owner, a man named E.M. Sloggy,[44] who lived above the store, came down to investigate. Heeney let loose a torrent of obscenity at the owner as he approached the front door, and then drew his service revolver from his pocket and waved it at the man. Sloggy slipped away from Heeney and telephoned the police. "This is not the first time Detective Heeney has felt his oats since his appointment to the detective force," the press noted.[45] Heeney skipped bail and was briefly a fugitive before turning himself in.[46] St. Paul removed him from the force in early 1900.[47]

John McGinn's behavior worsened, and one evening in September 1900 he confronted a neighbor, Edwin Brown. McGinn ran into Brown's yard, shouting at him and tackling him to the ground.[48] The commotion brought out over a dozen other neighbors, who watched Brown pin down the drunk detective. When Brown let him up, McGinn drew his silver gun and fired three quick shots at Brown; all missed. Another nearby officer quickly subdued McGinn.[49]

Like Heeney, McGinn also skipped bail, but McGinn's charge—attempted murder—was far more serious, and his failure to show caused a sensation.[50] McGinn remained at his house, debating whether to flee or face the charges. Several days passed. McGinn stayed home, he was a fugitive, but no one came for him. On September 21, after a grand jury indicted him for attempted murder, McGinn got word that he would be apprehended again that afternoon.[51] He decided what to do.

Cook County deputy sheriff Charles Kerten arrived at McGinn's house at 1:00 p.m. McGinn greeted him at the door and told him that he had chosen to surrender. Maggie McGinn was making lunch and asked if Kerten would stay to eat before leaving with McGinn. Kerten, a long-time friend of McGinn's, agreed, and he and McGinn sat and talked while Maggie finished preparing.[52]

When lunch was ready, McGinn asked if he could be excused for a second. He walked into the kitchen, kissed his wife, and then went into his bedroom, closing the door.⁵³ He calmly sat down and removed his silver revolver from his pocket. He relaxed on the green velvet chair and stared at the pistol, palming its smooth pearl handle. McGinn took one last look at its inscription from April 1893, still legible, though slightly tarnished around the edges of the letters. He brought the gun to his right temple, pointed the barrel exactly between his eye and ear, stared at the ceiling, and fired.

• • •

The decade seemed to start well for the Hornsbys, who were inching out of debt and had seven boarders living with them in their Tenth Street house.⁵⁴ After Rachel moved out, Marie decided to leave for an extended trip to England to spend the winter with her mother, arriving in Liverpool in September.⁵⁵ Soon after Marie's arrival, Augustus's older brother, Henry, died in the Canary Islands. He was still serving in the 102nd Royal Madras Fusiliers and had risen to lieutenant colonel, the same rank his father had held.

While Marie was in England, something happened to Augustus Hornsby's financial position. Whether it was another market downturn or a bad business decision that affected him is not known. By spring 1901, Hornsby had lost the family house, and the boarders dispersed. Marie had represented her husband at Henry's elaborate and well-attended funeral, having to tend most carefully Augustus's tattered reputation, putting the situation in the best light possible. She returned in June to rented rooms across town, the product of still another crisis. The pair eventually were forced to move in as boarders in their daughter and son-in-law's house, where they stayed for a year. The following two years saw Hornsby struggle to regain his position in real estate, while occasionally finding work as a proofreader.

Despite the setbacks, Hornsby's cynicism, cultivated during his years with the English army in India, diminished as he aged. He became more hopeful, more optimistic that people could change and willfully improve. Hornsby invoked Shakespeare: "'All the world's a stage,' sang the immortal William, and I would humbly add, hope is the quiet prompter that keeps the players on the boards of time."⁵⁶ Hornsby reflected on the despair of suicide: "Madness, suicide, death as a soulless brute, such is the heritage of those who cast adrift from hope."⁵⁷

Hornsby had achieved a unique perspective on hope, as one who had spent time in prison, or—as he called it—"reached seclusion from temptation to acquire what was not mine."⁵⁸ But he was mindful of the problems that America faced at the turn of the century, and he wrote grimly about them. "While it is undoubtedly a fact that the wealth of this country is gravitating into the hands of an ever numerically diminishing, yet power accumulating Few, it is also a fact that those who fret and fume at these acquisitions have made and are continuing to make them possible."[59] Hornsby had worked out many of his prejudices in prison, and saw race finally as a cultural and financial wedge: "By our greed we are each for himself; by the policy of a universal equality which we claim from those above us in society's stratification, but deny to such as we consider beneath us, as for instance the Indian, the Chinaman, and the Negro, we deliver ourselves into bondage by hopes that the politician will throw to us some insignificant stolen scrap."[60]

Hornsby, at last, was able to stabilize his finances and work his way out of debt in 1905, possibly with his son-in-law, Thaddeus Jameson's, help. The Hornsbys moved into a newly built, but more modest, home on George Street—they would live there the rest of their lives.[61] Gus and Marie planted a garden, and Gus settled down and devoted much of his remaining time to gardening, chess, and writing the occasional sports column in one of the St. Paul papers.[62]

• • •

For Frank Casseday, the move to the West Coast was a professional godsend. He left Minnesota in 1905 to follow his brother to the Pacific Northwest, taking his beloved mother with him. Casseday's medical practice took off at once in Oregon. After suffering the death of his wife Elizabeth, he eventually married a Portland physician named Flora Brown, and the two practiced medicine together in Portland from their Christmas Day 1911 wedding until her death in 1926.[63]

Frances Willard's influence on Casseday continued long after their friendship. In Portland, Casseday joined the Portland Woman's Club's Governmental Study Team, working to help the local juvenile court and addressing the problems of women and delinquent children.[64] Casseday and Flora also spoke to numerous organizations in Portland about women's suffrage. The Cassedays publicly supported one civic group's "Declaration of Principles ... equal rights of parents in guardianship of children, equal right of husband and wife to earnings of minor children, and calling attention to the rank injustice of master and servant statutes of certain states."[65] The declaration also called attention to the "absolute lack of laws for dealing with husbands who squander their wages and fail to provide for dependent wives and children."

A university alumni group gave Casseday a chance to recollect his time in Evanston publicly. "I would enjoy sitting under the old trees on the campus, visiting the old base-ball field, and strolling through the Prep

Chapter 12. The Precipice of the American Century 175

Building and the University Hall building, where Baldy invited us to read calculus, and Cumnock made orators of us all."[66] Casseday often gave detailed recollections of his time on Northwestern's champion baseball team. However, he never recorded his own detailed account of leading the school's first foray into football.

• • •

Hornsby, however, did eventually offer up his account of that first game. In 1909, Hornsby was sixty-three years old. He still dabbled in real estate but was semi-retired, occasionally writing opinion pieces for the St. Paul newspapers.[67] In December, he wrote a special column for the *Chicago Tribune*, headlined "Tells of Purple's Start," in which he told his story of the Chicago club, the first football team in the West. As always, Hornsby was not exactly the most reliable narrator. In his *Chicago Tribune* version of the game, Northwestern's twenty-five players swelled to fifty-two, a wild mob, and he attributes "five of seven touchdowns" to Curtis, "running on several occasions down the entire field, knocking aside the timid arms of would-be tacklers."[68]

The American football game of the early twentieth century was nearly unrecognizable from Hornsby's creation in Evanston. In 1905 Northwestern built its first proper football stadium, a 10,000-seat wooden colossus that was among the largest of the stadiums in the Midwest. It was dwarfed, however, by the football palaces that had sprung up in the East. Harvard's Soldiers Field was built two years earlier, a reinforced concrete stadium holding 20,000 fans. Yale Field, originally built in 1884, had by 1905 expanded to hold over 30,000 people. The violence of the original game remained, and, by 1900, it had intensified as wedge formations led to catastrophic injuries. The game's tactics had evolved to players linking arms, forgoing any attempt to pass, and using sheer brute force to move the ball forward. During the 1905 season, Northwestern Field's debut year, eighteen college players died and 159 were seriously injured throughout the nation.[69]

Northwestern had moved too fast and too aggressively. Its new athletic grounds had cost a small fortune, and when attendance did not meet expectations after the 1905 season, the school's athletic department was over $12,000 in debt, forcing it to hand over control of the athletic programs to Northwestern's trustees.[70] At the same time, the issue of the evolving sport's level of violence had attracted the attention of President Theodore Roosevelt, and several Midwest schools, including the University of Chicago and Wisconsin, considered eliminating football. In March 1906, Wisconsin proposed that all of the colleges in the Big Nine (later known as the Big Ten) suspend their football programs for two years, in order to address the injury issue and the increasing concern that college football had become "professionalized," with professional coaches instead of amateur instructors, alumni, or students coaching the teams.[71] Chicago backed down immediately, and Wisconsin's proposal failed to attract support from the other schools in the Big Nine, including Northwestern, which made Northwestern's next move all the more surprising.

Just two weeks after the Big Nine chose to keep college football, the Northwestern trustees voted without warning to eliminate its football program for at least five years.[72] The violence of the game was not the reason; instead, the trustees cited the program's debt, the specter of professionalism, and the elitism of having so few students able to take advantage of the sport's facilities and training. Instead of a varsity program, Northwestern chose to have class teams, which would play each other, more than quadrupling the number of students who would be involved in football, without the costs of a professional coach or road games.

The decision was a fiasco. Almost immediately after Northwestern's decision, President Roosevelt called for reform, and the NCAA was founded—an offshoot from William Curtis's Intercollegiate American Amateurs' Athletic Association. The new organization led to sweeping rules changes to football, including new play formations and the implementation of the forward pass. For two seasons, the sport evolved rapidly, but Northwestern's students played the old-style game with class teams, using plays no more advanced than the single "V" formation the team had used against Minnesota at the turn of the century. By 1908, the varsity ban was so unpopular among alumni and students that the Northwestern trustees had to reverse the decision, allowing a limited number of outside games that season. The damage, however, was done to Northwestern's program, which was still playing a style of football better suited to the 1890s with students who had come to the school for anything but playing football. It took Northwestern's program a decade to recover.

• • •

Northwestern's football team might have stalled at the start of the century, but the university itself was booming. The university's founders initially planned to locate the school in downtown Chicago before agreeing to place it north of the city in Evanston. By the beginning of the twentieth century, the school again looked to downtown Chicago. It decided to expand, situating its professional schools, including its dental and law programs, on a unified new campus within Chicago itself.

William Dyche, who had just stepped down from his post as Evanston's mayor, made the trek to downtown Chicago in February 1901 as a favor to Northwestern's finance manager. He needed to walk through the

Chapter 12. The Precipice of the American Century

building that the school was considering buying for its expansion. Dyche looked up at the structure's still-grand façade and the imposing mansard roof, which still sported oversized American flags. He walked into the Tremont House's vast, dark lobby, now noticeably shabbier than in the hotel's glory days. The previous decade had not been generous to the Tremont, and the hotel was steeped in debt.

Northwestern purchased the Tremont House for $500,000.[73] The hotel that had been resurrected after the Fire, played host to the birth of the Chicago Foot-Ball Club, and served as a hub for organized gambling finished its life as Northwestern University's anchor for the new century.

This ended the history of the Tremont House Hotel, which dated back to 1833. The various incarnations of the hotel (there were four buildings all called the Tremont; the last was the mammoth building constructed after the Great Fire) played host to some of the most important moments in nineteenth-century Chicago, including one of the landmark Lincoln-Douglas senate debates in 1858. General Grant welcomed back Union soldiers at the Tremont when the Civil War ended.[74] Elbridge Keith, the president of the Chicago Title and Trust Company, said of the Tremont in 1902 that "it seems to me that in no other spot in Illinois have there been so many associations with that which has made history."[75]

According to the Chicago *Inter-Ocean*, the Tremont corner lot in Chicago was valued in 1832 as being worth "a pair of boots. In 1833 it was refused when offered for a barrel of whiskey. The year 1834 saw it worth a yoke of steers and a barrel of flour. In 1835 it was rated at about $500. A few years later it was worth $5,000. In 1876 it was quoted at $500,000."[76]

By 1908, after Northwestern had settled into the Tremont, it wasn't worth quite that: the property was assessed at just under $100,000: $83,495 for the land and $12,500 for the improvements.[77] Buildings aside, the land alone where the Tremont once stood was worth at least $37 million by 2017.[78]

Game Day, 5:30 p.m.

No other city was doing more to celebrate Washington's birthday than Philadelphia. The holiday was the ultimate practice for the nation's July centennial party, during which Philadelphia would compete with Washington, D.C., to be the celebration's epicenter. Philadelphia festooned nearly every downtown building and house with flags, banners, and bunting, adding enormous flags to the ships docked in the river. The horses pulling carriages throughout the city had tiny wooden flagpoles attached to their heads, so that they too waved American flags as they moved through the streets. The nearby Keystone Battery fired artillery throughout the day to salute Washington. Residents followed suit, sporadically firing pistols and even small cannons. At noon bells throughout the city, including every church bell, rang out.[1]

By 6:20 Philadelphia time (cities kept their own time in 1876[2]), nearly an hour after sunset, the city exploded into illumination. Residents placed lanterns, fires, and other lights throughout their property, and some blocks were almost as bright as day. Independence Hall was lit, specially constructed lanterns throwing patriotic designs across the walls of the building, delighting the thousands of people outside.

Along Philadelphia's Arch Street, the throng of people was so large that carriages could not get through. The Arch Street Theatre had constructed an enormous display facing the street. Farther down Arch, past the other theaters and massive busts of Washington, Dr. Hatfield's Arch Street M.E. Church was just as decked out as the nearby restaurants and auditoriums. Hatfield was preparing to welcome Frances Willard to speak to an expected standing-room-only crowd. Hatfield had Methodist Bishop Matthew Simpson to thank for scheduling the event. Simpson, the religious confidante of President Grant—and Lincoln before him—had arranged the lecture just hours before.[3]

Willard was wrapping up a long, whirlwind tour of the East Coast, and she was looking forward to returning to Evanston. She had spent the last several days in Brooklyn and had given an impassioned lecture on Sunday night. Temperance supporters in Boston wanted Willard to speak there on Washington's birthday, offering her $10 a night and all expenses, but Willard declined.[4] She was looking forward to returning to Evanston instead.

Bishop Simpson, however, intervened. He had once been the president of the Garrett Biblical Institute on Northwestern's campus, and he and Willard were close colleagues—Willard was a family friend since childhood and was very close to Simpson's daughter, Ella.[5] He asked Willard to speak in Philadelphia during the holiday and stay at his residence afterward as his guest. She accepted. (Willard and Simpson would remain close for several more years; by 1880, however, the relationship between Willard and Simpson had become strained, as the church's leadership reined in its support of Willard when her cause became increasingly directed toward feminist and suffrage objectives.[6])

Frances E. Willard, Northwestern's dean of women, 1873–1874, and leader of the Woman's Christian Temperance Union, 1879–1898. This photograph was taken at Northwestern in 1877 (photograph by Alexander Hesler, courtesy Northwestern University Archives).

• • •

It was 5:30 p.m. in Evanston, and the sun was about to set, flinging shadow on the campus. The Chicago players had changed back to their street clothes, except for Curtis, who still wore his uniform, now ragged in spots from buffeting the rock-hard turf. Most of the Northwestern players had said their goodbyes. Remaining with the Chicago team, however, were Frank Casseday, William Arnold, Theo Hilton, and Theo's girlfriend Jessie Brown, who had stayed after the game. The group decided to dine together after the match, in the tradition of the East Coast teams. Jesse Cox, captain of the *Ben Drake*, joined them.

They walked south from campus down Davis Street, to Horner's, a restaurant specializing in "class and society suppers."[7] Considering the economic status of the Chicago crew, dinner would have likely come from the upper tier of the menu: pickled English walnuts, terrapin stew, oysters, fried frogs' saddles, roast turkey and duck, quail, pâté de foie gras, a selection of cakes, and vanilla or almond ice cream.

Of course, there would have been no wine, given the restaurant's proximity to Northwestern. Hornsby would not have cared, and Curtis was a teetotaler. (According to early twentieth-century athlete Archie Hahn, Curtis "never drank alcoholic beverages or tea or coffee.... When he became fifty years of age, he tried various drinks to see if he would really like them, but one of each was sufficient."[8]) However, it is a safe bet that most of the other Chicago team members would have been disappointed by the alcohol-free dinner.

There were more songs, then a dry toast to "the father of his country." Here the conversation took a turn: why was there no "mother" of the country? Why, indeed, were there so few mother figures in Western secular culture, in its history, its literature? Here, we can assume Jessie Brown would have held court on such a topic (though we have no record of her comments on this occasion): the W.C.T.U. would eventually name her the leader of its Mothers' Meetings, and she was already gaining a reputation as "a lady of culture and a speaker of rare ability."[9]

The cynical, prejudiced Hornsby of 1876 would also have much to say here, most of it probably unwelcome to relative progressives like Frank, Theo, and Jessie. Hornsby would say,

> The true mother in our culture has had her day and hour in the limelight. She has played the heroine on many a varied stage and now stands quietly back in the wings to come on when necessity demands her watchful energy.
>
> Dickens has given us many mothers of sorts: Of the several mothers in *Bleak House* Mrs. Bagonet stands out as filling to the brim the measure of motherly requirements.... She is the lioness standing dourly between her whelps and danger, then the gentle dove feeding her brood with such things that come her way.[10]

Hornsby continued. "But Dickens is not alone in mother delineation. Have you not read *Westward Ho*?" Hornsby smoothed his mustache and looked at the students pityingly.

> No? Then your education has been neglected *in several directions*.
>
> Mrs. Leigh is an aristocrat, but she shows herself a mother worthy of heroes. She combines the fortitude of the Spartan with the humility of the Christian. But she does no more than Mrs. Pegler. Both marvelous portraits are of women intensely motherly carrying self-sacrifice to the utmost limit.[11]

It is unlikely that Hornsby mentioned to the Northwestern students that, as a student himself, he had once played leapfrog with the book's author.

CHAPTER 13

1926: Evanston

On November 13, 1926, Northwestern formally dedicated a new, albeit still unfinished stadium during a game with the University of Chicago. The school named its new facility Dyche Stadium, in honor of the school's business manager, Evanston's former mayor. The $2 million structure, a grand, double-decked stadium bookended by two distinctive towers, was designed by James Gamble Rogers, the chief architect for both Northwestern and Yale Universities. It originally sat 47,000 spectators and was optimistically designed to last 500 years (it would end up lasting ninety-eight years).[1] The buildup to the dedication game was immense: the mayors of Chicago and Evanston attended, and WGN radio in Chicago broadcast the game live, on location at the stadium, a novelty in 1926. "A graphic picturization of the proceedings will be given, enabling listeners to follow every play," is how WGN tried to describe its upcoming experimental attempt at sports play-by-play broadcasting.[2]

The opening ceremonies did not skimp on pomp. A line of buglers played at the fifty-yard line, followed by the full marching band. Bearers carrying school pennants and American flags took their place beside the band. A larger American flag flew beyond the north end zone, and the band played the national anthem. William Dyche himself then raised an oversized Northwestern pennant beside the flag as the band played "Quæcumque Sunt Vera," the University Hymn.[3] Northwestern, on its way to its second-ever Big Ten football title, routed Chicago, 38 to 7. Wildcat junior Victor Gustafson opened the game by returning Chicago's kickoff nearly 90 yards for a touchdown. Afterward, Amos Alonzo Stagg, Chicago's legendary coach, refused to schedule Northwestern for any further games.

• • •

Earlier in the year, Northwestern recognized Fred M. Taylor, on the fiftieth anniversary of his graduation, by giving him an honorary doctorate. Taylor by then had taken over the University of Michigan's economic department and, at the age of seventy-four, he would eventually become president of the American Economic Association. The *American Economic Review* called his inaugural speech to the group "a milestone in the history of socialist economics and a partial demonstration of the superiority of socialism over capitalism."[4] Taylor's later work influenced a wide range of American economics and economists, from Roosevelt's New Deal to Henry Simons and the Chicago school of economics.[5]

• • •

Frances Willard had been dead for a generation by 1926, but the Woman's Christian Temperance Union was nearing the highest membership that it would ever have, topping 750,000 members throughout the world by the end of the year.[6] The work of Willard and the W.C.T.U. had been instrumental in getting women's suffrage ratified in the United States in 1920 and setting a standard for women's rights upon which succeeding generations of American women would build. Willard helped lead efforts to protect women and children, and to improve public education and workplace conditions. Her work helped to establish the PTA and led to improvements in the Pure Food and Drug Act.[7]

Willard's work to broaden human rights was not flawless, however. When civil rights activist Ida Wells, a former slave, moved to Chicago in 1893 and attempted to enlist Willard's help to press for anti-lynching laws, Willard initially turned her down. Willard brushed aside Wells as someone "whose zeal for her race has, it seems to me, clouded her perception."[8] Wells responded by writing, "During all the years prior to the agitation begun against the Lynch Laws, in which years men, women, and children were scourged, hanged, shot, and burned, the W.C.T.U. had no work, either of pity or protest; its great heart, which concerns itself about humanity the world over, was, toward our cause, pulseless as a stone."[9] The same year that Wells complained about Willard's perceived indifference to the Lynch Laws, Gus Hornsby had used the *Prison Mirror* to rail against lynching, printing pieces that called the practice "murder ... the effect of them is to lower the moral tone of the whole community. It is murder, neither more nor less."[10]

In a conference in London the following year, Wells confronted Willard about race and Willard's controversial statements that white women were imperiled in the American South, forcing Willard to "confess her ignorance of the matter. She said she was sorry she had made such statements and would do all she could to atone for the premature steps she had taken."[11]

The temperance movement's central objective, American prohibition, was enacted the same year as women's suffrage. Unlike suffrage, the group's work toward temperance proved dangerously naïve. The legal ban of alcohol in the United States did not end drinking; it gave power to an organized crime network beyond anything the nation had ever before witnessed. In Chicago, Al Capone, a gang member and bouncer at a brothel, rode a wave of bootlegging and illegal liquor to become a mob boss dramatically more powerful than "Big Mike" McDonald had ever been. It took nearly a decade for Chicago and federal law enforcement to bring an end to Capone's reign. In late 1931, as Capone stood trial for tax evasion, he sought refuge in public one final time—at Dyche Stadium, to watch Northwestern play Nebraska. By then, after over a decade of prohibition and nearly that long a period of mob rule in Chicago, the public had had enough of Capone. When Dyche Stadium's public address system informed the crowd that Capone had joined them for the game, fans mercilessly booed the crime boss. When Capone became fed up and left the stadium, the crowd cheered. The school's paper, *The Daily Northwestern*, felt brave enough in the face of the weakened Capone to mock him on its front page the following Wednesday:

> "Scarface Al" Capone, murderer and chief of murderers, brothel keeper and common procurer of women, has been a most distinguished guest at Northwestern's last two football games. At the Nebraska game, he and his party swept up to the stadium entrance, through the police barricades on Central Street, like an emperor arriving for his coronation. It is said that a motorcycle escort heralded his approach with screaming sirens.
> At the Notre Dame game, the pudgy bootlegger occupied one of the choice seats in the stadium box on the fifty-yard line. His presence was announced at both games over the loud speaker system. He was one of the stellar attractions of the day—in his own vulgar estimation.
> But—cheap gangsters and outlawed criminals are not wanted at any Northwestern function, athletic or social. Their presence is an insult to the dignity of a university.
> So get this, Capone! You're not wanted at Dyche Stadium or at Soldier Field when Northwestern is host. You're not getting away with anything, and you're only impressing a moronic few who don't matter anyway. Your kind doesn't belong in decent company.[12]

Four days later, Capone was convicted.

• • •

Hornsby was eighty years old when Northwestern built Dyche Stadium, but he still wrote occasional articles for the St. Paul press. As the fiftieth anniversary of the Chicago Foot-Ball Club's first games passed, Hornsby had opportunities to provide commentary about how the sport had changed. In October 1926, he covered the Minnesota-Notre Dame game in Minneapolis,[13] comparing the style of play by the Gophers and Irish to what he had learned in England and had later played in Chicago.

At Northwestern, there were a lot of football celebrations at the new stadium in 1926, but nothing to mark the half-century of the first game in Evanston. While the university had forgotten about its first football game by the 1920s, others had not. In late 1922, Jesse Leason, a reporter for the *Milwaukee Journal*, interviewed Hornsby about his experiences leading the first Midwestern football team and playing Northwestern, and newspapers syndicated his comments nationally. "Tucked away in an obscure section of St. Paul, Minn., lives an old, gray-haired man, A.H. Hornsby, who 47 years ago gave the middle west its first sight of a football game at Chicago, organized the old Chicago football club, helped establish the *American Field* sporting magazine, and in hundreds of other ways took a leading role in the fascinating romance and development of sports in this section of the country."[14]

Gus Hornsby continued to write columns and give interviews into his eighties. Here he is posing for the syndicated newspaper story in 1922. While the quality of the photograph is poor, it is one of only four known surviving images of Hornsby (originally published by Wide World Photos).

Hornsby's comments to Leason are his last recorded statements about the Northwestern game and the founding of American football in the Midwest. He again exaggerated the number of Northwestern players allowed on the field, and he name-dropped several of the most famous men who participated for Chicago, including Curtis, Pat Valentine, "who was an important associate of Phil Armour," and former Yale player William Hatch. Curiously, Hornsby mentioned neither Louis Sullivan nor William Hulbert, the team's two most famous members. In Hornsby's recollection by this point, Curtis had become a demigod, able to lift over

Chapter 13. 1926: Evanston

3,400 pounds using a harness. Hornsby described the Northwestern game as "a farce. Curtis was running wild and making touchdowns at will ... piling up scores." Leason's article characterized Hornsby as the "Daddy of Football in the Midwest."[15]

He might have been the Daddy of Football, but Hornsby's impression of himself was markedly humbler in later life. As an older man, he regretted his early choices, writing that

> had I continued in the wholesome, pious ways in which a good mother early taught me, I would not have once required the restraint of a penitentiary to bring me to my senses. Walking in God's highway I became well-to-do and prosperous till puffed up with overweening self-conceit. Then I tried rapid transit to wealth on the devil's reclining chair cars, self satisfied that my own smartness would enable me to put the brakes on in time to avert disaster. But, neglecting all danger signals, I ran into an open switch and ditched my train. Lying crippled in the ditch, with the wreck piled on top of me, I have yet the courage to wave the danger signal in the faces of others who are scheduled on the same track.[16]

Later still, Hornsby switched metaphors when describing his redemption as a man, going back to his days in the South African mines to write this poem about his transformation through loss:

> Forth to the sunlight Nature's ores conveying,
> Takes the strong hand its load of treasure trove;
> Nor for a moment ruthlessness delaying—
> Yet, must the furnace fire the richness prove.
>
> So within man—oft drear and rugged mountain,
> Lies garner'd deep a treasure all untold;
> Which shall flow forth, a pure and gushing fountain,
> Released from bondage of long winter's cold.
>
> But must the iron hand of grief and sorrow
> Rend the rough rock that would its wealth withhold,
> And from affliction's fires a purging borrow
> To loose from the dross the unalloyed gold.[17]

Hornsby's views toward other races, having changed so dramatically during his time at Stillwater, continued to evolve. As a young man, he had exploited the Indian people and had no qualms about keeping them indentured or even virtually enslaved as his servants, valets, and cargo bearers.[18] By the early twentieth century, Hornsby viewed England's behavior in India very differently, railing against his former country's attempts to keep Indians fighting among themselves, and therefore in a perpetually weakened state: "It is known much money is being spent throughout India to foment disturbances, without success."[19] He decried the outright theft conducted on India.

India was practically dominated by the Honorable East India Company [HEIC] for individual and collective profit, regardless of native sentiment. Under such conditions there was enormous wealth of the few and infinite poverty of the very many. The peasantry was practically enslaved to both the native landlord and the merchant who held the workers in the merciless bondage of usury.[20]

He did this while he cheered the Indian people's struggle against the caste system:

All of the Indian races are intelligent as well as patient and toiling. Gradually though very slowly the sun of righteousness forced its way through the density of caste prejudice. With growing frequency hither and yon right triumphed over might. Here one and there one arose and stood unshackled.... It may take another half century for the leaven of justice to permeate the caste-bound.[21]

To the end, Hornsby vigorously supported women's rights and suffrage. His last known column about suffrage, written *two decades* before American women achieved the vote, was his most earnest. "One of the strangest facts in our nation's history," Hornsby wrote, "is that, to this day, woman, who is equally subject to our laws, and who is taxed for the support of government, should have no voice in the laws that govern her."[22] Such a change in Hornsby's perspective and values—one that unfolded during the 1890s and left him so different in his last three decades of adulthood from who he was in his first three decades—merits inspection. Even in the twenty-first century, it is remarkable to observe a person raised in a nest of privilege and prejudice broaden his or her view past such a comfortable and narrow horizon. In the late nineteenth century, it was astonishing.

Gus Hornsby continued to write for the same St. Paul newspapers at which he had introduced sports journalism, and he remained in relatively good health, although he had stopped his daily one-mile runs once he was in his fifties and began, in his words, to "eat about twice as much as I should for my own good."[23] He played competitive chess into his eighties, and in the final years of his life he was best known as the local chess elder. The Minneapolis Chess Club referred to Hornsby as "a man whose very heart beat for the glory and promotion of Caissa,* and whose presence and work in every meeting ... made his name a loved one by all devotees who met him."[24]

On February 22, 1929, Hornsby, the oldest player in the Minneapolis-St. Paul chess organization, was named the group's honorary president. Two weeks later Hornsby was gone, dying in his home on George Street. His obituaries, published throughout the Midwest, featured his groundbreaking

---

*Caissa here refers to the goddess of chess.

The only known photograph of Marie Hornsby, in her garden of white flowers on George Avenue, St. Paul (author's collection, previously unpublished).

work in sports journalism, but said little about his football innovations. They said absolutely nothing about his past financial or legal problems, despite the national headlines that the scandals produced a generation before. By 1929 no one remembered or cared. Within the span of just a couple more years, even Hornsby's contributions to sport and journalism disappeared from memory.

Gus Hornsby, up to his death, had never stopped regretting the misery that he had brought to his wife throughout their marriage. He blamed his problems, in part, on being a man: "Men are vastly more to blame for the failure of marriage than women are," he wrote. "A pure, chaste man, these days, is almost as rare a bird as the passenger pigeon that once swarmed all over this continent."[25]

Marie Hornsby, Augustus's long-suffering wife, died in October 1929, also in the couple's home. Her obituary, likely written by their daughter Rachel, mentioned that since Gus's death, "it had been hard for [Marie] to live without her companion of many years. Mrs. Hornsby had a very sweet disposition and was loved by all who knew her."[26]

• • •

Frank Casseday retired from medicine just weeks before his death in 1932. Frank had served as a doctor for more than fifty years, starting as a country doctor, co-founding a medical school in Kansas City, and publishing the *Medical Argus* for more than ten years. His one regret as his life came to a close was that he never took an ocean voyage. He told a confidant that he would have liked to have seen the world by ship. When his friend asked Frank, just a few days before his death, "How is she heading, Skipper?" Frank "replied thickly, from his partially conscious mind, 'She is sailing in deep water—putting out to sea.'"[27]

Game Day, Night

As the dinner drew to its final courses, Jesse Cox left the group early to prepare his boat, the *Ben Drake*, for departure. The few remaining Northwestern students said goodbye, and the Chicago players told them that they hoped that they might arrange another match with the school, one that they might play on the superior grounds of the White Stockings.[1] Frank Casseday agreed.

Most of the Chicago men were eager to return to the city and get to the Tremont at a still-reasonable hour. In addition to the various parties the visiting Republicans were throwing, the Tremont was also playing host to a Freemason's ball, and several CFBC players were members.[2]

The Chicago team left Horner's Restaurant and began the eastward walk to the lake, down Evanston's Davis Street, passing the closed ice cream parlors, the storefront post office, and the now-dark Five Corners, the "V" intersection with Sherman and Orrington Avenues, which would soon become the centennial celebration Fountain Square. The group reached the end of Davis Street. To its left was a tiny plot of land called Bell Park. This lakeside strip was destined to become a monument to Evanston's war dead after World War I. By 1949, Fountain Square would be moved out of the intersection and onto the streetside, and it would also hold plaques with the names of local war dead. In the years to come, wars would sprout for each generation, and the town would add more plaques to its little fountain, seemingly inexhaustible slabs of faded metal crisscrossed with names. However, on this cold February night in 1876, the intersection offered no such reflection and showed no hint of what lay ahead. No streetlight, no sign, no memorial plaques, just cold wind.

Ahead of the group, reaching out into the inky black of Lake Michigan, stretched the Davis Street pier, Evanston's only dock of significance. The dock was enormous and had been expanded in the late 1860s to handle the ships that brought up the limestone used to build Northwestern's University Hall.[3] At the end of the pier, the *Ben Drake* waited. It was a light tug, a wooden steamer with a small stack and sidewheel, recently painted all-white, looking magnificent.⁴

• • •

Frank Casseday wanted to begin training immediately for the next opportunity at football, this time with a group of students fully aware of the rules and expectations of the new game. Sporting a batch of fresh bruises, he hobbled back to his mother's house.

• • •

Frances Willard made her way through the mass of people on Philadelphia's Arch Street, past the terrifyingly bright calcium lights that blazed across the theater district and down Broad Street. Hatfield's church was only a decade old. It was nearing completion when Abraham Lincoln's casket passed by the church steps on its way to Independence Hall,⁵ where Bishop Matthew Simpson gave his famous eulogy of the president. The resemblance of the towering neo–Gothic church spire to Northwestern's University Hall was likely not lost on Willard as she entered.

The church, as expected, was at capacity. Nine hundred Philadelphians⁶ came to celebrate the Tuesday holiday and listen to Willard's lecture, so many that Willard agreed to stay another night at Bishop Simpson's, return to the church Thursday evening and repeat her lecture, then leave immediately for Chicago on a late-night train.⁷

Willard wore a plain dark brown dress, as was her custom: in the 1870s many people had never before heard a woman speak in public, and she did not want to scandalize or provoke her audience. She wanted to project an acceptable public image, so that people would not be distracted by a woman addressing them, and could instead focus on her message.⁸

Alluding to the displays of patriotism and the forests of American flags that had risen throughout Philadelphia that night, Willard remarked:

> I do not believe there is one boy or girl here tonight that he or she does not revere the old flag, the red, white, and blue. I remember when I was a little girl, away up in Wisconsin, the 4th of July, I remember, when we had our little procession and flags made from a pillow case with red calico stripes sewed on and gold stars pinned on the corner. I was going to talk about the harm the liquor traffic does to the country and the flag we love so well, for I tell you I always loved the flag. Yes, it is a patriot's war because in our country we get up public opinion—everybody thinks one man's vote is as good as another even though he staggers up to the polls and drops in the ballot on election day. Our people are made to think you cannot change the habits and drinking customs they had over across the sea where one man is not as good as another on election day—where they have such a different government altogether. We should, I think, remember what difference there is between them and us....⁹

In her remarks on the night of February 22, Willard did not dwell on the ballot box or feminist concerns. However, she returned to Philadelphia in October 1876 to debut a new speech in front of the Women's Congress. "Home Protection" became a cornerstone address for Willard throughout the next decade. In it, she openly called for women's suffrage.[10] She did so shrewdly and pragmatically, appealing not only to progressive thought but to those Americans who were concerned about foreign influence and the increasing power of recent immigrants:

> Four fifths of the teachers in this land are women, whose thoughtful judgment expressed with the authority of which I speak [the ballot] would greatly help forward the victory of our cause. And finally by those who fear the effect of the foreign element in our country let it be remembered that we have six native for every one woman who is foreign born, for it is men who emigrate in largest number to our shores.[11]

Such an argument could be considered somewhat cynical, with its subtext of appealing to xenophobia in exchange for women's rights. It was an effective tactic, but it built on the cultural, immigration, and racial issues that would later haunt Willard.

Robert Hatfield, the leader of Philadelphia's Arch Street Church, would leave Philadelphia within a few weeks of Willard's presentation, moving to Evanston and joining Willard, Jessie Brown Hilton, and her husband, Theo. In 1878 Hatfield became a trustee of Northwestern University and a vital supporter of the school. He was an instrumental supporter of Willard and Brown Hilton's suffrage work.

• • •

In Evanston, the Chicago Foot-Ball Club boarded the *Ben Drake*, and Jesse Cox cautiously piloted the tug away from the unlit pier. One of the players pulled from his bundle a small bottle of Old Crow whiskey and passed it to the team. They might not yet be four miles from Northwestern's campus, but no one would stop them from having a round of drinks now. Cox let them, despite being leery about alcohol on board: he had recently fired a mate on the *Ben Drake* for drunkenness.[12]

> *We drink to our comrades' eyes.*
> *The world is a world of lies.*

Bundling his coat around his collar and swiftly taking a modest swig from the Old Crow bottle, Hornsby looked back at the shore. In the distance to his right, Evanston's lighthouse slit the dark. He could barely see the tip of University Hall against the darkness, marking where he and the team had made history that was nearly as fleeting as the game itself. To Hornsby's left, toward Chicago, he saw a few feeble fireworks propel skyward and briefly illuminate the night. The city no longer restricted fireworks after the Great Fire,[13] and several neighborhoods celebrated accordingly.

Hornsby watched as gold and silver streaked for a moment across the void. Each projectile hurtled upward, burst silently, and sent a glittering series of tendrils to battle the enveloping darkness. The darkness, each time, proved the victor in a single heartbeat. As the boat moved south, the sky returned to its emptiness, and Hornsby stood cold, moving into darkness, skirting the bounds of oblivion.

Chicago Foot-Ball Club
List of Known Members, 1875–1878

Player	Position (If Known)	Comments
Philip Beaumeier		Boxer
C.A. Booth		Joined Nov. 1876
Frank Booth		Joined Nov. 1876
§ William Vernon Booth	Halfback	Served as captain after Hornsby, fall 1876
* § William Borner	Three-Quarters Back	President, 1877–78. Boating Club & Chicago Athletic Club member
§ W. Brown	Forward	
* § Ralph D. Cleveland	Forward	Chicago Athletic Club member. Left Sept. 1876.
* Ira Couch, Jr.		
Edward F. Cragin	Reserve Halfback	
William P. Cragin		
* § William B. Curtis	Fullback	President, 1875–77. Co-founder, Lotus Club, New York and Chicago Athletic Clubs. Previous experience with association football only.
* William E. Day		Treasurer. Left Jan. 1876
John Ennis		Professional pedestrian athlete
§ Thomas S. Fauntleroy	Forward	Helped organize the Chicago White Stockings. Joined CFBC Nov. 1875. Took over as football captain in 1877.
* § John J. Flanders	Forward	Original Chicago Athletic Club member. Also played on the 1882 Chicago Foot-Ball Club rugby team.

Player	Position (If Known)	Comments
* R. Gardner		
Scott Hastings		
William Hatch	Halfback	Former Yale player; Briefly joined in 1877
* § Charles C. Hilton	Fullback	
* § Augustus H. Hornsby	Forward	Previous experience with rugby football; First captain and secretary of CFBC
* William A. Hulbert		Baseball National League co-founder
* John B. Jeffrey		Previous rugby football experience; Played in New York (and possibly Canada)
* § W.B. "Charles" Keith	Forward	Previous rugby football experience
C. Miller	Reserve	
* § Albert W. Sullivan	Forward	
* § Louis H. Sullivan	Forward	Took over as club secretary, fall 1876.
L. H. Sutherland		Joined in 1877
* G. "Pat" Valentine		
Walker		
* § W. Wallace	Forward	Had American football experience
* § Charles J. "C.J." Williams	Halfback	Had rugby football experience; London Athletic Club member; Final captain of the CFBC. Also captained Chicago's 1882 rugby team.
§ Dr. L. R. Williams	Forward	
* James Wood	Honorary Member	Former manager and second baseman, Chicago White Stockings (Chicago Cubs)

* Original member, attended the club's 11/15/1875 organizational meeting.
§ Played in the Feb. 22, 1876, game vs. Northwestern.

Chapter Notes

Epigraphs

1. Willard continued to use it into the 1890s (see *Minneapolis Star*, Oct. 14, 1954, p. 10).Frances Willard occasionally included this phrase when signing autographs. The phrase became a slogan for the temperance movement in the UK, fashioned by Lady Henry Somerset, who met Willard in the United States in 1891 and took the saying back to England (*Oxford Dictionary of National Biography*, Oxford University Press, 2004; see also *New York Tribune*, Nov. 29, 1897, p. 5).
2. Charles Kingsley, *Westward Ho!*, First Copyright Edition, Leipzig: Bernhard Tauchnitz, 1855, vol. 2, p. 26.

Preface

1. Walter Paulison, *The Tale of the Wildcats*, Evanston-Chicago: N Men's Club, Northwestern University Club of Chicago, Northwestern University Alumni Assoc., 1951, pp. 17–18.
2. Weyland, *The Saga of American Football*, 1955, p. 55.
3. *St. Paul Globe*, Feb. 18, 1904, p. 5.

Introduction

1. Melvin I. Smith, *Evolvements of Early American Foot Ball: Through the 1890/91 Season*, Bloomington: AuthorHouse, 2008, p. xi.
2. *Ibid.*
3. George H. Devol, *Forty Years a Gambler on the Mississippi*, Cincinnati: Devol & Haines, 1887 (Gutenberg.org, eBook #23587, Nov. 22, 2007).
4. John Philip Quinn, *Fools of Fortune, or Gambling and Gamblers*, Chicago: G.L. Howe & Co., 1890, p. 448.
5. Edward L. Glaeser, "A Nation of Gamblers: Real Estate Speculation and American History," *NBER Working Paper Series*, Cambridge: National Bureau of Economic Research, no. 18825, Feb. 2013, p. 26.

Game Day: 6:30 a.m.

1. Information from "Memoir of Frank Fisk Casseday," an unpublished manuscript, author unknown (Casseday provided portions; an unknown writer finished it), held in the Northwestern University Archives.
2. Details from 1870 census, Evanston, Illinois, p. 13, and from Frank Casseday's personal papers (Portland, OR, records of Northwestern Alumni Association, 1911–1949).
3. Phi Kappa Sigma Fraternity's public motto. "Equal to the stars in endurance."
4. *Semi-Centennial Register of the Members of the Phi Kappa Sigma Fraternity*, Philadelphia: private printing, 1900, p. 263.
5. *Ibid.*, p. 266.
6. Casseday's personal correspondence (Portland, OR, records of Northwestern Alumni Association, 1911–1949).
7. *Ibid.*
8. Casseday was enrolled in the Latin & Scientific program at Northwestern. His exact list of courses for February 1876 is taken from the 1875–76 *Catalogue of The Northwestern University*, p. 64.
9. *Chicago Tribune*, Feb. 22, 1876, p. 1.
10. *Chicago Evening Journal*, Feb. 23, 1876, p. 4.

11. *Evanston Index*, Feb. 26, 1876.
12. New York *Daily Herald*, Feb. 19, 1876, p. 10.
13. *Ibid.*
14. Northwestern *Alumni News*, 1926.
15. This is unsurprising: music and singing were very important to Willard, who stated, "Five minutes of beautiful singing or playing will change my entire mental attitude" (Anna A. Gordon, *The Beautiful Life of Frances E. Willard: A Memorial Volume*, Chicago: Woman's Temperance Publishing, 1898, p. 69).
16. Until he reached his fifties, Hornsby ran at least one mile each morning (*Morning Tulsa Daily World*, Dec. 17, 1922, p. 17).
17. St. Louis *Post-Dispatch*, Feb. 23, 1876, p. 2.
18. The Union was located on the corner of Canal and Madison.

The current building on this site is the windowless skyscraper AT&T 10 South Canal Building, a building designed to house telecommunications equipment, and built in 1970 to withstand a nearby nuclear blast. Its exact current purpose and content are unknown—AT&T won't divulge.

Chapter 1

1. Now called Chennai, the city averages temperatures in the nineties Fahrenheit in May. It has never dipped below seventy Fahrenheit during the month.
2. *The Asiatic Journal*, 1835, p. 49.
3. Eyre Chatterton, *A History of the Church of England in India Since the Days of the East India Company*, London: Macmillan, 1924.
4. *Asiatic Intelligence*, Nov. 1838, p. 164.
5. Stillwater, MN, *Prison Mirror*, Nov. 9, 1893, p. 1.
6. *Chicago Field*, Jan. 1, 1876, p. 305.
7. *Ibid.*
8. *Ibid.*
9. From documents held by Hugh Evans. According to photograph inscriptions, Eliza buried Rachel in Eliza's parents' tomb, located near Dublin.
10. The quotes from Hornsby in this chapter are courtesy of Wellington College. They come from correspondence Hornsby wrote to the school in 1927, when he was 80 years old.

11. *Ibid.*
12. *Ibid.*
13. Temple was also an emerging educational reformer and an early proponent of the theory of evolution. And, like Wellington's Edward Benson, Temple was also destined to become Archbishop of Canterbury, as was Temple's son, William, who served from 1942 to 1944.
14. Hornsby's correspondence with Wellington College, 1927.
15. For a full analysis and comparison of the two book series, see David K. Steege, "Harry Potter, Tom Brown, and the British School Story: Lost in Transit?" *The Ivory Tower and Harry Potter: Perspectives on a Literary Phenomenon*, ed. Lana A. Whited, Colombia: University of Missouri Press, 2002, pp. 141-143.
16. Parke H. Davis, *Football: The American Intercollegiate Game*, New York: Scribner, 1911, pp. 25-26.
17. Hornsby's correspondence with Wellington College, 1927.
18. *Ibid.*
19. *Ibid.*
20. Minneapolis *Star Tribune*, May 19, 1921, p. 7.
21. Stillwater, MN, *Prison Mirror*, Nov. 9, 1893, p. 1.
22. Hornsby's correspondence with Wellington College, 1927.
23. C.H. Gardiner, *Centurions of a Century*, London: F.V. Hadlow, 1911, p. 334.

Game Day: 9:00 a.m.

1. *Chicago Field*, Nov. 21, 1875, p. 12.
2. Chicago *Inter-Ocean*, Feb. 23, 1876, p. 1.
3. American Passenger Rail Heritage Foundation, "The Devil's Carriage Comes to Heavenston," www.trainweb.org/evrailfan/chap1.html.
4. See Jay Pridmore, *Northwestern University: Celebrating 150 Years*, Evanston: Northwestern University Press, 2000, p. 75.
5. As dutifully noted in the Evanston, IL, *Index* newspaper, Feb. 19, 1876.
6. *Catalog of the Northwestern University*, 1875-1876, p. 14, under the heading "Peculiarities."

Among the other listed peculiarities: "The University has no room for idlers" and "The University is not a reform school. The student is put on his manhood, rather than on his ability to avoid detection."

7. Taken from Frank Casseday's recollections in the Nov. 1928 Northwestern University *Alumni News* magazine, p. 19.

8. The honor of the first African American college football player is generally given to Harvard's William Henry Lewis. See *Boston Globe*, Dec. 12, 1893, p. 6.

9. Northwestern and the University of Michigan would honor Jewett over a century after his death by creating the George Jewett Football Trophy in 2021, awarded to the winner of the Northwestern–Michigan football game each year. It is the first FBS trophy named for an African American football player.

10. Description is from Frank Elliot, ed., *History of Omega Chapter and Reminiscences of Northwestern: A Brief Sketch of the Sigma Chi Fraternity, and a List of the Members of Omega, Etc., Etc.*, Chicago: Donohue & Henneberry, 1885, p. 92.

11. Recounted in Charles Lyford Logan, et al., eds., *Campus Fires of '77, The Fiftieth Anniversary Memorial of the Class of 1877, Northwestern University*. Evanston–Chicago: Privately Printed by Northwestern University, 1928.

12. *Chicago Tribune*, Feb. 20, 1876, p. 7.

13. *Campus Fires of '77*.

14. *Chicago Tribune*, Jan. 18, 1876, p. 8.

15. *New York Herald*, Dec. 18, 1876, p. 10.

16. *Harvard Crimson*, Oct. 29, 1875. The *Crimson* outlined the rules (and what brought them about) in preparation for the November 13, 1875, Harvard–Yale match, the first game to use the Concessionary Rules.

17. As printed in Hornsby's *Chicago Field*, Nov. 13, 1875—the day of the Harvard–Yale game (p. 197).

Chapter 2

1. *London Gazette*, Mar. 9, 1866.
2. *102nd Regiment of Foot Register*, 1870, p. 248.
3. *Chicago Field*, June 19, 1875, p. 273.
4. *Ibid.*
5. *Ibid.*
6. *Ibid.*
7. *Ibid.*
8. *Chicago Field*, July 10, 1875, p. 322.
9. *Ibid.*
10. Hornsby, "Tiger Shooting in India," *Field & Stream*, vol. 4, issue 3, January 1899, p. 130.
11. *Chicago Field*, July 31, 1875, p. 370.
12. *Ibid.*, Sept. 11, 1875, p. 50.
13. St. Paul *Pioneer Press*, Mar. 11, 1929, p. 10.
14. Passage is from Hornsby's column, written with the pen name "Bengalee," *Chicago Field*, Dec. 18, 1875, p. 273.
15. Minneapolis *Star Tribune*, May 19, 1921, p. 7. The operative word here is "claimed," since this statement by Hornsby is suspect. The Nawab of Awadh during Hornsby's period in India was a man named Birjis Qadr, who was exiled out of India at the time, returning only in 1887.
16. *Chicago Field*, Aug. 21, 1875, p. 1.
17. *Ibid.*
18. *Ibid.* (quote is Hornsby's).
19. *Ibid.*
20. Stillwater, MN, *Prison Mirror*, Nov. 9, 1893, p. 1.
21. *London Gazette*, June 12, 1868, p. 3304.
22. *Prison Mirror*, Nov. 9, 1893, p. 1.
23. *Ibid.*
24. *Register and Magazine of Biography*, Westminster: Nichols and Sons, v. 2, Nov. 1869, p. 267.
25. *West St. Paul Times*, Mar. 16, 1929.
26. *Ibid.*
27. Long after Hornsby's departure, the 102nd again served overseas, including a stint in Sri Lanka (then Ceylon) before being retitled the Royal Dublin Fusiliers.
28. The details of this game can be found on the BBC website: http://www.bbc.co.uk/scotland/sportscotland/asportingnation/article/0007/.
29. *Chicago Tribune*, Dec. 19, 1909, p. 29.
30. As recounted in *The Wellington*, Wellington, UK, 1871, p. 321.
31. *Ibid.*
32. "South Africa's Diamond Industry," *The Engineering News*, London, Feb. 21, 1908, p. 42.
33. *History Alive: Standard 9. South Africa*, Pietermaritzburg, South Africa: Shuter & Shooter, 1986, p. 237.
34. https://www.britannica.com/place/South-Africa/Diamonds-gold-and-imperialist-intervention-1870-1902.
35. London *Morning Post*, Nov. 6, 1871, p. 5.

36. *Washington Post*, July 10, 1994, Travel Section, p. 1.
37. The comments by Hornsby here are taken from his book *The South African Diamond Fields*, Chicago: Inter-Ocean, 1874, p. 63.
38. *Ibid.*
39. *Ibid.*
40. *Ibid.*, p. 68.
41. *cf., Ibid.*, pp. 10, 25, 35, 47.
42. *Ibid.*, p. 46.
43. London *Gazette*, Jan. 9, 1872, p. 116.
44. Bristol *Mercury and Daily Post*, Feb. 10, 1872, p. 8.
45. From Marie Hornsby's personal correspondence, author's collection.
46. *The Wellington*, 1872, p. 435.
47. *Ibid.*
48. *Guernsey Star*, Mar. 1, 1873, p. 4.
49. Cf. *South African Diamond Fields*, p. 52.
50. Hampshire *Advertiser*, Southampton, England, May 17, 1873, p. 8.
51. See Edward Scot Skirving, *Cheltenham College Register, 1841–1927*, p. 608.
52. Hampshire *Advertiser*, May 17, 1873, p. 8.
53. *Ibid.*
54. *Ibid.*
55. Words by Monk Lewis, music by Henry Russell, published by Oliver Ditson & Co., 1840.
56. Hampshire *Advertiser*, May 17, 1873, p. 8.

Game Day: A Glimpse of Evanston, Illinois at High Noon

1. The population went from 4,000 in 1873 (Everett Chamberlin, *Chicago and Its Suburbs*, Chicago: T.A. Hungerford, 1874, p. 378) to 6,000 in 1875 (William Sennett, *The Northwest Illustrated for Tourists of 1875*, Chicago: Chicago & Northwestern Railway, 1875, p. 8).
2. *London Morning Post*, Oct. 17, 1870, p. 3; Nov. 7, 1870, p. 2; Apr. 10, 1871, p. 2.
3. *Chicago Tribune*, July 16, 1875, p. 7.
4. *Ibid.*, Jan. 19, 1877, p. 8.
5. Chicago *Inter-Ocean*, Oct. 25, 1879, p. 8.
6. *Ibid.*, Aug. 31, 1884, p. 7; *Chicago Tribune*, Sept. 1, 1884, p. 8. In a truly bizarre finale to the Adam Mares saga, a grand jury opted not to indict Mares for attempting to murder the four officers he shot at. According to the *Chicago Tribune*, after the grand jury voted not to indict, "two of the members of this same grand jury took a buggy and drove up to Adam Mares' place and told him they had refused to indict him, but there was a motion to reconsider the vote, and asked him for $100 if he did not want to be indicted. To Mares' credit he not only refused to pay the money, but came down and informed his lawyer" (*Chicago Tribune*, Oct. 10, 1884, p. 8).
7. 1879 Evanston town directory.
8. *Ibid.*
9. Hornsby mentions this in his 1922 syndicated recollections of the 1876 game (*Morning Tulsa Daily World*, Dec. 17, 1922, p. 17).
10. *Ithaca Journal*, July 22, 1986, p. 20.
11. *Ibid.*
12. Clyde D. Foster, *Evanston's Yesterdays: Stories of Early Evanston and Sketches of Some of Its Pioneers*, Evanston: privately published, 1956, p. 20.
13. Graduation rate information from Robert Seaman, "Items from the [1877] Class History," *Campus Fires of '77: The Fiftieth Anniversary Memorial of the Class of 1877*, Northwestern University, 1928, p. ix.
14. *Evanston Index*, Mar. 4, 1876.
15. *Registers of Deaths of Volunteers, 1861–1865*, ARC ID: 656639, National Archives.
16. Gordon Berg, "Battle of Chickamauga and Gordon Granger's Reserve Corps," HistoryNet.com.
17. Isaac H.C. Royse, *History of the 115th Regiment, Illinois Volunteer Army*, published by Royse, 1900, p. 139.
18. This quote is taken from the account posted by William L. Baran on the genealogy website ILGenWeb (https://civilwar.illinoisgenweb.org/photos/kinmanw.html).
19. *Registers of Deaths of Volunteers, 1861–1865*.
20. *Evanston Index*, Feb. 5, 1876.
21. *Ibid.*, Feb. 12, 1876.
22. *Ibid.*, Feb. 19, 1876.
23. Paulison, p. 22.
24. *Chicago Tribune*, Nov. 16, 1924, part 2, p. 1.

Chapter 3

1. *England & Wales Civil Registration Marriage Index*, 1837–1915.
2. *St. Paul Globe*, June 22, 1899, p. 8.
3. U.S. Census records, 1880.
4. Robert J. Kelly, Ko-lin Chin, Rufus Schatzberg, eds., *Handbook of Organized Crime in the United States*, Westport, CT: Greenwood Press, 1994, p. 172.
5. *Chicago Tribune*, Apr. 17, 1874, p. 7.
6. Ibid.
7. Ibid., Aug. 1, 1874, p. 11.
8. Ibid.
9. *Journal of Criminal Law and Criminology*, Chicago: Northwestern University School of Law, vol. 40, 1949, p. 272.
10. *Chicago Evening Mail*, July 22, 1872, p. 4.
11. T.J. English, *Paddy Whacked: The Untold Story of the Irish American Gangster*, New York: Harper, 2005, pp. 75–76.
12. Ibid.
13. Hornsby, *The South African Diamond Fields*, Chicago Inter-Ocean, p. 5.
14. The copy in private hands belonged to F.W. Hosken (Preface to the Kimberly Reprint, *The South African Diamond Fields*, Northern Cape Printers).
15. S. Stuntz, *List of Agricultural Periodicals*, Washington, D.C.: U.S. Dept. of Agriculture, 1941, p. 9.
16. From a February 1874 print advertisement for the Chicago *Field & Stream*.
17. *Chicago Tribune*, May 24, 1874, p. 4.
18. Ibid., May 31, 1874, p. 5.
19. Ibid.
20. *Chicago Field*, Nov. 20, 1875, p. 209.
21. *Canadian Patent Office Record*, June 1875, p. 70: Patent 4604. Augustus H. Hornsby, Chicago, Ill., U.S. 9th April, 1875, for 5 years: "Extension Arm Chair."
22. Ibid.
23. Northwestern University *Tripod*, May 21, 1874, p. 54.
24. *Chicago Tribune*, July 18, 1869, p. 3.
25. The Haas Park mentioned here is not the present Haas Park in Chicago's Logan Square neighborhood but a much older Haas Park farther south in the city.
26. *Chicago Tribune*, Oct. 28, 1873, p. 5. See also *New York Sun*, Oct. 20, 1873, p. 1.
27. Details from "Hazing at Cornell: A Tradition?" at ithacating.com.
28. University of Michigan, *The Chronicle*, Ann Arbor, May 1874.
29. *Chicago Tribune*, May 20, 1874, p. 5.
30. *Detroit Free Press*, Oct. 23, 1874, p. 3.
31. Cornell University Football's Record Book, 2017 Edition, p. 1.
32. *Chicago Field*, Oct. 23, 1875, p. 152.
33. *Chicago Tribune*, Oct. 24, 1875, p. 12.
34. Lowell Seida, *William Buckingham "Father Bill" Curtis: Founder of the U.S. Olympic Committee*, published by Seida, 2017 edition, p. 6.
35. Curtis's correspondence with several members of the eventual Chicago Foot-Ball Club has survived in the Ryerson and Burnham Archives, Art Institute of Chicago.

Game Day: 1:00 p.m.

1. In 1876, the street cutting through the Northwestern campus from south to north was called Chicago Street (or Avenue). In 1889, however, most of this stretch was renamed Sheridan Road, after Civil War general Philip H. Sheridan, who had died the previous year.
2. See Paul DeLoca, "William Curtis," *American National Biography*, New York: Oxford University Press, 2005 edition, p. 120.
3. *Morning Tulsa Daily World*, Dec. 17, 1922, p. 17.
4. Seida, p. 6.
5. Emily Ann Donaldson, *The Scottish Highland Games in America*, Gretna, LA: Pelican, 1986, p. 39.
6. "Sketch of the Life of William B. Curtis," *Proceedings of the American Association for the Advancement of Physical Education, 1892*, Springfield, MA: Springfield Printing, 1893, p. 69.
7. Seida, p. 224.
8. Arthur H. Wilde, *Northwestern University: A History, 1855–1905*, New York: University Publishing Society, 1905, vol. 2, p. 345.
9. The students of the class of 1879 would add the tower's clock; its bell would be added the following year (https://maps.northwestern.edu/txt/facility/120).
10. *Evanston Index*, Feb. 19, 1876.
11. See *Evanston Index*, Feb. 26, 1876, which mentioned that "the gym is killing the billiard halls, and saving money for some of our wayward boys."

12. Northwestern University *Tripod*, Mar. 22, 1875, p. 33.
13. *History of Omega*, 1885, p. 150.
14. *Ibid.*, Sept. 28, 1876, p. 66.
15. *Chicago Tribune*, Mar. 7, 1875, p. 14.
16. Gabriel Rollenhagen, *Nvclevs Emblematvm Selectissimorvm*, Arnhem, 1611.
17. George Wither, *A Collection of Emblemes, Ancient and Moderne*, London: Richard Royston, 1635, p. 5.
18. *Chicago Tribune*, Dec. 12, 1875, p. 7.
19. Northwestern University *Tripod*, Apr. 24, 1875.
20. Northwestern's first football field was located where the Northwestern University Jacobs Center now stands on the campus. Before the school cleared this field in the early 1870s, Northwestern had used a small field south of campus to play baseball and other games, but moved its athletic grounds to be closer to the other university activities. The new field's northern end zone overlapped with what is now Lunt Hall's southern tip. The university used this location for football until about 1886, when building construction necessitated that the school relocate the field. The next location was about 200 feet south, where Deering Meadow is now. Northwestern continued to play its games in the meadow through 1890.
21. This building was located roughly where Northwestern's Deering Library now stands. Heck Hall was destroyed by fire in 1914.
22. Northwestern University *Tripod*, Nov. 20, 1871, p. 11, describes "what, for courtesy's sake, may be called our college band. The aforesaid band meet twice a week, for practice.... Noise is made by the following instruments: two violins, one violoncello, one flute, one piccolo, one guitar, and six male voices."
23. For examples, see Northwestern University *Tripod* issues:
- July 20, 1872, p. 5;
- April 20, 1873, p. 8;
- July 15, 1873, p. 4; and
- July 20, 1873, p. 6.

24. This military-style band formed from a merger of two other bands in Chicago in 1864. Eugen Seeger, *Chicago, the Wonder City*, Chicago: Gen. Gregory Printing Company, 1893, p. 217.

25. Philadelphia *Inquirer*, Dec. 13, 1990, p. 57.
26. Pattiani's biographical details come from Daniella Thompson's "Historic Pattiani House Emerges from a 20-Year Restoration," posted at http://berkeleyheritage.com/eastbay_then-now/pattiani-sadler.html, May 22, 2006.
27. Ernst Kohler, *Volksbrauch, Aberglauben, Sagen und andre alte Ueberlieferungen im Boigtlande*, Leipzig: Berlag von Fr. Fleischer, 1867, pp. 28–32.
28. Thompson.
29. *Ibid.*
30. Margaret D. Ericson, *Women and Music: A Selective Annotated Bibliography on Women and Gender Issues in Music*, Boston: G.K. Hall, 1996, p .333.
31. Oakland, CA, *Tribune*, Nov. 9, 1880, p. 2.
32. *The Daily Northwestern*, May 9, 1933, p. 1; May 11, 1933, p. 1.
33. See Pamela Y. Dees, *A Guide to Piano Music by Women Composers: Vol. 1, Composers Born Before 1900*, Westport, CT: Greenwood Press, 2002.
34. Northwestern University *Tripod*, June 30, 1874, p. 12.

Chapter 4

1. *Book of Chicagoans: A Biographical Dictionary of Leading Living Men of the City of Chicago*, edited by Albert Nelson Marquis, Chicago: A.N. Marquis & Co., 1905 & 1911 editions.
2. No relation to the vastly more famous hotelier Conrad Hilton. Charles Hilton eventually did manage multiple hotels in the Midwest, including the Tremont Hotel itself, in 1881.
3. Albert N. Marquis, *Marquis' Hand-Book of Chicago*, Chicago: A.N. Marquis & Co., 1887, p. 270.
4. The list of Chicago Foot-Ball Club players is compiled from a variety of sources, primarily the newspaper accounts of the February 22, 1876 game, as well as multiple accounts of the club's meetings during 1875–1878. A list of all known players is included in this book.
5. *Home and Abroad*, Boston, vol. 61, no. 27, July 8, 1905, p. 14. The article also gives details about Hilton's leadership of the Hotel Men's Mutual Benefit Association, as

does the Chicago *Inter-Ocean*, Jan. 18, 1879, p. 8.

6. See J. Bryan Lowder's article, "Anything Short of Breaking the Law" on Slate.com (Aug. 18, 2015, https://slate.com/human-interest/2015/08/hotel-concierge-history-and-origins-of-the-hospitality-profession.htm) for more detail about *Les Clefs d'Or* and its connection to "The Society of Crossed Keys."

7. Bankers Life and Casualty press release, Chicago, Dec. 2, 2004.

8. William Connely, *Louis Sullivan as He Lived: The Shaping of American Architecture*, New York: Horizon Press, 1960, p. 51. Connely, while having pieced together solid details about Sullivan's experience with Curtis in the Lotus Club, seems unaware of Sullivan's membership in the Chicago Foot-Ball Club or his participation in early football games.

9. Robert Twombly, *Louis Sullivan: His Life and Work*, New York: Viking, 1986, p. 52.

10. *Chicago Tribune*, Nov. 16, 1875, p. 2.

11. Daniel Okrent and Steve Wulf, *Baseball Anecdotes*, Oxford: Oxford University Press, 1989, p. 11.

12. *Chicago Tribune*, July 11, 1874, p. 7.

13. *Chicago Field*, Nov. 20, 1875, p. 216.

14. Ibid.

15. Jack Bales, *Before They Were Cubs: The Early Years of Chicago's First Professional Baseball Team*, Jefferson, NC: McFarland, 2019, p. 61.

16. *Manufacturers' News*, Chicago, vol. XX, no. 20, Nov. 17, 1921, p. 28.

17. *Chicago Evening Post*, Oct. 13, 1869, p. 4.

18. Ibid.

19. Bales, p. 61.

20. Ibid.

21. Ibid.

22. *Inter-Ocean*, Nov. 11, 1875, p. 8.

23. Ibid., Nov. 16, 1875, p. 5.

24. Ibid., Nov. 19, 1875, p. 2.

25. *Chicago Tribune*, Nov. 21, 1875, p. 12.

26. Ibid.

27. Ibid., Nov. 25, 1875, p. 8.

28. Ibid., Nov. 30, 1875, p. 8.

29. Ibid., Dec. 9, 1875, p. 8.

30. Ibid., Feb. 20, 1876, p. 10.

31. *The Field*, Jan. 1, 1876, p. 308.

32. *Chicago Tribune*, Jan. 21, 1876, p. 8.

33. Port Huron, MI, *Times Herald*, Mar. 24, 1876, p. 4.

34. Ibid.

35. *Detroit Free Press*, Mar. 24, 1876, p. 1.

36. Ibid.

37. Ibid.

38. *Chicago Tribune*, Mar. 26, 1876, p. 5, also citing *Detroit Free Press*.

39. *Chicago Field*, Nov. 13, 1875, p. 197.

40. See Melvin I. Smith, p. 18.

41. *New York Herald*, Dec. 18, 1875, p. 10.

42. Michael MacCambridge, *ESPN College Football Encyclopedia*, New York: ESPN Books, 2005.

43. *Chicago Tribune*, Feb. 8, 1876, p. 2.

44. *Chicago Tribune*, Apr. 29, 1909.

45. Details from *The Official Railway Guide: North American Freight Service Edition*, Philadelphia: National Railway Publication Co., 1876 edition, p. 340; *Chicago Tribune*, May 11, 1873, and Sept. 11, 1875.

46. *Chicago Tribune*, Apr. 29, 1909.

47. *Chicago Tribune*, Feb. 20, 1876, p. 10.

48. *Evanston Index*, Feb. 19, 1876.

Game Day: 2:00 p.m.

1. The content of "Game Day: 2:00 p.m." through "Game Day: 4:05 p.m." entails a reconstruction of the February 22, 1876 game between the Chicago Foot-Ball Club and Northwestern University. Each detail, including the players and their appearance, the field conditions, the time of each play and who was involved, and the specifics of the scoring, comes from a combination of all available primary sources that described the game.

The sources for the game details include:
- The Northwestern University *Tripod*, Feb. 26, 1876, p. 10;
- *Evanston Index*, Feb. 26, 1876;
- *Evanston Herald*, Feb. 25, 1876;
- *Chicago Tribune*, Feb. 23, 1876, p. 8;
- *Chicago Tribune*, Dec. 19, 1909, p. 29 (Hornsby's brief recollection of the game, provided in 1909 directly to the *Tribune*);
- *Chicago Times*, Feb. 23, 1876, p. 2;
- *Chicago Daily News*, Feb. 23, 1876, p. 1;
- *Chicago Evening Journal*, Feb. 23, 1876, p. 4;

- *Chicago Field* Magazine, Feb. 26, 1876 (this is the main source for the details of the game and was written by Hornsby); and
- Hornsby's 1922 recollection of the game, which was syndicated throughout the United States and published in different edited forms in dozens of newspapers throughout December 1922 and January 1923. The full set of 1922 recollections is compiled from
  ° *Tulsa Daily World*, Dec. 17, 1922, p. 17;
  ° Franklin, PA, *News Herald*, Dec. 11, 1922, p. 6;
  ° Santa Ana, CA, *Register*, Dec. 18, 1922, p. 13 and
  ° Honolulu, HI, *Star-Bulletin*, Jan. 6, 1923, p. 30.

2. *Peck & Snyder's Encyclopædia and Price List*, 1873, p. 20, provides more details of the "Taylor Safety Spike" system that the Chicago team used.

3. Donaldson, p. 39.

4. *Chicago Field*, Feb. 26, 1876.

5. *Campus Fires of '77*, p. 11.

6. Dempster Hall started out in the 1850s as the Garrett Biblical Institute building, and Garrett actually finished it before Northwestern built any structures on its own campus. Garrett used Dempster until 1868, when it swapped the building with Northwestern for the use of Heck Hall. Northwestern used Dempster until its destruction. Garrett eventually retook the area where Dempster had stood, and this is Garrett's current location.

7. *Chicago Tribune*, Jan. 3, 1879, p. 5.

8. Carl W. Condit, *The Chicago School of Architecture*, Chicago: University of Chicago Press, 1964, p. 59.

9. *Ibid.*

10. *Evanston Index*, Feb. 23, 1876.

11. Later known as Northwestern Academy, then Evanston Academy. It closed in 1917.

12. Frances Willard, *A Classic Town: The Story of Evanston*, Chicago: Woman's Temperance Publishing Assoc., 1891, p. 416. Later, David Dyche founded the Evanston Law and Order Society, to enforce Evanston's prohibition laws.

13. *Ibid.*, p. 175.

14. *Chicago Field*, Feb. 26, 1876.

15. *Chicago Field*, Feb. 26, 1876; *Chicago Times*, Feb. 23, 1876, p. 2.

16. richardlindon.co.uk.

17. *Ibid.*

18. *Peck & Snyder's Encyclopædia and Price List of All Out and Indoor Sports and Games*, 1873, p. 26.

Chapter 5

1. *Evanston Index*, Feb. 26, 1876.
2. *Ibid.*
3. *New York Sun*, Feb. 25, 1876, p. 2.
4. *The Cornellian*, Ithaca: Secret Societies of the Cornell University, 1876, p. 106.
5. *Ibid.*, p. 70.
6. University of Michigan, *The Chronicle*, Nov. 18, 1876, p. 60.
7. *Ibid.*, March 3, 1877, p. 153.
8. *Ibid.*, Feb. 3, 1877, p. 120.
9. *Ibid.*, Jan. 20, 1877, p. 109.
10. *Chicago Tribune*, Mar. 26, 1876, p. 5.
11. *Chicago Field*, Mar. 18, 1876, p. 77.
12. *Ibid.*
13. *Chicago Tribune*, March 26, 1876, p. 5. The location is nearly halfway between downtown Chicago and Hyde Park. The block on which the Chicago Foot-Ball Club built its field now holds fraternity houses for the Illinois Institute of Technology.
14. Oakland, CA, *Oakland Tribune*, Mar. 13, 1910, p. 29.
15. Bloomington, IL, *Pantagraph*, Oct. 31, 1913, p. 13.
16. *Ibid.*
17. "Printers and the Great Chicago Fire," *The Printer and Bookmaker*, New York: Howard Lockwood & Co., vol. xxv, no. 4, Dec. 1897, p. 216.
18. Here Jeffrey is referring to the same Civil War General (Philip H. Sheridan) for whom Illinois's Sheridan Road is named. During the Chicago Fire, Sheridan commanded the city after Mayor Roswell Mason declared martial law. Sheridan dispatched troops to provide security and relief.
19. Bloomington, IL, *Pantagraph*, Oct. 31, 1913, p. 13.
20. UPI story syndicated nationally, Nov. 10, 1924, here quoted from the Santa Maria, CA, *Times*, p. 1.
21. *Chicago Tribune*, Oct. 8, 1911, p. 1.
22. Santa Cruz, CA, *Evening News*, Sep. 21, 1925, p. 1.
23. Based on a description in Chicago *Inter-Ocean*, Feb. 22, 1879, p. 6.

24. Chicago *Inter-Ocean*, Oct. 7, 1876.
25. Based on the official Chicago Foot-Ball Club program, which Jeffrey had printed at the *Evening Journal*.
26. *Chicago Field*, May 27, 1876.
27. *Chicago Field*, Dec. 9, 1876.
28. A.H. Hornsby, "The Battle of the Breeds: A Reminiscence of the National Field Trials of 1877," *Field & Stream*, vol. 2, no. 7, Dec. 1897, p. 196.
29. *Chicago Field*, April 28, 1877.
30. *The Japan Mail*, Dec. 12, 1878, p. 645.
31. R.F. Johnston, "James H. Stewart Lockhart," *Journal of the Royal Asiatic Society of Great Britain and Ireland*, London, no. 2 (1937): 391–93. http://www.jstor.org/stable/25201540.
32. Shiona Airlie, *Thistle and Bamboo: The Life and Times of Sir James Stewart Lockhart*, Hong Kong: Hong Kong University Press, 2010, p. 7. First published Oxford: Oxford University Press, 1989.
33. Fort Scott, KS, *Daily Monitor*, Nov. 3, 1881, p. 4.
34. *St. Paul Globe*, Aug. 24, 1881, p. 1.
35. See Carole Zellie and Garneth Peterson, *Pioneer Houses: 1854–1880*, St. Paul Heritage Preservation Commission, 2001, p. 1.

Game Day: 3:05 p.m.

1. *Campus Fires of '77*, p. 10.
2. *Chicago Tribune*, June 24, 1894, p. 11.
3. Northwestern University *Alumni News*, November 1928, p. 19.
4. Pridmore, p. 44.
5. Frances Willard, *Glimpses of Fifty Years: The Autobiography of an American Woman*, Chicago: H.J. Smith & Co., 1889, p. 235.
6. *Ibid.*, p. 356.

Chapter 6

1. *St. Paul Globe*, Nov. 15, 1897, p. 2. When Hornsby arrived in St. Paul, his house was on Caroline Street. The city changed the name of the street to Dearborn soon afterwards, and that name remained for the rest of the time that the Hornsbys lived there. The Dearborn neighborhood is now gone, and Dearborn Street has been replaced by a small street called Stevens.
2. *St. Paul Globe*, May 14, 1882, p. 5.
3. *Chicago Tribune*, Feb. 25, 1883, p. 15.
4. Ramsey Co. 1928 map, published by G.M. Hopkins Co. Hornsby's addition was in the wedge of land between George Street and the present-day Cesar Chavez Street. The area is now home to small businesses of the local Hispanic community.
5. *Minneapolis Star Tribune*, Sept. 24, 1882, p. 7.
6. *Ibid.*
7. *Ibid.*
8. Quinn, p. 528.
9. *Ibid.*, p. 529.
10. *St. Paul Globe*, Nov. 20, 1886, p. 3.
11. *Chicago Field*, Dec. 9, 1876, p. 269.
12. Seida, pp. 7–8.
13. *Morning Tulsa Daily World*, Dec. 17, 1922, p. 17.
14. *Chicago Tribune*, Nov. 5, 1876, p. 10.
15. Described in the *San Francisco Examiner*, May 4, 1887, p. 2.
This article proved false several claims appearing in various genealogies, including some on Ancestry.com, that Arthur Hornsby died in Pajaro, California, in 1884. In fact, he had not yet left St. Paul in 1884.
16. *St. Paul Daily Globe*, May 22, 1886, p. 8.
17. Correspondence with Patty Conroy, a relative of Hornsby.
18. *St. Paul Daily Globe*, May 22, 1886, p. 8.
19. *Ibid.*, May 23, 1886, p. 9.
20. *Illustrated London News*, vol. 89, July 10, 1886, p. 40.
Hornsby mentions the 1881–82 Winnipeg real estate bubble in this ad. More information about this event can be found here: http://www.mhs.mb.ca/docs/mb_history/53/greatwinnipegboom.shtm.
21. *New York Times*, Aug. 16, 1886, p. 8.
22. *St. Paul Globe*, Aug. 31, 1886, p. 2.
23. *Ibid.*, Dec. 18, 1892, p. 3.
24. *Ibid.*, Nov. 18, 1885, p. 2.
25. *Ibid.*, Jan. 20, 1887, p. 7.
26. *Ibid.*, Nov. 18, 1885, p. 2.
27. *St. Paul Globe*, May 12, 1887, p. 2. This order was founded in 1871 in Pennsylvania. It should not be confused with the (still surviving) Society of the Sons of St. George, which was founded much earlier in Philadelphia.
28. Cf. C.W. Heckethorn, *The Secret Societies of All Ages & Countries*, London: Richard Bentley & Son, 1875, vol. 2, p. 275.

29. Details of the initiation are based on *Ritual and Book of Forms of the American Order, Sons of St. George*, George T. Watts et al., Brockton, MA: Keystone Print, revised 1895, pp. 21–28.
30. *St. Paul Globe*, Feb. 20, 1887, p. 10.
31. *Ibid.*, Nov. 21, 1888, p. 2.
32. *Ibid.*, May 12, 1887, p. 2.
33. *Atlanta Constitution*, Dec. 21, 1892, p. 5.
34. *St. Paul Globe*, Oct. 23, 1887, p. 12.
35. A description of "Ajeeb's" history can be found here: https://web.archive.org/web/20081008033803/http://batgirl.atspace.com/automaton.html.
36. *St. Paul Globe*, Oct. 25, 1887, p. 3.
37. *Ibid.*, Oct. 31, 1887, p. 1.
38. *Ibid.*, Nov. 29, 1887, p. 2.
39. *Ibid.*, Apr. 15, 1888, p. 3.
40. *Columbia Chess Chronicle*, New York: Columbia Chess Club, vol. 2, No. 17, Apr. 28, 1888, pp. 126–127.

The 1888 match in which Moehle played blindfolded and beat Hornsby appears to have taken place just a couple of weeks after Hornsby's disastrous trip to Chicago (described in the next chapter), so it is safe to assume that Hornsby might not have been playing his best chess at the time.

41. Richard A. Proctor, Esq., "Mechanical Chess," *Mephisto, the Marvellous Automaton, Exhibited at the International Teatre, Exposition Universelle, Paris*, London: T. Pettitt & Co., 1889, p. 51. This book detailed several chess automatons of the nineteenth century, including Mephisto and Ajeeb. The text refers to the objects as "androids."
42. *Atlanta Constitution*, Dec. 21, 1892, p. 5.

Game Day: 3:10 p.m.

1. Elmira, NY, *Star-Gazette*, Dec. 6, 1923, p. 8.
2. Denese Neu, *Chicago by the Pint: A Craft Beer History of the Windy City*, Charleston, SC: The History Press, 2011, p. 43.
3. Tom Melville, "A League of His Own: William Hulbert and the Founding of the National League," *Chicago History*, Fall 2000, p. 46.
4. *Ibid.*
5. Charles W. Alcock, *Football: Our Winter Game*, London: Imperial Press, 1874, pp. 65, 74.
6. Cf., Jerry Roberts, *Pass Receiving in Early Pro Football: A History to the 1960s*, Jefferson, NC: McFarland, 2016, p. 61.
7. Rudolf A. Hofmeister, *The Germans of Chicago*, Champaign, IL: Stipes Publishing, 1976, p. 194.
8. Edward Esher transferred to the old Chicago University. He eventually practiced law in Chicago, establishing the firm of Ritchie, Esher & Judd (Alfred Andreas, *History of Chicago*, Chicago: A.T. Andreas Co., 1886, vol. 3, p. 558).

Chapter 7

1. *Atlanta Constitution*, Dec. 21, 1892, p. 5; Chicago *Inter-Ocean*, Dec. 18, 1892, p. 24.
2. "A 'King' Who Had Us in His Back Pocket," *Chicago Tribune*, Oct. 2, 1988.

This story is likely apocryphal. The phrase, made popular by W.C Fields, has been attributed to many people, several of whom have a more realistic claim than McDonald.

3. As described (somewhat surprisingly) in the New York journal *Tobacco Leaf*, vol. 44, Aug. 14, 1907, p. 22.
4. *Chicago Tribune*, Oct. 2, 1988.

Here we have another potentially apocryphal story, which has been attributed to John L. Sullivan and others. However, this quote does seem to have originated with McDonald. Most of the sources of this joke throughout the twentieth century eventually trace the line back to him.

5. The details of Room 177 and the hotel's gambling operation are given in the *Chicago Tribune*, Mar. 13, 1888, p. 1.
6. *Ibid.* The assistant greeted all the initiated in the same manner.
7. The same article in the *Chicago Tribune* (Mar. 13, 1888) that detailed the operation in Room 177 also gave Rice's reaction when police raided the operation. Rice's quotes here are all taken from the *Tribune* article (and not, as one might have assumed, lifted from *Casablanca*).
8. *Chicago Tribune*, Dec. 25, 1890, p. 3.
9. Chicago *Inter-Ocean*, Mar. 21, 1888.
10. English, pp. 81–82.
11. For a more detailed description of faro, please see *The Cyclopædia of Card and*

Table Games, Prof. Hoffmann, ed., London: George Routledge & Sons, 1891 edition, pp. 111–114. This provides a view of the game contemporary with Hornsby's experience.

12. See www.legendsofamerica.com/we-faro/.

13. A nearly contemporary view of cheating at faro and a description of brace boxes can be found in S.W. Erdnase's *Artifice, Ruse, and Subterfuge at the Card Table: A Treatise on the Science and Art of Manipulating Cards*, Chicago: Frederick J. Drake & Co., 1902, p. 18.

14. *St. Paul Globe*, Jan. 3, 1888, p. 8.
15. Ibid., Oct. 23, 1888, p. 7.
16. Concord, NH, *Granite Monthly*, June 1906, p. 190.
17. *St. Paul Globe*, Oct. 23, 1888, p. 7.
18. Minneapolis *Star Tribune*, Sep. 3, 1889, p. 3; *Engineering and Building Record*, New York, vol. 20, Nov. 1889, p. 224.
19. *St. Paul Globe*, Jan. 14, 1890, p. 3.
20. Ibid., Sep. 13, 1890, p. 2.
21. *West St. Paul Times*, Sept. 14, 1929.
22. Later printed in *The Prison Mirror*, May 24, 1894, p. 1.
23. *St. Paul Globe*, Apr. 18, 1891, p. 2.
24. Details from *Records and Briefs in Cases Decided by the Supreme Court of Minnesota*, 1893, pp. 151–159.
25. Ibid.
26. *Atlanta Constitution*, Dec. 21, 1892, p. 5.
27. Ibid.
28. *Records and Briefs in Cases Decided by the Supreme Court of Minnesota*, 1893, pp. 151–159.
29. *St. Paul Globe*, Dec. 18, 1892, p. 3.
30. *St. Paul Pioneer Press*, May 1, 1893.
31. Chicago *Inter-Ocean*, Dec. 18, 1892, p. 24.

Game Day: 3:25 p.m.

1. Northwestern University *Alumni News*, November 1928, p. 18.
2. Frank Scott's biographical entry in *A Biographical History of Prominent Men of the Great West* (John Campbell, ed., Chicago: Western Biographical and Engraving Co., 1902, p. 288) contains a string of legal accomplishments. He served on the Illinois bar for over fifty years.
3. *Chicago Tribune*, Oct. 18, 1931, p. 16.

4. *Alumni Record of the College of Liberal Arts, Northwestern University*, Charles B. Atwell, editor, Evanston–Chicago: Northwestern University, 1903, p. 110.

5. Archibald Shaw, editor, *History of Dearborn County, Indiana: Her People, Industries, and Institutions*, Indianapolis: B.F. Bowen & Co., 1915, pp. 318–319.

6. Evanston *Index*, Feb. 23, 1876.
7. Connely.

Chapter 8

1. *History of an Attempt to Steal the Body of Abraham Lincoln*, edited by John Carroll Power, Springfield, IL: Rokker, 1890, p. 45.
2. Ibid.
3. Ibid.
4. "The Lincoln Tomb Robbers," Washington, D.C., *Sunday Star*, June 18, 1905, p. 2.
5. Chicago *Inter-Ocean*, Dec. 9, 1887, p. 7.
6. *Chicago Tribune*, Jan. 30, 1888, p. 6.
7. *St. Paul Globe*, July 19, 1888, p. 1.
8. Correspondence between McGinn and Pinkerton, 1890, personal collection.
9. *St. Paul Globe*, Nov. 18, 1892, p. 2.
10. Chicago *Inter-Ocean*, Sep. 22, 1900, p. 1.
11. *New York Times*, Dec. 18, 1892, p. 1.
12. *Chicago Tribune*, Dec. 18, 1892, p. 2.
13. For an example of both mistakes in the same article, see the *Indianapolis Journal*, Dec. 19, 1892, p. 3.
14. Syndicated column, printed in the Hawarden, IA, *Independent* (Dec. 22, 1892, p. 3) and several other papers. It is possible, though unlikely, that this account (printed here nearly in its entirety) was intended to be satire, and the article's writer assumed that the readers of the time would naturally view it as such.

"'Ansom" refers (with mock cockney accent) to a hansom cab, considered inferior to a full carriage.

The reference to the Palmer's "hostelry" and putting "suppers" and "bank" in quotes can be inferred as references to Hornsby enjoying vice of a different sort during his stay.

The anonymous writer's use of the word "syndicate" referring to organized crime in 1892 is actually one of the earliest known such uses of the term.

"Lun'non" soda is another parody of Hornsby's assumed accent, a mocking version of London soda. Here, the author seems to imply that Hornsby's drinking affected his libido.

15. *Chicago Field*, Aug. 7, 1875, p. 389.
16. Ann Fabian, *Card Sharps, Dream Books, & Bucket Shops: Gambling in 19th-Century America*, Ithaca: Cornell University Press, 1990, p. 66.
17. Princeton, MN, *Princeton Union*, Aug. 31, 1893, p. 2.
18. Sioux Falls, SD, *Argus-Leader*, Mar. 18, 1893, p. 2; *St. Paul Globe*, Mar. 17, 1893, p. 2.

Details of the case are found in *Records and Briefs in Cases Decided by the Supreme Court of Minnesota*, 1893, pp. 151–159.

Lamprey and C.W. Clark were eventually found not liable.

19. *St. Paul Globe*, Dec. 2, 1892, p. 2.
20. Hornsby's trail from December 1892 through March 1893 is outlined in St. Paul *Pioneer Press*, May 1, 1893.
21. *Los Angeles Times*, Aug. 26, 1893, p. 6.
22. St. Paul *Daily News*, March 13, 1893, p. 2.
23. *St. Paul Globe*, Dec. 2, 1892, p. 2.
24. St. Paul *Daily News*, Apr. 18, 1893.
25. *Ibid*.
26. St. Paul *Pioneer Press*, May 2, 1893.
27. *Ibid*.
28. *St. Paul Globe*, May 1, 1893, p. 2. The Thiel agency was started by a former Pinkerton detective.
29. St. Paul *Pioneer Press*, May 1, 1893.
30. *St. Paul Globe*, May 2, 1893, p. 2.
31. *Chicago Tribune*, May 2, 1893, p. 9.
32. St. Paul *Pioneer Press*, May 2, 1893.
33. *St. Paul Globe*, May 1, 1893, p. 2.
34. St. Paul *Pioneer Press*, May 2, 1893.
35. The St. Paul, Minnesota, *Pioneer Press* ran a very detailed account of the train trip from Chicago on its May 2, 1893, front page. In the account, the *Pioneer Press* reporter included direct quotes from both John McGinn and Augustus Hornsby.

There were several conflicting accounts of Hornsby's train trip. In the days that followed the train escapade, it became evident that the *Pioneer Press*'s initial account was not only the most detailed, it was the most accurate. For this reason, I based most of my account of the train ride on the *Pioneer Press*'s excellent article.

36. Chicago *Inter-Ocean*, May 1, 1893, p. 1.
37. St. Paul *Pioneer Press*, May 2, 1893, p. 1.
38. *Ibid*.
39. *Chicago Tribune*, May 2, 1893, p. 9.
40. St. Paul *Pioneer Press*, May 2, 1893, p. 1.
41. *New York Times*, May 2, 1893, p. 2.
42. *Ibid*.
43. St. Paul *Pioneer Press*, May 2, 1893, p. 1.
44. *Chicago Tribune*, May 2, 1893, p. 9; St. Paul *Pioneer Press*, May 2, 1893, p. 1.
45. *New York Times*, May 2, 1893, p. 2.
46. As with the rest of the time spent on the train to St. Paul, there are various and conflicting accounts of Hornsby's last moments before escaping. The account presented here is based on the two most reliable versions—the details of which correspond the closest to McGinn and Hornsby's later accounts: the *St. Paul Globe*, May 2, 1893, and the St. Paul *Pioneer Press*, May 2, 1893.

Game Day: 3:30 p.m.

1. As stated by Hornsby, *Chicago Field* magazine, Feb. 26, 1876.
2. "A Student Prank," Foster, p. 21.
3. *Ibid*.
4. *History of Omega Chapter*, 1885, p. 199.
5. *Ibid*., p. 189.
6. *Chicago Tribune*, Nov. 9, 1877, p. 3.
7. Chicago *Inter-Ocean*, July 28, 1903, p. 3.
8. *History of Northwestern University and Evanston*, edited by Sheppard and Hurd, Chicago: Munsell Publishing, 1906, p. 395.
9. Atwell, p. 110.
10. Personal correspondence, Jessie Brown, 1873. Author's collection.

Brown's signature as a student:

Brown's signature as a student (image scanned from personal correspondence, Jessie Brown. Author's collection).

11. Frances Willard, *A Wheel Within a Wheel: How I Learned to Ride the Bicycle*, London: Hutchinson & Co., 1895, p. 13.
12. Maury Z. Levy and Barbara Jane Walder, "Frances Willard and Amelia Bloomer: The Bicycle Was the First Vehicle of Women's Liberation," *WomenSports*, San Mateo, CA: WomenSports Publishing, July 1974, vol. 1, issue 2, pp. 23–24.
13. Willard, *Wheel Within a Wheel*, p. 73.
14. *Ibid.*, p. 12.
15. Diedre M. Moloney, "Combatting Whiskey's Work: The Catholic Temperance Movement in Late Nineteenth-Century America," *U.S. Catholic Historian*, vol. 16, no. 3, 1998, pp. 15, 17.
16. *Ibid.*
17. *Peabody Enterprise*, Peabody, MA, Mar. 26, 1920, p. 4.
18. Frances Willard, "A Helpful Husband," *The Union Signal*, Feb. 17, 1898, p. 4.
19. *Ibid.*
20. Sheppard and Hurd, p. 400.
21. *Topeka State Journal*, Sept. 19, 1898. The battleship at issue was the USS *Illinois* (BB-7).
22. Hornsby, *The South African Diamond Fields*, p. 14.
23. Jessie Brown Hilton, as printed in the McCune, KS, *Weekly Transcript*, May 12, 1899, p. 13.
24. Ian Tyrrel, "Temperance, Feminism, and the W.C.T.U.: New Interpretations and New Directions," *Australasian Journal of American Studies*, vol. 5, no. 2, Dec. 1986, p. 27.

Chapter 9

1. As with the previous chapter, most of the details of the incident on the Burlington train are from the St. Paul, Minnesota, *Pioneer Press* coverage, May 2, 1893, p.1.
2. *Ibid.*
3. Bill Wolston, "Hastings Heritage Map," Hastings Area Tourism Bureau. Printing date unknown. The ferry had been toll-free since 1867. It would be scrapped just two years later, when Hastings built its unique Spiral Bridge across the Mississippi.
4. *Pioneer Press*, May 2, 1893.
5. *Ibid.*, May 3, 1893.
6. *Ibid.*, May 2, 1893.
7. Some locations mentioned are based on the account in the *Pioneer Press*; others are based on plat maps of Hastings from 1879 and 1896 (Dakota Co. Outline Map, 1896, Union Publishing).
8. *Pioneer Press*, May 3, 1893.
9. *The Irish Standard*, Minneapolis, MN, May 6, 1893, p. 8.
10. *Chicago Tribune*, May 2, 1893, p. 9.
11. Princeton, MN, *Princeton Union*, Aug. 31, 1893, p. 2.
12. St. Paul *Pioneer Press*, May 2, 1893.
13. Located on the town's west side, the fair grounds were a big attraction in the 1880s and 1890s. The site is currently the Hastings Middle School.
14. *St. Paul Globe*, May 2, 1893, p. 2.
15. *Minneapolis Star Tribune*, May 3, 1893, p. 3.
16. St. Paul *Pioneer Press*, May 2, 1893.
17. *St. Paul Globe*, May 2, 1893, p. 2.
18. *Ibid.*
19. St. Paul *Pioneer Press*, May 2, 1893.
20. *Ibid.*
21. *Ibid.*
22. *Ibid.* Hasting's Gardner House was a beautiful brick hotel built in 1884 just a couple of blocks from the river. The building survives today as the Hastings Beauty School.
23. *Ibid.*
24. *Ibid.*
25. *Ibid.*
26. West St. Paul *Broad Axe*, May 4, 1893.
27. St. Paul *Pioneer Press*, May 2, 1893.
28. *Minneapolis Star Tribune*, May 3, 1893, p. 3.
29. *St. Paul Globe*, May 3, 1893, p. 8.
30. St. Paul *Pioneer Press*, May 3, 1893.
31. *Ibid.*
32. *St. Paul Globe*, May 11, 1893, p. 4.
33. Princeton, MN, *Princeton Union*, Aug. 31, 1893, p. 2.
34. Mower, MN, *Mower County Transcript*, May 24, 1893, p. 8.
35. *St. Paul Globe*, May 20, 1893, p. 2.
36. *Ibid.*
37. Stillwater, MN, Prison Commitment Papers, 1891–1899, archived at Gale Family Library, Minnesota History Center, St. Paul, Minnesota.

Game Day: 3:45 p.m.

1. *Chicago Field*, Feb. 26, 1876.
2. Marcus Aurelius, *Helpful Thoughts*

from the Meditations of Marcus Aurelius Antoninus, edited by Walter Lee Brown, Chicago: A.C. McClurg & Co., 1902.
   3. *31st Annual Report of the Free Public Library of Evanston, Ill.*, May 31, 1904, p. 4.
   4. *The Sigma Chi Quarterly*, Vol. IX, No. 1, Nov. 1889, p. 68.
   5. *Ibid.*
   6. *Ibid.*

Chapter 10

   1. Stillwater, MN, *Prison Mirror*, May 25, 1893, p. 2.
   2. William C. Heilbron and Cole Younger, *Convict Life at the Minnesota State Prison, Stillwater, Minnesota*, St. Paul–Minneapolis: W.C. Heilbron / Murphy-Travis Co., 1909, p. 7.
   3. *Ibid.*
   4. John Koblas, *When the Heavens Fell: The Youngers in Stillwater Prison*, St. Cloud, MN: North Star Press, 2002, p. 23.
   5. Ted Genoways, ed., *Hard Time: Voices from a State Prison, 1849–1914*, St. Paul: Minnesota Historical Society Press, 2002, p. 18.
   6. Heilbron and Younger, p. 8.
   7. *Prison Mirror*, June 29, 1893, p. 3.
   8. *Ibid.*
   9. *Ibid.*, June 29, 1893, p. 1.
   10. *Ibid.*, July 20, 1893, p. 2.
   11. *Ibid.*, Aug. 10, 1893, p. 3.
   12. *Ibid.*, Nov. 2, 1893, p. 2.
   13. *Ibid.*, Aug. 10, 1893, p. 3.
   14. From a print advertisement for Stillwell Prison Binder Twine, 1894.
   15. See Mental Floss for a fascinating article about the creation of *The Prison Mirror* (mentalfloss.com/article/502636/colorful-history-prison-mirror-americas-oldest-continuously-operated-prison-newspaper).
   16. Cole Younger, *The Story of Cole Younger, by Himself*, Chicago: Press of the Henneberry Company, 1903, p. 89.
   17. Koblas, p. 24.
   18. Heilbron and Younger, p. 146.
   19. Hornsby was also anonymous, as mentioned in this book's preface. The following is some of the evidence that establishes Hornsby as the new editor of *The Prison Mirror*.
   Just three weeks after Hornsby's arrival at the paper, the old editor announced that he had found a successor and that the successor was a former newspaperman. The new editor, in various issues during the following six months, mentioned that he: was English, balding, and older; had spent his youth in India; was a follower of author Charles Kingsley; had squandered a fortune as a young man; and had edited several publications before being a prisoner. All these facts pointed directly to Hornsby. To be sure, I looked at the Stillwater, Minnesota, prison records for all inmates received at the facility from 1892 through June 1893, the time during which Hornsby had arrived. No one except Hornsby matched the criteria set out by the new editor.
   20. *Prison Mirror*, June 22, 1893, p. 2.
   21. Heilbron and Younger, p. 92.
   22. *Prison Mirror*, June 8, 1893, p. 1.
   23. *Ibid.*, May 4, 1893, p. 2.
   24. *Ibid.*, Aug. 3, 1893, p. 3.
   25. Heilbron and Younger, p. 8.
   26. *Prison Mirror*, June 29, 1893, p. 1.
   27. *Ibid.*
   28. *Ibid.*
   29. Frank F. Casseday, "Our National Handicap," *Wisconsin Medical Recorder*, Janesville, WI, Aug. 1911, vol. xiv, no. 8, p. 195.
   30. *Prison Mirror*, June 29, 1893, p. 1.
   31. *Ibid.*, Aug. 24, 1893, p. 3.
   32. *Ibid.*, Sept. 21, 1893, p. 2.
   33. *Ibid.*
   34. Minneapolis *Star Tribune*, Sept. 9, 1893, p. 4.
   35. *Prison Mirror*, Aug. 31, 1893, p. 2.
   36. *Ibid.*
   37. *Ibid.*, Aug. 17, 1893, p. 2.
   38. *Ibid.*
   39. Hornsby, *The South African Diamond Fields*, p. 14.
   40. *Prison Mirror*, Aug. 17, 1893, p. 2.
   41. As early as the 1860s, Americans had organized against woman's suffrage. The most influential anti-suffrage organization, the Massachusetts Association Opposed to Further Extension of Suffrage to Women, began in the 1880s. The opposition included large numbers of men *and* women (Allison Lange, "National Association Opposed to Woman Suffrage," www.crusadeforthevote.org/naows-opposition).
   42. *Prison Mirror*, Aug. 10, 1893, p. 1.
   43. *Ibid.*

44. *Ibid.*
45. Heilbron and Younger, pp. 117.
46. *Ibid.*, pp. 67.
47. *Ibid.*, pp. 28–29.
48. *Prison Mirror,* Jan. 11, 1894, p. 1.
49. *Ibid.*
50. Princeton, MN, *Princeton Union,* Aug. 16, 1894, p. 2.
51. *St Paul Globe,* Nov. 15, 1897, p. 2.
52. *St. Paul City Directory,* 1894.
53. *The Prison Mirror,* June 28, 1894, p. 1.

Game Day: 3:55 p.m.

1. See *Montreal Star,* Dec. 23, 1896, p. 3, for an example of Booth's polo and fox hunt exploits.
2. John N. Booth, *Booths in History,* Los Alamitos, CA: Ridgeway Press, 1982, p. 82.
3. *St. Louis Globe-Democrat,* Jan. 15, 1899, p. 29.
4. *A History of the City of Chicago, Its Men and Institutions,* author uncredited, Chicago: Inter-Ocean, 1900, p. 279.
5. *St. Louis Globe-Democrat,* Jan. 15, 1899, p. 29.
6. *Salt Lake Tribune,* Feb. 28, 1909, p. 1.
7. Syndicated comment appearing in multiple newspapers, including the Fairmount, IN, *Fairmount News,* July 2, 1909, p. 2.

Chapter 11

1. Marie controlled the remaining properties in Hornsby's Rearrangement. *St. Paul Globe,* Feb. 11, 1895, p. 8.
2. *St. Paul Globe,* July 5, 1896, p. 11; *St. Paul City Directory,* 1897. It appears that Henry's ball career did not extend past 1897. He did, however, play one game as a member of the minor league baseball team Kansas City Blues in 1897 (*St. Paul Globe,* Aug. 2, 1897, p. 5).
3. *Minneapolis Star Tribune,* Dec. 11, 1908, p. 6.
4. *St. Paul Globe,* Feb. 8, 1891, p. 11.
5. Sam Pickering, *One Grand, Sweet Song,* College Station: Texas A&M University Press, 2016. The book is not paginated.
6. *St. Paul Globe,* May 8, 1898, p. 26.
7. *Ibid.*
8. *Minneapolis City Directory,* 1881.

9. *Minneapolis Star Tribune,* Jan. 5, 1883, p. 8.
10. *Minneapolis City Directory,* 1881.
11. *Minneapolis Star Tribune,* Feb. 26, 1880, p. 4.
12. *Ibid.,* Dec. 16, 1885, p. 4.
13. *Ibid.,* Sept. 4, 1881, p. 3.
14. *Ibid.,* Oct. 8, 1889, p. 5.
15. *Ibid.,* March 13, 1899, p. 7.
16. *St. Paul Globe,* Mar. 14, 1899, p. 8.
17. *St. Paul City Directory,* 1902.
18. *St. Paul Globe,* June 22, 1899, p. 8.
19. *Chicago Tribune,* Nov. 5, 1899, p. 18.
20. *Ibid.*
21. *Ibid.*

Game Day: 4:05 p.m.

1. Given his prior experience with football, it's a bit of a mystery as to why Jeffrey did not participate in the February game. No source mentions the reason.
2. *Chicago Tribune,* Aug. 30, 1876, p. 5.
3. *Ibid.,* July 13, 1874, p. 3; May 18, 1877, p. 7.
4. *Ibid.,* Apr. 28, 1874, p. 5.
5. *Ibid.,* July 21, 1876, p. 8.
6. Northwestern University *Tripod,* Mar. 23, 1876, p. 22.
7. "To the Rubicon," *Tripod,* May 20, 1873, p. 4. Students sang the song into the 1880s, eventually changing "Rubicon" to the more general "river." The song's student composer is not known.
8. Lyrics from *The Northwestern Song Book: A Collection of College and Other Music,* edited by George Muir, New York: Athenaeum, 1879, p. 100.
9. A favorite song in the 1870s at many American colleges, including Northwestern.
10. Quoted by Ron Wanttaja in "The Songs They Sang: A World Full of Lies," http://www.bowersflybaby.com/stories/songs/02_lies.html.
11. *The Cheltenham Chronicle and Gloucestershire Advertiser,* July 6, 1837, p. 4.
12. Salinas, *The Californian,* Mar. 8, 1900, p. 4.
13. Northwestern University *Tripod,* Mar. 23, 1876, p. 22.
14. The lyrics quoted are from the version included in *The Northwestern Song Book,* 1879, p. 77.

Chapter 12

1. *Chicago Tribune*, June 10, 1900, p. 4.
2. See Emporis.com.
3. The extended passages presented here from Sullivan's speech are excerpts of "The Young Man in Architecture," a speech he drafted earlier in 1899, revised in a manuscript June 8, 1900, and presented to the League in Chicago on June 9.

These quotes are taken directly from the manuscript that Sullivan used for the June 9, 1900, speech (and which now is held by the Ryerson and Burnham Library Archives at the Art Institute of Chicago). It differs slightly from the versions later revised and published, cf. *Louis Sullivan: The Public Papers*, Robert Twombly, editor, 1988.

4. Ibid.
5. Ibid.
6. Ibid.
7. As characterized and supported by Vanessa Chase in "Edith Wharton, *The Decoration of Houses*, and Gender in Turn-of-the-Century America," from *Architecture and Feminism*, Elizabeth Danze, Carol Henderson, and Debra Coleman, editors, New York: Princeton Architectural Press, 1996, pp. 133–134.
8. Seida, p. 250.
9. Ibid.
10. *The Literary Digest* (quoting *The Interior*, Chicago), New York: Funk & Wagnalls, March 12, 1898, p. 320.
11. *The Union Signal: A Journal of Social Welfare*, 1898, p. 233.
12. *St. Paul Globe*, Nov. 6, 1898, p. 13.
13. *Report of the National Woman's Christian Temperance Union*, Chicago, 1898–1899, p. 279.
14. *American National Biography*, Supplement 2, Oxford University, 2005, p. 119.
15. Some of Bill Curtis's surviving correspondence with Albert Sullivan is kept in the Ryerson and Burnham Library archives at the Art Institute of Chicago. In an early letter from 1876, Curtis gives Sullivan his forwarding address and signs the letter, "Until further orders, W.C."
16. William Curtis, "The Increase of Gambling and Its Forms," published in *The Forum*, New York, vol. XII, Oct. 1891, pp. 281–284.
17. Ibid.
18. *St. Paul Saturday Evening News*, May 27, 1893.
19. Curtis, *The Forum*, Oct. 1891, pp. 281–284.
20. Ibid.
21. "Curtis," *American National Biography*.
22. Nicholas Howe, *Not Without Peril: 150 Years of Misadventure on the Presidential Range of New Hampshire*, Boston: Appalachian Mountain Club Books, 2000, p. 61.
23. Ibid., p. 62.
24. Ibid.
25. *New York Tribune*, July 7, 1900, p. 7.
26. Hornsby's syndicated comments in 1922, here quoted from the Tulsa, OK, *Daily World*, Dec. 17, 1922, p. 17.
27. "A Notable Lawsuit," *The American Stationer*, New York, vol. xxiv, no. 18, Nov. 1, 1888, p. 1083.

In later life, Jeffrey was indicted on various occasions for perjury and fraud. The courts dismissed the cases against him each time.

28. *Oakland Tribune*, Mar. 13, 1910, p. 29.
29. Ibid.
30. *San Francisco Call*, July 10, 1908, p. 16; *Oakland Tribune*, July 9, 1908, pp. 1–2.
31. *Oakland Tribune*, Mar. 13, 1910, p. 29.
32. The company still exists, now titled the Moline Bearing Co.
33. Beverly Rae Kimes, *Standard Catalog of American Cars, 1805–1942*, Iola, WI: Krause, 1989, p. 14.
34. Ibid.
35. *Motor Age*, Chicago, vol. 15, no. 16, April 22, 1909, p. 43
36. Atwell, 1903, p. 115.
37. F.M. Taylor's doctoral thesis, *The Right of the State to Be*, Ann Arbor: University of Michigan, 1891, p. 1.
38. Ibid., p. 2.
39. St. Paul *Daily News*, Sept. 19, 1893.
40. *St. Paul Globe*, Nov. 7, 1893, p. 2.
41. *Chicago Tribune*, Jan. 16, 1896, p. 4.
42. Ibid., Dec. 20, 1899, p. 1.
43. *St. Paul Globe*, Nov. 6, 1899, pg. 4.
44. Yes, really. (*Ibid*.)
45. Ibid.

46. *Ibid.*, Nov. 14, 1899, p. 2.
47. *Ibid.*, Feb. 26, 1900, p. 2.
Unfortunately, Heeney's removal worsened his condition. He spent the next three years drinking before his former colleagues had him sent to jail—not for a specific crime, but so that he could receive medical attention (*St. Paul Globe*, Feb. 27, 1903, p. 2).
48. Chicago *Inter-Ocean*, Sep. 13, 1900, p. 6.
49. *Ibid.*
50. *Chicago Tribune*, Sep. 14, 1900, p. 3.
51. Chicago *Inter-Ocean*, Sep. 22, 1900, p. 1.
52. The details of McGinn's suicide are taken from Chicago *Inter-Ocean*, Sep. 22, 1900, p. 1; *St. Paul Globe*, Sep. 22, 1900, p. 1; *Chicago Tribune*, Sep. 22, 1900, p. 1; *Minneapolis Star Tribune*, Sep. 23, 1900, p. 20; Cook County Coroner's Report, Sep. 22, 1900.
53. *Ibid.*
54. 1900 Census; *St. Paul City Directory*, 1900.
55. *Minneapolis Star Tribune*, Sept. 30, 1900, p. 16; *St. Paul Globe*, Sept. 30, p. 22.
56. Hornsby's quote comes from his past recollection in *The Prison Mirror*, Nov. 9, 1893, p. 1.
57. *Ibid.*
58. *Ibid.*, May 31, 1894, p. 1.
59. *Ibid.*
60. *Ibid.*
61. The Hornsby house on George Street still stands.
62. *West St. Paul Times*, March 16, 1929.
63. Frank Casseday's personal correspondence, Northwestern University Archives.
64. Portland, OR, *Oregon Daily Journal*, Oct. 20, 1907, p. 9.
65. *Ibid.*, Feb. 25, 1912, p. 49.
66. Frank Casseday's personal correspondence, Northwestern University Archives.
67. In 1909, the Hornsbys no longer had boarders, but Bertha Stackpole moved back into the Hornsby house that spring, after an absence of several years.
68. *Chicago Tribune*, Dec. 19, 1909, p. 29.
69. Craig Lambert and John T. Bethell, "First and 100," from *Harvard Magazine*, Sept. 2003, citing *College Football: History, Spectacle, Controversy*, John Sayle Watterson.
70. Chicago *Inter-Ocean*, Mar. 4, 1906, p. 9.
71. *Chicago Tribune*, Mar. 9, 1906, p. 10.
72. *Ibid.*, Mar. 24, 1906, p. 10.
73. Chicago *Inter-Ocean*, Mar. 17, 1901, p. 7.
74. Northwestern University, "Description of the New Quarters of the School," university report, 1902, p. 2.
75. *Ibid.*
76. *Inter-Ocean*, Sept. 4, 1901, p. 6.
77. Letter to William A. Dyche, personal correspondence, April 8, 1908, Northwestern University Archives.
78. Bloomberg: https://www.bloomberg.com/news/articles/2017-11-02/america-s-urban-land-is-worth-a-staggering-amount.

Game Day: 5:30 p.m.

1. Details of Philadelphia's celebration are based on the report in the *Philadelphia Inquirer*, Feb. 23, 1876, p. 2.
2. Many cities in 1876 used a time based on John Mayo's signal from Chicago. Philadelphia Time was 49½ minutes ahead of Chicago Time in 1876 (see "Diagram of Difference of Time Between Places," *Johnson's New Illustrated Family Atlas of the World*, A.J. Johnson, New York: Johnson and Ward, 1874, p. 2).
3. Described in good detail by the *Pittsburgh Press*, Feb. 12, 1956, p. 68.
4. Details of Willard's trip and the events leading up to her lecture in Philadelphia are recorded in Willard's personal correspondence, Feb. 23, 1876, Frances E. Willard Memorial Library and Archives, Evanston, IL.
5. Willard, *Glimpses*, pp. 174–175.
6. Darius Salter, *God Cannot Do Without America: Matthew Simpson and The Apotheosis of Protestant Nationalism*, Wilmore, KY: First Fruits Press, 2017, pp. 582–583.
7. As described in an 1875 advertisement.
8. Archie Hahn, *How to Sprint: The Theory of Sprint Racing / Spalding's Athletic Library*. New York: American Sports Publishing Company, 1929, p. 222.

Chapter 13

1. From the Nov. 13, 1926, game program for NU vs. Chicago: "During the period of construction a force of 400 carpenters and laborers were employed. The stadium contains 16,000 cubic yards of concrete. Nearly 153,000 feet of lumber was used for the seats and 12,000 cast iron brackets were used to fasten down the seats. Engineers state that under ordinary circumstances the stands will last from 500 to 1,000 years."
2. *Chicago Tribune*, Nov. 13, 1926, p. 19.
3. *Daily Northwestern*, Evanston, IL, Nov. 16, 1926, p. 1.
4. *American Economic Review*, New Haven, CT, vol. xix, 1929, pp. 1–8.
5. Details of this influence can be found in the Sherry Davis Kasper essay, "Why Was Henry Simons Interventionist: The Curious Legacy of a Chicago Economist," 2011, pp. 6–7. Retrieved from scribd.com.
6. Ian Tyrrell, *Woman's World / Woman's Empire: The Woman's Christian Temperance Union in International Perspective 1880-1930*, Chapel Hill: University of North Carolina Press, 1991, p. 2.
7. See www.wctu.org/history.html.
8. Frances Willard, "Fifteenth Presidential Address," 1894, as cited in *Let Something Good Be Said: Speeches and Writings of Frances E. Willard*, Carolyn DeSwarte Gifford and Amy R. Slagell, editors, Urbana: University of Illinois Press, 2007, p. 204.
9. Ida Wells, "The Red Record: Tabulated Statistics and Alleged Causes of Lynching in the United States," 1895, as quoted by Leslie Harris and Lori Osborne, "Ida B. Wells vs. Frances Willard: Getting to the Truth of a Failure to Fight Racial Injustice," *Chicago Sun-Times*, Mar. 11, 2019.
10. *The Prison Mirror*, May 17, 1894, p. 1.
11. *Baltimore Sun*, Sept. 15, 1894, p. 10.
12. *Daily Northwestern*, Oct. 14, 1931, pp. 1–2.
13. For the St. Paul *Pioneer Press*.
14. First printed in Dec. 10, 1922 in the *Milwaukee Journal*, the article appeared in various forms throughout the country until late January 1923.

The quotes used here are taken from a full version of the article printed in the *Morning Tulsa Daily World*, Dec. 17, 1922, p. 17.
15. Ibid.
16. *Prison Mirror*, Aug. 3, 1893, p. 2.
17. Ibid., Mar. 22, 1894, p. 1.
18. As noted throughout Hornsby's commentary for much of his time with the *Chicago Field*, particularly his columns about his Indian travels, which he wrote for the *Chicago Field* from 1875 through 1877.
19. Minneapolis *Star Tribune*, Nov. 29, 1915, p. 9.
20. Ibid.
21. Ibid.
22. *Prison Mirror*, May 3, 1894, p. 1.
23. *Morning Tulsa Daily World*, Dec. 17, 1922, p. 17.
24. *Minneapolis Journal*, Feb. 18, 1934, p. 11.
25. Ibid., Oct. 26, 1893, p. 2.
26. *West St. Paul Times*, Sept. 14, 1929.
27. This information and the proceeding quote come from "Memoir of Frank Fisk Casseday," an unpublished manuscript, author unknown (Casseday provided portions; an unknown writer finished it), held in the Northwestern University Archives.

Game Day: Night

1. There is no evidence that the two teams played each other again, despite Hornsby's later, vague recollection that the CFBC played Northwestern once more in 1877.
2. Chicago *Inter-Ocean*, Feb. 23, 1876, p. 3.
3. See digital.library.northwestern.edu/architecture/building.php?bid=26.

4. *Chicago Tribune*, May 4, 1875, p. 6.

5. Arch Street UMC Website: archstreetumc.org/who-we-are/our/story/.

6. *Ibid.*

7. Willard's correspondence, Frances E. Willard Memorial Library and Archives, Evanston, IL.

8. As detailed in *Let Something Good Be Said: Speeches and Writings of Frances E. Willard*, Carolyn De Swarte Gifford and Amy R. Slagell, 2007, pp. xxvi–xxvii.

9. Passage from Willard's speech, "Everybody's War," which she initially wrote in Fall 1874, as transcribed in De Swarte Gifford and Slagell, 2007, p. 6.

10. Philadelphia *The Times*, Oct. 6, 1876, p. 1.

11. Gifford and Slagell, 2007, pp. 22–23.

12. *Chicago Tribune*, Aug. 11, 1875, p. 7.

13. Not only did Chicago allow fireworks again just a couple of years after the 1871 Fire, for the 1893 World's Fair, Chicago staged a massive fireworks show that commemorated the Great Fire. The blazing spectacle was titled "The Burning of Chicago" (Chicago *Inter-Ocean*, Oct. 9, 1893, p. 13).

Bibliography

Books

Airlie, Shiona. *Thistle and Bamboo: The Life and Times of Sir James Stewart Lockhart*. Oxford: Oxford University Press, 1989.

Alcock, Charles W. *Football: Our Winter Game*. London: Imperial Press, 1874.

Andreas, Alfred T. *History of Chicago*. Chicago: A.T. Andreas Co., 1886.

Atwell, Charles B., ed. *Alumni Record of the College of Liberal*. Evanston–Chicago: Northwestern University, 1903.

Bales, Jack. *Before They Were Cubs: The Early Years of Chicago's First Professional Baseball Team*. Jefferson, NC: McFarland, 2019.

Booth, John N. *Booths in History*. Los Alamitos, CA: Ridgeway Press, 1982.

Campbell, John, ed. *A Biographical History of Prominent Men of the Great West*. Chicago: Western Biographical and Engraving Co., 1902.

Chamberlin, Everett. *Chicago and Its Suburbs*. Chicago: T.A. Hungerford, 1874.

Chase, Vanessa. "Edith Wharton, *The Decoration of Houses*, and Gender in Turn-of-the-Century America." *Architecture and Feminism*. Elizabeth Danze, Carol Henderson, and Debra Coleman, editors. New York: Princeton Architectural Press, 1996.

Chatterton, Eyre. *A History of the Church of England in India Since the Days of the East India Company*. London: Macmillan, 1924.

Condit, Carl W. *The Chicago School of Architecture*. Chicago: University of Chicago Press, 1964.

Connely, William. *Louis Sullivan as He Lived: The Shaping of American Architecture*. New York: Horizon Press, 1960.

Cornellian. Ithaca: Secret Societies of the Cornell University, 1876.

Davis, Parke H. *Football: The American Intercollegiate Game*. New York: Scribner's, 1911.

Dees, Pamela Y. *A Guide to Piano Music by Women Composers: Vol. 1, Composers Born Before 1900*. Westport, CT: Greenwood Press, 2002.

DeLoca, Paul. "William Curtis." *American National Biography*. New York: Oxford University Press, 2005.

Devol, George H. *Forty Years a Gambler on the Mississippi*. Cincinnati: Devol & Haines, 1887.

Donaldson, Emily Ann. *The Scottish Highland Games in America*. Gretna, LA: Pelican, 1986.

Elliot, Frank M., ed. *History of Omega Chapter and Reminiscences of Northwestern: A Brief Sketch of the Sigma Chi Fraternity, and a List of the Members of Omega, Etc., Etc*., Chicago: Donohue & Henneberry, 1885.

English, T.J. *Paddy Whacked: The Untold Story of the Irish American Gangster*. New York: Harper, 2005.

Erdnase, S.W. (pseudonym). *Artifice, Ruse, and Subterfuge at the Card Table: A Treatise on the Science and Art of Manipulating Cards*. Chicago: Frederick J. Drake & Co., 1902.

Ericson, Margaret D. *Women and Music: A Selective Annotated Bibliography on Women and Gender Issues in Music*. Boston: G.K. Hall, 1996.

Fabian, Ann. *Card Sharps, Dream Books, & Bucket Shops: Gambling in*

19th-Century America. Ithaca: Cornell University Press, 1990.
Foster, Clyde D. Evanston's Yesterdays: Stories of Early Evanston and Sketches of Some of Its Pioneers. Evanston: privately published, 1956.
Gardiner, Charles Henry. Centurions of a Century. London: F.V. Hadlow, 1911.
Genoways, Ted, ed. Hard Time: Voices from a State Prison, 1849-1914. St. Paul: Minnesota Historical Society Press, 2002.
Gifford, Carolyn DeSwarte, and Amy R. Slagell, eds. Let Something Good Be Said: Speeches and Writings of Frances E. Willard. Urbana: University of Illinois Press, 2007.
Gordon, Anna A. The Beautiful Life of Frances E. Willard: A Memorial Volume. Chicago: Woman's Temperance Publishing, 1898.
Hahn, Archie. How to Sprint: The Theory of Sprint Racing / Spalding's Athletic Library. New York: American Sports Publishing Company, 1929.
Heckethorn, Charles William. The Secret Societies of All Ages & Countries. London: Richard Bentley & Son, 1875.
Heilbron, William C., and Cole Younger. Convict Life at the Minnesota State Prison, Stillwater, Minnesota. St. Paul-Minneapolis: W.C. Heilbron / Murphy-Travis Co., 1909.
A History of the City of Chicago, Its Men and Institutions. Chicago: Inter-Ocean Publishing, 1900.
Hoffmann, Professor (Angelo John Lewis), ed. The Cyclopædia of Card and Table Games. London: George Routledge & Sons, 1891 edition.
Hofmeister, Rudolf A. The Germans of Chicago. Champaign, IL: Stipes Publishing, 1976.
Hornsby, A.H. The South African Diamond Fields: A Practical Matter-of Fact Account, to the Latest Date. Chicago: Inter-Ocean Steam Book and Job Print, 1874.
Howe, Nicholas. Not Without Peril: 150 Years of Misadventure on the Presidential Range of New Hampshire. Boston: Appalachian Mountain Club Books, 2000.
Johnson, A.J. Johnson's New Illustrated Family Atlas of the World. New York: Johnson and Ward, 1874.
Kelly, Robert J., Ko-lin Chin, and Rufus Schatzberg, eds. Handbook of Organized Crime in the United States. Westport, CT: Greenwood Press, 1994.
Kingsley, Charles. Westward Ho! Leipzig: Bernhard Tauchnitz, First Copyright Edition, 1855.
Koblas, John. When the Heavens Fell: The Youngers in Stillwater Prison. St. Cloud, MN: North Star Press, 2002.
Kohler, Ernst. Volksbrauch, Aberglauben, Sagen und andre alte Ueberlieferungen im Boigtlande. Leipzig: Berlag von Fr. Fleischer, 1867.
LaTourette, Larry. Northwestern Wildcat Football. Charleston, SC: Arcadia, 2005.
Logan, Charles Lyford, Charles Wesley Thornton, Frederick A. Ingalls, eds. Campus Fires of '77, The Fiftieth Anniversary Memorial of the Class of 1877, Northwestern University. Evanston-Chicago: privately printed by Northwestern University, 1928.
MacCambridge, Michael. ESPN College Football Encyclopedia. New York: ESPN Books, 2005.
Marcus Aurelius. Helpful Thoughts from the Meditations of Marcus Aurelius Antoninus. Walter Lee Brown, ed. Chicago: A.C. McClurg & Co., 1902.
Marquis, Albert Nelson, ed. Book of Chicagoans: A Biographical Dictionary of Leading Living Men of the City of Chicago. Chicago: A.N. Marquis & Co., 1905 & 1911 editions.
_____. Marquis' Hand-Book of Chicago. Chicago: A.N. Marquis & Co., 1887.
Muir, George W., ed. The Northwestern Song Book: A Collection of College and Other Music. New York: Athenaeum Publishing, 1879.
Neu, Denese. Chicago by the Pint: A Craft Beer History of the Windy City. Charleston, SC: The History Press, 2011.
Official Railway Guide: North American Freight Service Edition. Philadelphia: National Railway Publication Co., 1876 edition.
Okrent, Daniel and Steve Wulf. Baseball Anecdotes. Oxford: Oxford University Press, 1989.
Oxford Dictionary of National Biography. New York: Oxford University Press, 2004.
Paulison, Walter Merryman. The Tale of the Wildcats. Evanston-Chicago: N Men's Club, Northwestern University Club

of Chicago, Northwestern University Alumni Assoc., 1951.

Pickering, Sam. *One Grand, Sweet Song*, College Station: Texas A&M University Press, 2016. The book is not paginated.

Power, John Carroll, ed. *History of an Attempt to Steal the Body of Abraham Lincoln*. Springfield, IL: Rokker, 1890.

Pridmore, Jay. *Northwestern University: Celebrating 150 Years*. Evanston: Northwestern University Press, 2000.

Proctor, Richard A., Esq. "Mechanical Chess." *Mephisto, the Marvellous Automaton, Exhibited at the International Teatre, Exposition Universelle, Paris*. London: T. Pettitt & Co., 1889.

Quinn, John Philip. *Fools of Fortune, or Gambling and Gamblers*. Chicago: G.L Howe & Co., 1890.

Roberts, Jerry. *Pass Receiving in Early Pro Football: A History to the 1960s*. Jefferson, NC: McFarland, 2016.

Rollenhagen, Gabriel. *Nvclevs Emblematvm Selectissimorvm*. Arnhem, 1611.

Royse, Isaac H.C. *History of the 115th Regiment, Illinois Volunteer Army*. Privately published, 1900.

Salter, Darius. *God Cannot Do Without America: Matthew Simpson and the Apotheosis of Protestant Nationalism*. Wilmore, KY: First Fruits Press, 2017.

Seeger, Eugen. *Chicago, The Wonder City*. Chicago: Gen. Gregory Printing Company, 1893.

Seida, Lowell. *William Buckingham "Father Bill" Curtis: Founder of the U.S. Olympic Committee*. Privately published, 2017 edition.

Sennett, William. *The Northwest Illustrated for Tourists of 1875*. Chicago: Chicago & Northwestern Railway, 1875.

Shaw, Archibald, ed. *History of Dearborn County, Indiana: Her People, Industries, and Institutions*. Indianapolis: B.F. Bowen & Co., 1915.

Sheppard, Robert D., and Harvey B. Hurd, eds. *History of Northwestern University and Evanston*. Chicago: Munsell Publishing, 1906.

Smith, Melvin I. *Evolvements of Early American Foot Ball: Through the 1890/91 Season*. Bloomington: AuthorHouse, 2008.

Steege, David. "Harry Potter, Tom Brown, and the British School Story: Lost in Transit?" *The Ivory Tower and Harry Potter: Perspectives on a Literary Phenomenon*. Edited by Lana A. Whited. Colombia: University of Missouri Press, 2002.

Stuntz, Steven Conrad. *List of Agricultural Periodicals*. Washington, D.C.: US Dept. of Agriculture, 1941.

Taylor, F.M. *The Right of the State to Be*. Ann Arbor: University of Michigan, 1891.

Twombly, Robert. *Louis Sullivan: His Life and Work*. New York: Viking, 1986.

_____, ed. *Louis Sullivan: The Public Papers*. Chicago: University of Chicago Press, 1988.

Tyrrell, Ian. *Woman's World / Woman's Empire: The Woman's Christian Temperance Union in International Perspective 1880–1930*. Chapel Hill: University of North Carolina Press, 1991.

Watts, George T., et al. *Ritual and Book of Forms of the American Order, Sons of St. George*. Brockton, MA: Keystone Print, revised 1895.

Weyland, Alexander. *The Saga of American Football*. New York: Macmillan, 1955.

Wilde, Arthur H. *Northwestern University: A History, 1855–1905*. New York: University Publishing Society, 1905.

Willard, Frances E. *A Classic Town: The Story of Evanston*. Chicago: Woman's Temperance Publishing Assoc., 1891.

_____. *Glimpses of Fifty Years: The Autobiography of an American Woman*. Chicago: H.J. Smith & Co., 1889.

_____. *A Wheel Within a Wheel: How I Learned to Ride the Bicycle*. London: Hutchinson & Co., 1895.

Wither, George. *A Collection of Emblemes, Ancient and Moderne*. London: Richard Royston, 1635.

Younger, Cole. *The Story of Cole Younger, by Himself*. Chicago: Press of the Henneberry Company, 1903.

Zellie, Carole, and Garneth Peterson. *Pioneer Houses: 1854–1880*. St. Paul Heritage Preservation Commission, 2001.

Newspapers, Journals, and Periodicals

Advertiser (Hampshire, UK)
American Economic Review (New Haven)
The American Stationer (New York)
Annual Report of the Free Public Library of Evanston, Ill.

Bibliography

Argus-Leader (Sioux Falls)
Asiatic Intelligence (London)
The Asiatic Journal and Monthly Register for British and Foreign India, China, and Australasia (London)
Atlanta Constitution
Australasian Journal of American Studies
The Baltimore Sun
Boston Globe
Broad Axe (West St. Paul, MN)
The Californian (Salinas)
The Cheltenham Chronicle and Gloucestershire Advertiser (Cheltenham, UK)
Chicago Daily News
Chicago Evening Journal
Chicago Evening Mail
Chicago Field (also titled *The Field, American Field*, and *Field and Stream*)
Chicago History
Chicago Sun-Times
Chicago Times
Chicago Tribune
Columbia Chess Chronicle (New York)
Daily Herald (New York, NY)
Daily Monitor (Fort Scott, KS)
Daily News (St. Paul)
The Daily Northwestern (Evanston, IL)
Detroit Free Press
Engineering and Building Record (New York)
The Engineering News (London)
Evanston Herald (Evanston, IL)
Evanston Index (Evanston, IL)
Evening News (Santa Cruz, CA)
Fairmount Semi-Weekly News (Fairmount, IN)
Field & Stream
The Forum (New York)
Granite Monthly (Concord, NH)
Guernsey Star (also titled *Guernsey Evening Press and Star*) (Vale, Guernsey)
Harvard Crimson (Cambridge)
Harvard Magazine (Cambridge)
History Alive: Standard 9. South Africa (Pietermaritzburg, South Africa)
Home and Abroad (Boston)
Illustrated London News
Independent (Hawarden, IA)
Indianapolis Journal
Inquirer (Philadelphia)
Inter-Ocean (Chicago)
The Irish Standard (Minneapolis)
Ithaca Journal (Ithaca)
The Japan Mail (also titled *The Japan Weekly Mail*) (Yokohama)
Journal of Criminal Law and Criminology (Chicago)
Journal of the Royal Asiatic Society of Great Britain and Ireland (London)
The Literary Digest (New York)
London Gazette
Los Angeles Times
Mercury and Daily Post (Bristol, UK)
Milwaukee Journal
Minneapolis Star
Minneapolis Star Tribune
Montreal Star
Morning Post (London)
The Morning Tulsa Daily World
The Mower County Transcript (Mower, MN)
NBER Working Paper Series (Cambridge, MA)
New York Herald
New York Sun
New York Times
New York Tribune
News Herald (Franklin, PA)
Northwestern University, *Alumni News*
Northwestern University, *Catalogue of the Northwestern University, 1875–1876*
102nd Regiment of Foot Register (London)
Oregon Daily Journal (Portland)
Pantagraph (Bloomington, IL)
Peabody Enterprise (Peabody, MA)
Peck & Snyder's Encyclopædia and Price List, 1873
Pioneer Press (St. Paul)
Pittsburgh Press
Plain Dealer (McHenry, IL)
Post-Dispatch (St. Louis)
Princeton Union (Princeton, MN)
The Printer and Bookmaker (New York)
Prison Mirror (Stillwater, MN)
Proceedings of the American Association for the Advancement of Physical Education, 1892
Register (Santa Ana, CA)
Register and Magazine of Biography (Westminster)
Report of the National Woman's Christian Temperance Union (Chicago)
St. Louis Globe-Democrat
St. Paul Globe (also titled *St. Paul Daily Globe*)
St. Paul Saturday Evening News
Salt Lake Tribune (Salt Lake City)
San Francisco Call
San Francisco Examiner
The Sigma Chi Quarterly
Star-Bulletin (Honolulu)
Star-Gazette (Elmira, NY)
Sunday Star (Washington, D.C.)
The Times (Philadelphia)

Times (Santa Maria, CA)
Times Herald (Port Huron, MI)
Tobacco Leaf (New York)
Topeka State Journal (Topeka)
The Tribune (Oakland)
The Tripod (Evanston, IL)
The Union Signal: A Journal of Social Welfare
University of Michigan Chronicle (Ann Arbor)
U.S. Catholic Historian
Washington Post
Weekly Transcript (McCune, KS)
The Wellington (Wellington, UK)
West St. Paul Times
Wisconsin Medical Recorder
WomenSports July 1974

Records, Archives, and Censuses

Canadian Patent Office Record, June 1875.
Census Records, US, 1870, 1880.
Cook County, IL, Coroner's Reports, 1900.
Cornell University Football's *Record Book*, 2017 edition.
England & Wales Civil Registration Marriage Index, 1837–1915.
Evanston, IL, Town Directory, 1879.
Frances E. Willard Memorial Library and Archives, Evanston, IL. Personal correspondence and records of Frances Willard.
Minneapolis, MN, City Direction, 1881.
National Archives. *Registers of Deaths of Volunteers, 1861–1865*. ARC ID: 656639.
Northwestern University Archives. Records of the Portland, OR, Northwestern Alumni Association, 1911–1949.
_____. "Description of the New Quarters of the School." 1902.
_____. Personal correspondence archives of Frank Casseday and William A. Dyche.
Records and Briefs in Cases Decided by the Supreme Court of Minnesota, 1893.
Ryerson and Burnham Library Archives at the Art Institute of Chicago
St. Paul, MN, City Directory, 1894, 1897, 1900, 1902.
Stillwater, MN, Prison Commitment Papers, 1891–1899, archived at Gale Family Library, Minnesota History Center, St. Paul, MN.
Wellington College Archives.

Websites

American Passenger Rail Heritage Foundation. "The Devil's Carriage Comes to Heavenston." www.trainweb.org/evrailfan/chap1.html.
Ancestry.com.
Arch Street UMC Website: archstreetumc.org/who-we-are/our/story/.
Baran, William L. https://civilwar.illinois genweb.org/photos/kinmanw.html.
BBC. http://www.bbc.co.uk/scotland/sport scotland/asportingnation/article/0007/.
Berg, Gordon. "Battle of Chickamauga and Gordon Granger's Reserve Corps," HistoryNet.com.
Bloomberg: https://www.bloomberg.com/news/articles/2017-11-02/america-s-urban-land-is-worth-a-staggering-amount.
Britannica. https://www.britannica.com/place/South-Africa/Diamonds-gold-and-imperialist-intervention-1870-1902.
Emporis.com.
"Hazing at Cornell: A Tradition?" ithacating.com.
https://web.archive.org/web/2008 1008033803/http://batgirl.atspace.com/automaton.html.
Kasper, Sherry Davis. "Why Was Henry Simons Interventionist: The Curious Legacy of a Chicago Economist." 2011, pp. 6–7. Retrieved from scribd.com.
Legends of America. "Faro." www.legendsofamerica.com/we-faro/.
Lindon, Richard. http://www.richardlindon.co.uk.
Mental Floss. mentalfloss.com/article/502636/colorful-history-prison-mirror-americas-oldest-continuously-operated-prison-newspaper.
Northwestern University. digital.library.northwestern.edu/architecture/building.php?bid=26.
_____. https://maps.northwestern.edu/txt/facility/120.
Slate.com. https://slate.com/human-interest/2015/08/hotel-concierge-history-and-origins-of-the-hospitality-profession.html.
Thompson, Daniella. "Historic Pattiani House Emerges from a 20-Year Restoration." http://berkeleyheritage.com/eastbay_then-now/pattiani-sadler.html.
Woman's Christian Temperance Union. https://www.wctu.org/history.

Index

Numbers in **_bold italics_** refer to pages with photographs

Abbey, Wallace 45
Academical Cricket Club (Edinburgh, Scottland) 35
Adler, Dankmar 163, **_165_**
Ahern, Michael 82
"Ajeeb" (chess automaton) 98–99
Aldershot, England 35–36, 74, 160
Alexandria, Egypt 35
American Economic Association 182
American Field see *Chicago Field*
Appalachian Mountain Club 168
Appleton, Alanson 139
Architectural League of America 163
Armour, Philip, Jr. 151, 184
Armour Packing Co. 151
Arnold, Matthew 19
Arnold, Thomas 19
Arnold, William 113–114, 159, 161, 179
Auditorium Hotel (Chicago) 163
Averill, H.R. 170

Barrington, Joseph 47, 49
baseball 65, 101–102
A Basket of Chips 153
Bell Park (Evanston, Illinois) 189
Ben Drake (passenger boat) 159, 179, 189–191
Benson, Edward White 18
Beta Theta Pi Fraternity 44
"The Big Hole" (diamond mine) 36
Big Ten Conference (also Big Nine) 175–176, 181
The Book of Chicagoans 63
Booth, Alfred 151–152
Booth, William Vernon 84, 93, 101, 151–152, 158, 160
Booth & Co. 151
Borner, William 63, 93, 102, 152
Boston, Massachusetts 69
Brown, Abbie 127
Brown, Andrew 127, **_130_**
Brown, Edwin 172
Brown, Flora 174

Brown, Walter Lee 25, **_71_**–72, 138
Brown Hilton, Jessie 127, 129–131, 159, 165–166, 179–180, 191
Burnham, Daniel 163

Camp, Walter 85, 93, 102–103
Capone, Alphonse G. "Al" 183
A Car Without a Name (FAL automobile) 170
Casseday, David 10, 12, 154–155
Casseday, Ellen 10
Casseday, Frank 7, 10–12, 25, 27, 42–45, 60, 67, 78, 89, **_114_**, 146, 157, 187–188; friendship with Frances Willard 24, 127, 155, 189; game vs. CFBC 57, 71–72, 113, 126, 131, 158, 161, 179, 190; medical practice **_155_**, 174; proponent of feminism 24, 174; real estate in St. Paul 154–155
SS *Celtic* 95
Chennai, India see Madras
Chicago, Illinois 6, 23, 53, 55, 64, 81, 113, 116, 181; architecture 73; 1893 World's Fair 63, 121–124, 139; football games in 51–52; gambling and crime in 7, 46–47, 105–106, 183; see also Chicago Fire of 1871
Chicago Athletic Club 53, 56, 63, 66, 70
Chicago Barge Club 66–67
Chicago Cardinals see Morgan Athletic Club
Chicago Field (magazine; also called *Field & Stream*, *Field*, and *American Field*) 13, 30, 48–49, 52, 67, 84–86, 120, 184
Chicago Fire of 1871 6, 12, 23, 48, 55, 65, 70, 81, **_105_**, **_122_**, **_130_**, 159, 177, 192; O'Leary legend 82
Chicago Foot-Ball Club (American football team) 1, 54, 66–67, 74, 93–94, **_105_**, 113, 151, 191; athletic grounds 65, 80; creation of 7, 64–65; track and field events 70, 79, 84
Chicago Football Club (soccer team) 94
Chicago Tribune 1, 45, 51–53, 58, 68, 70, 82, 85, 122, 133, 145, 175

219

220 Index

Chicago Wanderers 94
Chicago Water Tower 56
Chicago White Stockings (Chicago Cubs)
  63, 65, 101, 169; athletic field 65–66, 79, *80*,
  84, 189
Chillicothe, Ohio 60
Cincinnati Red Stockings 65
Civil War 25, 53, 55, 116, *122*, 177; Battle of
  Chickamauga 43, 114
Cleveland, Grover 123–124
Cleveland, Ralph 63
Columbia University 5, 46, 69
Colvin, Harvey 46
Concessionary Rules 26–27, 69, 79
Cornell University 51–52, 78–79
Couch, Ira, Jr. 63–64
Cox, Jesse 159, 179, 189, 191
Cumnock, Robert 24–25, 88
Curtis, William Buckingham 68, 71, 85, 159,
  167, 180; athletic clubs and organizations
  55–56, 66, 93, 165–166, 176; and the CFBC
  3, 53, 63–64, 70, 78–79, 84; Civil War
  service *54*–55, 114; death 167–168; vs.
  Northwestern 56–57, 69, 74, 102–103, 131,
  175, 179, 185
Custer, Gen. George Armstrong 13

The Daily Northwestern (newspaper) 183
Dalrymple, Abner 150
Dana, Charles 81
Dartmouth College 69
Davis, Parke 20
Davis Street Pier (Evanston, Illinois) *73*,
  189
Day, William 63
Detroit, Michigan 68
Detroit Free Press 68
Devol, George H. 7
Douthart, Simon 25, 125–126, 138–139
Dublin, Ireland 18
Duluth, Minnesota 111, 118, 120
Dyche, Dr. David 74
Dyche, William 74, 176–177, 181
Dyche Stadium 181, 183

Early, Frank 72, 88–89
Edison, Thomas 50
Egan, Hon. James J. 137, 140
Ellis, William Webb 20
England Rugby Football Union 40
English, T. J. 47
Esher, Edward 103, 113, 152
Esher, Bishop John Jacob 103
Evanston, Illinois 6, 23–24, 40–42, 60, *71*,
  73, 74, 127, 138, 165 179; Fountain Square
  41–42, 157, 189; temperance within 41–42,
  57, 74, 180, 191
Evanston College for Ladies 24
Evanston Historical Society 42
Evanston Index 43, 74

Evening Journal (Chicago) 6, 63, 81–83
Eversley, England 19

Fabian, Ann 120
faro *see* gambling
"The Father's Responsibility" 130
Fauntleroy, Thomas 65, 78, 88, 93, 169–170
feminism, nineteenth-century "first wave"
  127–131, 148, 182, 190–191
Ferguson, John 107–109
Ferris, John 106
Field & Stream see Chicago Field
The Fighting Methodists 44
Findley, Sam 155
First National Bank (Northfield, Minnesota)
  143
Fisher, Arthur 134–135
Fisk, Herbert F. 89
"Fizzle Club" 153
The Flamingoes (rugby club) 40
Flanders, John J. 63, 73–74
Fleming, Alice 41–42
football (American sport) 51; ball used for
  games 75–77; origins and evolution of 5–6,
  26, 46, 52, 69, 90, 102–103, 175–176; *see also*
  Concessionary Rules; rugby (game)
football (association, or soccer) 5–6, 20, 26,
  69, 86
football (Canadian sport) 46, 52
football (rugby) *see* rugby (game)
Football: Our Winter Game 102–103
The Four Hundred 142
The Four Million 142
Fowler, the Rev. Charles 89–90
Frend, John 15
Fresh Air Club 166–168

Galesburg, Illinois 55
gambling 7, 101, 144; faro 7, 92, 106–108;
  history in America 120, 167; poker 7, 33,
  92, 107
Gardner House Hotel (Hastings, Minnesota)
  135–137
Garrett Biblical Institute 60, 74, 157, 179
Garvin, Albert 121, 134; at Stillwater Prison
  141
The Gentlemen's Own (gambling hall) 92
Grant, Ulysses S. 11, 23, 177–178
Great Western Light Guard 60–61
Gustafson, Victor 181

Hahn, Archie 180
Harvard University 5–6, 26, 46, 52, 69,
  76–77, 84, 93, 175
Hastings, Minnesota 120, 132–136, 171
Hatch, Alfrederick Smith 93
Hatch, Rufus 144–145
Hatch, William 85, 93, 145, 184
The Hatch Family (painting) 93
Hatfield, the Rev. Robert Miller 178, 190–191

Index

Hattabaugh, Margaret 165
Heeney, James 134–136, 172
Henry, O. (William Sydney Porter) 98, 142
Hilton, Charles 63–64, 66, 102–103, 105, 114
Hilton, Theophilus 59, 66–67, 72, 103, 113, 125–127, 129, 166, 179, 191
Home Insurance Building 73
"Home Protection" 172, 191
Hong Kong Football Club 85–86
Horan, Dan 82
Horner's (restaurant) 179, 189
Hornsby, Arthur (Augustus's brother) 16, *17*, 85, 91, 94, 121
Hornsby, Arthur (Augustus's son) 85, 110
Hornsby, Augustus Henry "Gus": arrest and escape 122–124, 132–136; athletic abilities and habits 13, 32, 79–80, 84, 96, 120; books authored by 48, 85; chess play 21, 33, 153, 186 (game with "Ajeeb" 98–99); childhood 16–*17*; diamond mining 36–37, 48; financial problems 37–38, 49, 109, 150, 157, 173–174; football (American) play 1, 46, 52, 65–66, 78–79, 83, 93 (vs. Northwestern 6, 56–57, 69–70, 75–77, 88, 90, 103, 113–115, 125, 131, 138, 151–152, 158, 175); gambling addiction 7, 33–34, 49–50, 67–68, 86, 91–92, 100, 104–109, 118, 166; hunting 17, 29–31, 37; inventing 50; journalist career ([in Chicago] 48–49, 85–86; [in prison] 144; [in St. Paul] 91, 94, 109, 183–184); legal problems 49, 97, 110–112, 120, 137; military career 29, 34–35, 38; Minnesota Supreme Court case 120; period as a fugitive 111–112, 118–121; photography stint 109; poetry by 110, 148, 185; real estate career 91, 94–95, 109–111, 150, 153; rugby play 20, 22, 31–32, 35–36, 38; Stillwater Prison incarceration 140–149; teaching football in Japan and Hong Kong 85; views on feminism, race, and society 37–38, 129, 145–147, 173–174, 180, 182; views on India 31, 185–186; Wellington ([as an alumnus] 36, 38; [as a student]) 18–21; wrestling referee 68–69
Hornsby, Eliza Frend 15–18
Hornsby, Henry (Augustus's son) 50, 149–150, 153, 156
Hornsby, Henry, Jr. (Augustus's brother) 15–18, 29–31, 33, 38–39, 160, 173
Hornsby, Henry, Sr. (Augustus's father) 15–18
Hornsby, Marie Blackmore 38, 46, 50, 85–86, 91, 97, 104, 109–111, 118–119, 149–150, 153–154, 156, 173–174, 187
Hornsby, Rachel (Augustus's daughter) 85, 149, 153, 156, 173, 187
Hornsby, Rachel (Augustus's sister) 18
Hornsby, Raymond 16, 34
horse racing 7, 33–34, 49, 85, 92
Hotel Men's Mutual Benefit Association 64
How I Learned to Ride the Bicycle 127

The Hub (Chicago tavern) 116–117
Hulbert, William 63, 65, 84, 101–102, 184
Hyde Park, Illinois 49, 67

USS *Illinois* 129
Independence Hall 178, 190
Indianapolis News 81
Inter-Ocean (Chicago newspaper) 13, 41, 48, 81, 127, 177
Interstate Exposition Building 47
The Irish Standard (Minneapolis) 133
Ithica, New York 42
Ithica Journal 42
"It's a Way We Have at Northwestern" 159–160

James, Frank 143
James, Jesse 143
Jameson, Thaddeus Ferguson 156, 174
Jaynes, Cy 106–107
Jeffrey, John 6, 63, 81–84, 159, 168–169
Jenney, William LeBaron 13, 73
Jewett, George 25
Jones, Sir Harry 21

Kappa Alpha Society fraternity 51
Keene, Jim 167
Keith, Charles 79, 88, 90
Keith, Elbridge 177
Kellogg, Julius "Baldy" 88–89
Kelly, Patricia 42
Kensington, England 46
Kenwood, Illinois 119–120
Kerten, Charles 172
Kingsley, Charles vi, 19–20, 141, 145
Kinman, Cyrus 43
Kinman, Edward 42–45, 57, 67, 71–72, 74, 77, 113–114, 126, 131, 158
Kinman, Newton 43
Kinman, William 43
Knox College, Illinois 55
Koblas, John 141

Lake Forest College 78
Lamprey, Uri 109, 111, 120
Leason, Jesse 184
Leggett, Mortimer 51
Levy, Maury 127–128
Lighter, Jonathan 161
Lincoln, Abraham 23, 178, 190; attempt to rob Lincoln's grave 116–117
Lincoln, Robert Todd 116
Lincoln-Douglas debates 177
Lindon, Richard 75–77
London Athletic Club 40
London News 94
London Times 154
Lotus Club 56, 64, 115, 168
Lowe, E.H. 170
Löwenthal, Johan 21

Loyola University *see* St. Ignatius College
Lunt, Orrington 127
Lynch Laws 182

Madras (Chennai, India) 15, 29
Maller's Building 73
"The Maniac" 38-39
Mares, Adam 40-41
Markham, William 117-118
Martin, Benjamin 111, 118, 120, 137
Mason, John 117
Mayo, John B. 70, 81; John Mayo Cup trophy 80
McDonald, Michael 46, 104-107, 183
McFetridge, William 134, 171
McGinn, John C.: captures Lincoln grave robbers 116-117, 143; escorts and pursues Hornsby 123-124, 132-134, 136, 145; Pinkerton detective 117; St. Paul detective 118, 120-*122*; suicide 171-173
McGinn, Maggie 172
Medical Argus 155
Melville, Tom 102
The Merchandise Mart (Chicago) 23
Milwaukee Journal 184
Minneapolis, Minnesota 92, 98, 154
Minneapolis Chess Club 98
Minneapolis Daily Herald 154
Moehle, Charles 98-99
Molly Maguires 96
Morgan Athletic Club 94
Mount Washington, New Hampshire 167-168
Munroe, Edwin 72, 78, 152

Naperville, Illinois 103
National Association of Amateur Athletes of America 93, 166, 168, 176
National Collegiate Athletic Association (NCAA) 176
National League (baseball) 101-102
Nawab of Awadh 33
Nelson, James 169
The New Awakening 139
New Rush Mine 36, 48
New York, New York 46, 53, 55, 81, 93, 101, 171
New York Athletic Club 7, 40, 53, 55, 93, 168
New York Daily Herald 11
New York Sportsman 86
New York Sun 78, 81
New York Times 95, 118
Newberry Library (Chicago) *130*
Nixon, William 48
noms de plume 49, 144, 146
North American Kennel Club 49
North Central College (formerly North-Western College) 103
"The North-Western University March" 60-61

Northern Pacific Railway 111, 150, 153
Northfield, Minnesota, bank raid 143
Northrop Field (University of Minnesota stadium) 156
Northwestern Field 175
Northwestern Preparatory School (also known as Northwestern Academy) 74, 89, 127, 129
Northwestern University 24-25; baseball at *43*, 44, 65, 113-*114*; Dempster Hall 72, *160*; football at 1, *43*, 51, 78, 156-157, 175-176, 181, 183; fraternities 10, 44, 58, 157; game vs. CFBC 66-67, 69-70, 75, 88-90 101-103, 113-115, 125-127, 131, 138, 151-152, 158-159; gymnasium 25, 56-57, 71, 170; Heck Hall 60, 72-74; history 24, 42, 44-45, 72, 127; Mann Prize 25; University Hall 24, 56, 60-62, *73*, 126, 189-191; *see also* Spade and Serpent Society; Willard, Frances

102nd Regiment of Foot 29, 35, 38, 173
115th Illinois Volunteers 43
Order of Sons of St. George 96-97, 111-112
Ormsbee, Allan 167-168
The Owls 60

Pajaro, California 94
Palmer, Potter 65
Palmer House Hotel 65, 70, 119, 172
Panic of 1893 155, 163, 168
paper chases 20-21
Pattiani, Alfred W. 60
Pattiani, Madame Eliza (née Elisabeth von Bergen) 60-61
Paulison, Walter 1
Paul's (gambling hall) 91-92
Phi Kappa Sigma fraternity 10
Philadelphia, Pennsylvania 178-179, 190-191
Pierson, J.P. 125-126
pigsticking 30-31
Pinkerton, Robert A. 121
Pinkerton, William A. 117, 121
Pinkerton Detective Agency 116-117, 120, 122, 134, 171
Pioneer Press (St. Paul) 86, 91, 94, 109, 135, 137
Pitts, Charles 143
poker *see* gambling
Portland, Oregon, Woman's Club 174
Princeton University 5, 26, 46, 69, 85
The Prison Mirror (Stillwater newspaper) 143-149, 182

"Quæcumque Sunt Vera" 181
quarterback (American football position) 102-103
Quinn, John Philip 92

Racine College 1
"Revelry of the Dying" *see* "Stand to Your Glasses"

Index

Rice, John 106
Riley, James Whitcomb 81
Rogers, James Gamble 181
Rollenhagen, Gabriel 59
Roosevelt, Franklin D. 182
Roosevelt, Theodore 98, 175–176
Rowe, Dr. Nicholas 48
Rowling, J.K. 19–20
"The Rubicon" 74, 159–*160*
rugby (game) 5–6, 19–20, 22, 27, 31, 35–36, 52, 69, 75–76, 102
Rugby (school in England) 18–20, 75
"Rule Britannia" 160
Russell, Henry 38–39
Rutgers University 5, 46, 69, 120

The Saga of American Football 2
St. George Club 95–96, 112
St. Ignatius College (Loyola University Chicago) 67
St. Paul, Minnesota 13, 86, 116, 118, 136, 149, 166; gambling in 91–92; real estate 94–95, 109, 154
St. Paul Chess Club 98
St. Paul Daily News 121, 171
St. Paul Globe 86, 91, 94, 97, 117–118, 136, 153–154
Sanborn, Gen. John B. 137
Sandhurst, England 18, 21
Sandhurst Royal Military College 21–22, 29, 34
Say's Law *170*
Scott, Frank H. 59, 113
HMS *Serapis* 35
Sharkwell, Frank 31
Sheedy, Tom 106
Sheridan, Gen. Philip 65, 82
Sheridan Guards 51
"Sic Transit Gloria Mundi" 110
Sigma Chi Fraternity 127
Simons, Henry 182
Simpson, Bishop Matthew 178–179, 190
Skull and Bones 58
Sloggy, E.M. 172
Smith, William 120, 133, 137
soccer *see* football (association, or soccer)
Soldier Field (Chicago) 183
South Africa 36–37, 48
The South African Diamond Fields 48
Spade and Serpent Society 57–59, 66, 127, 170
Spalding, Albert 65, 101–*102*
Spanish-American War 169
The Sportsmen's Record 85
Springfield, Illinois 116–117
Stackpole, Bertha 153
Stagg, Amos Alonzo 181
"Stand to Your Glasses" 160–162
Stewart Lockhart, James 85–86
Stillwater Prison, Minnesota 121, 140–149,
153; conditions in 143, 148–149; race relations at 146–147; visit from W.C.T.U. 147–148
Stoady, John 35
The Store (gambling hall) 47, 107
suffrage (American movement) 6, 131, 148, 165, 182, 186, 191
Sullivan, Albert 61–62, 64, 84, 115
Sullivan, Louis 62, 64, 73, 79, 84, 93, 115, 151, 163–165, 184

Tale of the Wildcats 1
Tamil Nadu, India 16
Taylor, Fred Manville 57–59, 127, 158, 170–171, 181–182
temperance and prohibition 129; gateway to organized crime 183; means of safety for women 130; ties to athletics 57, *114*, 127–128
Temple, Frederick 19–20
Thiel Detective Service 122
Thompson, William 161
three-quarters back (rugby and American football position) 102–103
time (nineteenth-century systems of measuring) 70, 178
Tom Brown's School Days 19
Tremont House Hotel 6, 12, 63, 66–67, 189; gambling at 13, 104–107; history of 177; Northwestern's purchase 177
Tufts University 6, 69
Turf Exchange (gambling hall) 92
Twain, Mark 81

Union House Hotel 13, 23
United States Olympic Team 166
University of Chicago 175–176, 181
University of Michigan 1, 25, 51–52, 79, 170, 181
University of Minnesota 156–157, 183–184
University of Nebraska 183
University of Notre Dame 183–184
University of Wisconsin 175–176
The Utah Review *126*

Valentine, G. "Pat" 63, 184
Vestibuled Express 104
Victoria, Queen of England 18, 21, 38
Vivian, Gen. Sir Robert 29
von Bergen, Elisabeth *see* Pattiani, Madame Eliza

Walder, Jane 127–128
Washington's birthday (holiday) 11, 24, 69, 74, 178
The Water-Babies 19
WCTU *see* Woman's Christian Temperance Union
Wellington College, England 18–21, 36, 38, 141

Wells, Ida 182
Westward Ho! vi, 19, 145, 180
Weyland, Alexander 2
WGN Radio 181
White, Andrew 52
Willard, Clara 12, 154–155
Willard, Frances vi, 6, 74, 127, 129, 131, 148, 155, 165–166, 172, 178–179, 190–191; in England 147, 182; at Northwestern 11, 24, 89–90; support of athletics *114*, 127–128
Willard, Thomas 154–155
Williams, Charles J. "C.J." 40–42, 55, 63, 67, 79, 84, 115, 151–152, 158, 161; starts rugby club 94
Wilmette, Illinois 11
Wilson, Charles (newspaper owner) 82
Wilson, Charles (Northwestern student) 44
Windsor, Ontario 94, 122
Wither, George 58
Woman's Christian Temperance Union 11, 89, 127, 129, 131, 147–148, 155, 166, 172, *179*–180, 182
Women's Temperance Alliance 40, 127
Wood, James "Jimmy" 65
Wortman, Antonia 111, 118, 137
Wright, Frank Lloyd 163

Yale University 5, 26, 46, 58, 69, 76–77, 85, 93, 175, 181, 184
Younger, Cole 143–144
Younger, James 143–145
Younger, Robert 143–144

Zouaves militia 51, 53, *54*

www.ingramcontent.com/pod-product-compliance
Lightning Source LLC
Chambersburg PA
CBHW032040300426
44117CB00009B/1129